Language in Use

Georgetown University Round Table on Languages and Linguistics series
Selected Titles

Discourse and Technology: Multimodal Discourse Analysis
PHILIP LEVINE AND RON SCOLLON, EDITORS

Language in Our Time: Bilingual Education and Official English, Ebonics and Standard English, Immigration and Unz Initiative
JAMES E. ALATIS AND AI-HUI TAN, EDITORS

Linguistics, Language, and the Professions: Education, Journalism, Law, Medicine, and Technology
JAMES E. ALATIS, HEIDI E. HAMILTON, AND AI-HUI TAN, EDITORS

Linguistics, Language, and the Real World: Discourse and Beyond
DEBORAH TANNEN AND JAMES E. ALATIS, EDITORS

LANGUAGE IN USE

Cognitive and Discourse Perspectives on Language and Language Learning

Andrea Tyler, Mari Takada, Yiyoung Kim, and Diana Marinova, *Editors*

GEORGETOWN UNIVERSITY PRESS
Washington, D.C.

Georgetown University Press, Washington, D.C.

Printed in the United States of America

10 9 8 7 6 5 4 3 2 1 2005

This book is printed on acid-free paper meeting the requirements of the American National Standard for Permanence in Paper for Printed Library Materials.

Library of Congress Cataloging-in-Publication Data

Language in use : cognitive and discourse perspectives on language and language learning / Andrea E. Tyler . . . [et al.], editors.
p. cm. — (Georgetown university round table on languages and linguistics series)
Includes bibliographical references and index.
Summary: "This book explores how language is shaped by the nature of human cognition and social-cultural activity, by studying how language is used in context in interactions between at least two people in order to achieve some purpose. It brings together perspectives from cognitive linguistics, discourse analysis, and first and second language acquisition research"—Provided by the publisher.
ISBN 1-58901-044-2 (pbk. : alk. paper)
1. Language acquisition. 2. Cognitive grammar. 3. Discourse analysis. I. Tyler, Andrea. II. Georgetown University round table on languages and linguistics series (2004).
P118.L3638 2005
401′.93—dc22 2004023166

Contents

Figures and Tables

Figures

Tables

Acknowledgments

This volume contains a selection of papers from the 2003 Georgetown University Round Table on Languages and Linguistics, widely known either as GURT or the Round Table. The theme for GURT 2003 was "Language in Use: Cognitive and Discourse Perspectives on Language and Language Learning." The papers were selected by peer review from among more than 120 presentations and 5 plenary addresses. The editors of this volume are Andrea Tyler, Mari Takada, Yiyoung Kim, and Diana Marinova.

The chair for GURT 2003 was Andrea Tyler, professor of linguistics at Georgetown University. Mari Takada, doctoral student in Georgetown's Department of Linguistics, was the conference coordinator. We also want to acknowledge the invaluable service of Ken Petersen, our webmaster, and Yiyoung Kim and Diana Marinova, the assistant coordinators who helped ensure that the conference ran smoothly. Our thanks also go to the members of Washington CogLink who enthusiastically provided intellectual support, in particular Joe Grady and Michael Israel. A special thanks to the organizers of the four invited colloquia—Kendall King, Debby Schiffrin, Deborah Tannen, and Sarah Taub—and the phenomenal group of scholars who agreed to participate in the colloquia. We want to acknowledge the many graduate students and faculty members of the Department of Linguistics who volunteered to assist in organizing and running the conference. Finally, we thank the faculty of languages and linguistics for its generous financial support.

Introduction

ANDREA TYLER
Georgetown University

IN RECENT YEARS there has been growing awareness of the importance of studying language and language learning in its context of use. Researchers who identify themselves as taking a cognitive approach (broadly defined) and those who take various discourse perspectives have sounded the theme, often independently of each other, that an accurate understanding of the properties of language requires an understanding of how language is used to create meaning. Moreover, an increasing number of researchers in language learning have argued that in acquiring a language the learner experiences the language in context. This perspective emphasizes the importance of studying language learning as it is embedded in meaningful communication and recognition that language learning is crucially shaped by the particular language patterns to which a learner is exposed. The aim of GURT 2003 was to bring together research from various perspectives that emphasize the shared notions that the properties of language and the process of language learning crucially involve how language is used in context and how these patterns relate to cognition more generally.

The presentations at GURT 2003 adhered to a shared set of tenets concerning language as it occurs in natural contexts. These shared tenets include the following: when humans use language, they do so for a purpose; with very few exceptions, the purpose is to communicate with other humans beings; communication always occurs in a context; language is created by humans who are unique not only in their language using ability but also in their particular physical and neurological anatomy, as well as many aspects of their social organization and culture making; and language is inevitably shaped by the nature of human cognition and social-cultural activity. In spite of the fact that these attributes stem from basic, commonsensical observations, for many linguists and language acquisitionists they have not been of central concern. Placing this particular perspective on language at the center of our inquiries has profound consequences in terms of the questions we ask, the data we consider, the patterns we discover, and our interpretation of the import of those patterns.

Although cognitive researchers, discourse analysis researchers, and language acquisition researchers share the foregoing assumptions about language, the particular areas of inquiry and emphases of these subfields are diverse enough that many of us have tended to remain unaware of the interrelations among these approaches. Thus, we also have remained unaware of the possibilities for research from each of these perspectives to challenge, inform, and enrich the others. A key goal of GURT 2003, the success of which is admirably reflected in this collection of papers, was to begin to make these connections more transparent.

The essays collected in this volume represent a rich range of frameworks within a usage-based approach to language and language learning. They can be grouped into four strands that were central to the conference.

Language Processing and First-Language Learning

The first strand of essays examines the nature of language through the lens of language processing and first-language learning. Goldberg and Bencini present an impressive body of language processing evidence in support of a construction grammar model of language—that is, a model that represents syntactic patterns as independently meaningful. From the area of language comprehension, they present evidence that suggests that comprehenders recognize that basic sentence patterns are directly linked to meaning, independently of the main verb. Reviewing priming studies, Goldberg and Bencini also provide evidence that units of the type and size of constructions can be primed in language production. Thus, the psycholinguistic evidence offers support for a constructional approach to grammar. Presenting new experimental findings, Casenhiser shows that young children tend to disprefer homophony. He argues that patterns of one-to-many mappings between form and meaning potentially reduce communicative efficiency and concludes that children's dispreference for homophones supports the hypothesis that communicative goals of language are reflected in learning biases. Matsui, McCagg, and Yamamoto examine the development of young Japanese children's use of *datte*, a discourse marker that roughly translates to *but-because*. Using both experimental and longitudinal observational data, they conclude that children as young as three years begin to use *datte* as a justification marker in communicative situations in which they sense opposition to their statements and only later in response to why questions. They argue that this development of the suasive marker reflects the children's growing awareness of the particular contexts in which adults use *datte,* in conjunction with their growing theory of mind. Kyratzis also examines children's use of a suasive discourse marker: the English *because*. Incorporating gender into her analysis of the discourse of preschool play groups, Kyratzis finds that young girls tend to use *because* more often than boys of the same age. Using the construct of participation network and considering both the contextualized presence and absence of a linguistic feature, Kyratzis concludes that when these young girls use *because,* it tends to work as a marker of collaborative stance. In contrast, the absence of *because* that is characteristic of boy's discourse is used to convey either urgency or disagreement with the partner.

Issues in Second-Language Learning

The second group of essays addresses insights that discourse and usage-based models provide into issues of second-language learning (L2). Bardovi-Harlig offers a comprehensive review of the literature on interlanguage pragmatics. She argues that interlanguage pragmatics research would benefit from a "recontextualization" into the larger framework of communication and communicative competence. She advocates reorienting L2 pragmatic research to emphasize language learning embedded in social interaction and the importance of contextual constraints on appropriate language use and interpretation of utterances. Davies' study offers a window into a natural process of language socialization—language coaching—with a focus (created and articulated by the participants themselves) on particular cognitive dimensions of the contextualized speech activity. Analyzing language-coaching discourse between two friends who speak different varieties of English, Davies demonstrates the need to incorporate the cognitive dimension of collaboratively constructed intersubjectivity into a model of interactional competence. Niemeier provides a general overview of key points of cognitive linguistics and how they might apply to second-language teaching. In particular, she emphasizes the tenet that there are no discrete boundaries between the lexicon and syntax; this perspective allows the L2 teacher to exploit the recurrent patterns, or operational uniformity, found at all "levels" of linguistic organization. Taking a Vygotskyan perspective, Iddings and McCafferty examine naturally occurring interactions of third-grade children who do not share a mutual language. The interactions show how, through language play, the children created a hybrid functional system for making meaning that afforded them scaffolded opportunities to communicate, as well as to develop metalinguistic knowledge of their first languages (L1s). Scarcella and Zimmerman present a series of experiments focusing on L2 learners' use of L1 cognates in L2 writing. They offer the surprising finding that native Spanish speakers use relatively few academically appropriate English lexemes that have cognates in Spanish. They conclude that cognate knowledge does not transfer automatically. They suggest that explicit teaching of cognates in the particular context of academic writing may be necessary before most L1 Spanish speakers will be able to effectively produce English cognates in written discourse.

Discourse Resources and Meaning Construction

Using a diverse array of methodologies, the third group of essays examines how speakers employ various discourse-level resources to structure interaction and create meaning. Wennerstrom considers the contribution of "contrast" and "given" intonation patterns to meaning construction and how prosodic analysis might contribute to cognitive models such as mental space theory (Fauconnier and Turner 2002) and Clark's (1992) model of community membership. Wennerstrom concludes that discourse-level prosodics provide a rich resource for creating meaning and that analysis of their patterns of use can shed new light on cognitive constructions and processes. Using multidimensional analysis, Csomay provides a linguistic characterization of the lexically coherent discourse units found in university classroom discourse. Combining elements of quantitative and qualitative analysis, the methodology allows classification of lexical episodes into episode types (involved narrative, procedural, content-oriented), based on their shared linguistic characteristics and association of these lexical episode types with varying communicative purposes. Waring presents evidence that speakers in graduate seminars use other-initiated repair as an interactional resource both to advance their potentially disaffiliative claims and to find a way out of interactional deadlock once a stalemate is reached. Rather than always employing repair initiations to address problems in speaking, hearing, or understanding, English speakers in this particular context use repairs as vehicles for conveying speaker stance. In the final paper in this group, Thepkanjana and Uehara add a diachronic dimension by considering how speakers' contextualized uses of linguistic resources give rise to implicatures that subsequently become entrenched (or grammaticalized) and eventually shape the language. They examine a set of polysemous Thai lexemes that synchronically function as both directional verbs and success markers. They argue that these lexemes express notions of motion and direction (coming from the earlier, core meaning of the directional verbs), while also expressing the meaning of success that arises from pragmatic inferences linked to the general human conceptualization of forward motion along a path correlating with reaching a goal. The authors argue that the multiple meanings associated with these directional verbs/success markers indicate they are in an early stage of grammaticalization, in which meaning shift rather than semantic bleaching has occurred.

Language and Identity

The final set of essays addresses issues of language use and creation of social identity. Gordon analyzes parent-child discourse involving a three-year-old's narratives concerning her yet-to-be-born brother. The analysis reveals how the interactions allow the young child to rehearse the future role of being a big sister and thus to actively shape her identity through imaginative (or hypothetical) discourse. This discourse is a stunning example of a young child, in collaboration with her parents, actively creating multiple, complex conceptual blends. Premilovac investigates the ways in which the discursive construction of local identity (i.e., identity tied to place such as town versus country) is used at a reunion among old, ethnically diverse friends from Bosnia-Herzegovina to reassert a multiethnic community in the wake of radical, exclusionary nationalism. She argues that because the construction of local identity can cut across ethnic and national boundaries, this discursive construct allows accentuation of similarities among the groups and can serve as a basis for rebuilding communities' multiethnic composition. Reynolds offers an ethnographic study of language maintenance and social identity among the contemporary Igbo diaspora living in the United States. Unlike many historical immigrant groups, the Igbo have not settled in distinct neighborhoods. Nevertheless, through specific cultural organizations and special gatherings, which constitute "key sites" for language use, the group creates contexts in which Igbo verbal arts and identity are performed and transmitted to a new generation.

This volume presents a glimpse into the rich, intersecting lines of research represented at GURT 2003. For language researchers who are unfamiliar with usage-based approaches to language, they offer a vibrant introduction to the range of research currently being undertaken within this framework. For those working within usage-based models, they demonstrate the challenges and potential rewards when—to paraphrase Proust—we seek discovery not by simply searching for new landscapes but in seeing the familiar with new eyes.

REFERENCES

Clark, Herbert H. 1992. *Arenas of language use*. Chicago: University of Chicago Press.

Fauconnier, Gilles, and Mark Turner. 2002. *The way we think: Conceptual blending and the mind's hidden capacities*. New York: Basic Books.

I

Language Processing and First-Language Learning

1

Support from Language Processing for a Constructional Approach to Grammar

ADELE E. GOLDBERG AND GIULIA M. L. BENCINI
Princeton University and New York University

A KEY TENET of Construction Grammar (CxG) (e.g., Goldberg 1995; Kay and Fillmore 1999; Michaelis and Lambrecht 1996) is that the basic units of language are learned pairings of form and function: *constructions*. CxG strives to characterize the knowledge that underlies a native speaker's capacity to understand and produce an indefinite number of sentences and discriminate between the acceptable and unacceptable sentences in his or her native language. It departs from classical generative approaches in the Chomskian tradition in several crucial ways, however.[1]

Perhaps the most far-reaching difference stems from CxG's additional commitment to account for the entirety of a language. This commitment to full coverage entails that problematic data cannot be set aside as irrelevant to the theory. Over the past ten to fifteen years, linguists working within the CxG framework have provided analyses of a large number of constructions traditionally relegated to the "periphery" (or "residue") of grammar. Systematic exploration of these seemingly noncore phenomena has led to the discovery that these cases involve a greater degree of systematicity and generalization than previously assumed (e.g., Goldberg 1995; Kay and Fillmore 1999; Michaelis and Lambrecht 1996). Importantly, CxG scholars have demonstrated that the theoretical machinery that is used to account for seemingly more idiomatic cases (e.g., the WXDY construction that licenses expressions such as "What are they doing resurrecting constructions?") is the same as that needed to account for more general patterns, (e.g., subject auxiliary inversion, which is found in yes/no and main clause wh- questions, as well as several other more specific constructions). This finding, in turn, has led to a blurring of the boundary between lexicon and grammar and between "core" and "periphery." The vision of grammar that emerges is a cline of linguistic phenomena from the more idiomatic to the more abstract and general.

In the following section, we review some of the linguistic evidence for a constructional account of argument structure, which is uncontroversially part of traditional core grammar. We provide evidence for this approach from language comprehension. Specifically, we review evidence that suggests that comprehenders recognize that basic sentence patterns such as the transitive (*Pat threw the ball*), ditransitive (*Pat gave Kim a ball*) and resultative (*Pat took the box apart*) are directly linked to meaning, independently of the main verb. We provide evidence from language production in the third section. In particular, we report evidence that indicates that units of the size and kind of constructions can be primed in language production. Thus, the psycholinguistic evidence complements the growing body of traditional linguistic evidence accrued over the past fifteen years for adoption of a constructional approach to grammar (e.g., Abbott-Smith, Lieven, and Tomasello 2004; Croft 2001; Gleitman et al. 1996; Goldberg 2003; Jackendoff 2002; Kay and Fillmore 1999; Lambrecht 2001; Langacker 1988a, 1988b; Michaelis 2001; Zwicky 1994). Additional evidence comes from the area of child language (e.g., Bates and Goodman 1997; Chang and Maia 2001; Childers and Tomasello 2001; Diessel and Tomasello 2001; Tomasello 2003).

Theoretical Motivation for a Constructional Approach to Argument Structure

What aspects of a sentence convey contentful meaning? Verbal predicates seem to play a privileged role in determining a sentence's meaning and overall form (Chomsky 1981; Fillmore 1968; Lakoff 1970). For example, in the sentences in (1) there seems to be a natural correspondence between the number and types of actors in the scene and the number and types of actors typically associated with the predicate.

(1) a. She sneezed.
b. She kicked the table.
c. She gave him a beer.
d. She threw her glass across the room.

Sneezing typically is conceived of as a one-argument predicate, with one participant role: "the sneezer." A kicking event consists of two arguments—the "kicker" and the "kickee"—whereas *give* is a trivalent predicate expressing a "giver," a "given," and a "givee." This observation has led to the traditional view that the overall meaning of a sentence—the information about "who does what to whom"—is a projection of the lexical specifications of its verbal head. Under this lexical-projectionist account, part of the lexical entry of *give* is that it requires three arguments: *give* [NP [V NP NP]].

Unlike the predicates in formal logic however, natural language predicates typically occur in more than one (often many) alternative syntactic frames. For example, *give* can occur in two alternate forms that seem to express roughly the same propositional meaning:

(2) NP V NP PP (dative)
a. Pat gave a cookie to the child.
NP V NP NP (ditransitive)
b. Pat gave the child a cookie.

This property is not exclusive to *give,* of course. Languages typically provide more than one way of saying roughly the same thing, and accounting for these structural alternatives has been a central preoccupation of linguistic theory.

Early accounts of argument structure alternations relied on the rough paraphrasability of the members of an alternation to posit the existence of a transformational rule between them (e.g., Partee 1965, 1971; Fillmore 1968). Thus, linguists assumed that if two sentences were semantically (truth-functionally) identical, they should be structurally identical at some level of syntactic representation—specifically at the level of D-structure, where semantic relations were believed to be read off of syntactic configurations. Yet even the early proponents of transformations also noted that argument structure configurations are associated with subtle but systematic variations in meaning (e.g., Anderson 1971; Partee 1965; Fillmore 1968; Wierzbicka 1988).

The recognition of differences in (3) and (4), for example, led Partee (1965) to note that the ditransitive argument structure requires that the meaning be "X causes Y to receive Z":

(3) a. Pat sent a package to the boarder.
    b. Pat sent the boarder a package. (ditransitive)

(4) a. Pat sent a package to the border.
    b. *Pat sent the border a package. (ditransitive)

Additional semantic differences occur in the so-called spray/load alternation in (5):

(5) a. Pat loaded hay onto the truck.
    b. Pat loaded the truck with hay.

Sentence 5a differs semantically from 5b in that only 5b entails that the truck is somehow affected by the hay-loading (Anderson 1971). A natural interpretation of 5b is that the truck is completely loaded; in contrast, 5a may refer to a situation in which only one bale of hay has been placed onto the truck.

The recognition that differences in syntactic form are associated with subtle semantic differences led other theorists to abandon a syntactic account of alternations. In addition, some linguists also observed that many argument structure alternations appear to be licensed by semantically defined classes of verbs (e.g., Levin 1993; Pinker 1989). A broad variety of lexicalist accounts of alternations were therefore proposed as alternatives to syntactic accounts (e.g., Pinker 1989; Pollard and Sag 1994). For example, in the lexicalist account of the dative alternation proposed by Pinker (1989), a lexicosemantic rule is assumed to take as input a dative verb with the meaning "X causes Y to go to Z" and produce as output a ditransitive verb with the meaning "X causes Z to have Y." Under this argument, the syntax of the ditransitive alternant derives from quasi-universal linking rules that map thematic roles onto grammatical functions. Central to Pinker's account is the assumption that the surface syntax is in one-to-one correspondence with the thematic properties of the verb. To account for the fact that a given verb stem can appear in more than one argument structure, different verb senses were posited; the different senses were associated with different thematic structures and were related to one another via generative lexical rules. We refer to this account of argument structure as the *multiple-sense view*.

The two senses for the verbal stem *bring,* as it occurs in the prepositional dative and ditransitive frames, are represented in (6).

(6) Example Lexical rule:
bring-1 (sem: X causes Y to go to Z) → bring-2 (sem: X causes Z to have Y)

The constructional solution to argument structure shares with the lexicosemantic accounts an emphasis on the meaning distinctions associated with different argument structure patterns. As we will see, however, the constructional account has both theoretical and empirical advantages over lexical accounts that stipulate the existence of different verb senses.

Instead of positing different verb senses without independent evidence for them, the constructional approach assigns meaning directly to various abstract argument structure types, thereby recognizing the argument structure patterns as linguistic units in their own right (Goldberg 1995; Michaelis and Lambrecht 1996; Rappaport-Hovav and Levin 1996). Examples of English argument structure constructions with their forms and proposed meanings are shown in table 1.1.

On the constructional view, argument structure patterns contribute directly to the overall meaning of a sentence, and a division of labor can be posited between the meaning of the construction and the meaning of the verb in a sentence. Although the constructional meaning may be redundant—perhaps prototypically—with that of the main verb, the verb and construction may contribute distinct aspects of meaning to the overall interpretation. For example, the ditransitive construction has been argued to be associated with the meaning of transfer or "giving" (Goldberg 1995; Green 1974; Pinker 1989). When this construction is used with *give*, as in *Kim gave Pat a book*, the contribution of the construction is wholly redundant with the meaning of the verb. The same is true when the construction is used with *send*, *mail*, and *hand*. As is clear from these latter verbs, lexical items typically have a richer core meaning than the meanings of abstract constructions.

In many cases, however, the meaning of the construction contributes an aspect of meaning to the overall interpretation that is not evident in the verb in isolation. For example, the verb *kick* need not entail or imply transfer (cf. *Kim kicked the wall*). Yet when *kick* appears in the ditransitive construction, the notion of transfer *is* entailed. The ditransitive construction itself appears to contribute this aspect of meaning to the

Table 1.1.
English argument structure constructions

Construction	Form	Meaning	Example
Transitive	Subject Verb Object	X acts on Y	*Pat opened the door.*
Ditransitive	Subject Verb Object1 Object2	X causes Y to receive Z	*Sue faxed her a letter.*
Resultative	Subject Verb Object RP	X causes Y to become Z	*Kim talked himself silly.*

sentence. That is, the sentence *Kim kicked Pat the ball* can be roughly paraphrased as "Kim caused Pat to receive the ball by kicking it." The construction contributes the overall meaning of "X causes Y to receive Z" and the verb specifies the means by which the transfer is achieved (i.e., the act of kicking).

The multiple-verb-sense approach to argument structure may run into problems that the constructional approach avoids (Goldberg 1995). For example, consider the sentences in (7):

(7) a. Pat sneezed.
b. She sneezed the foam off the cappuccino. (Ahrens 1995)
c. She sneezed a terrible sneeze.
d. She sneezed herself silly.
e. She sneezed onto the computer screen.
f. She sneezed her way to the doctor's office.

To account for examples 7b–7f, the multiple-sense approach would require positing multiple special senses of the verb *sneeze.* For example, to license sentence 7b the following implausible sense of *sneeze* would be required:

(8) Sneeze-2: "to cause something to move by sneezing"

Sneeze is not unusual in this respect. Additional examples of verbs for which the multiple-verb sense account requires implausible senses are given in (9).

(9) a. The truck rumbled down the road.
b. She baked him a cake.
c. Pat eyebrow'd her surprise.
d. We will overnight you that package.
e. He kissed her unconscious.
f. They were unable to pray the little boys home.
g. The soldiers starved them out of their hiding place.
h. They wined, dined, and golfed their way into millions of yen.

In a constructional approach, stipulation of these implausible verb senses is avoided by recognizing that phrasal patterns themselves can be associated with meaning. The constructional meaning integrates with the more specific verb meaning in particular ways. For example, in 7b sneezing causes the transfer; in 9a rumbling is an effect of the motion, and in 9b baking is a precondition of transfer.

In light of such cases, even some early proponents of the multiple-verb-sense approach have recognized certain instances in which it seems preferable to view verb meaning as entering into composition with an independently existing construction or template (Pinker 1994; Rappaport-Hovav and Levin 1998). Additional arguments appear in Goldberg (1995). In the following section we provide arguments for an advantage of a constructional account over a multiple-sense account from language comprehension.

Evidence for Constructional Meaning from Comprehension

What types of linguistic information do people use to construct the meaning of a sentence? Most psycholinguistic models of sentence comprehension follow linguistic theory and assume that the main determinant of sentence meaning is the verb. It does seem to be true that of all the words in a sentence, verbs carry the most information about the syntax and semantics of the sentence. Because of the high predictive value of verbs, it is reasonable to assume that people use this information during comprehension to predict other lexical items in the sentence and the overall meaning of the sentence. Experimental evidence has demonstrated that in fact the main verb is a critical factor in sentence comprehension (e.g., Ahrens 2003; Garnsey et al. 1997).

In this section, however, we review studies that provide evidence for the existence of sentence-level generalizations that are used in language comprehension to construct an interpretation of an unknown predicate as well as the overall meaning of the sentence. Studies by Ahrens (1995) and Kaschak and Glenberg (2000) show that the way comprehenders interpret novel verbs depends on the sentence patterns in which the verbs occur.

Ahrens (1995) conducted an experiment with a novel verb form. She asked 100 native English speakers to decide what *moop* meant in the sentence *She mooped him something.* Sixty percent of subjects responded by saying that *moop* meant "give," despite the fact that several verbs have higher overall frequency than *give* and could be used in that frame, including *take* and *tell.*

Kaschak and Glenberg (2000) show that subjects rely on constructional meaning when they encounter nouns used as verbs in novel ways (e.g., *to crutch*). In particular, they show that different constructions differentially influence the interpretations of the novel verbs. For example, *She crutched him the ball* (ditransitive) is interpreted to mean that she used the crutch to transfer the ball to him, perhaps using the crutch as one would a hockey stick. On the other hand, *She crutched him* (transitive) might be interpreted to mean that she hit him over the head with the crutch. They suggest that the constructional pattern specifies a general scene and that the "affordances" of particular objects are used to specify the scene in detail. It cannot be the semantics of the verb that is used in comprehension because the word form is not stored as a verb but as a noun.

Bencini and Goldberg (2000) conducted an experiment with the aim of directly comparing the semantic contribution of the construction with that of the morphological form of the verb. As shown in table 1.2, the stimuli were sixteen sentences created by crossing four verbs with four different constructions.[2]

Seventeen University of Illinois undergraduate students were asked to sort the sixteen sentences, which were provided in random order, into four piles on the basis of "overall sentence meaning." Subjects could sort equally well by verb: For example, all instances of throw (1a–d) could have been grouped together, regardless of construction. Subjects also could sort by construction: For example, all instances of the VOO or ditransitive construction (1a, 2a, 3a, and 4a) could have been grouped together.

It would be possible, of course, to design stimuli with a great deal of overlapping propositional content so that we could a priori predict either a verb or constructional sort. For example, the sentences *Pat shot the duck* and *Pat shot the duck dead* would

Table 1.2.
Stimuli for sorting experiment

Example sentences	Construction types
1a. Pat threw the hammer.	(VO) Transitive
b. Chris threw Linda the pencil.	(VOO) Ditransitive
c. Pat threw the key onto the roof.	(VOL) Caused Motion
d. Lyn threw the box apart.	(VOR) Resultative
2a. Michelle got the book.	(VO) Transitive
b. Beth got Liz an invitation.	(VOO) Ditransitive
c. Laura got the ball into the net.	(VOL) Caused Motion
d. Dana got the mattress inflated.	(VOR) Resultative
3a. Barbara sliced the bread.	(VO) Transitive
b. Jennifer sliced Terry an apple.	(VOO) Ditransitive
c. Meg sliced the ham onto the plate.	(VOL) Caused Motion
d. Nancy sliced the tire open.	(VOR) Resultative
4a. Audrey took the watch.	(VO) Transitive
b. Paula took Sue a message.	(VOO) Ditransitive
c. Kim took the rose into the house.	(VOL) Caused Motion
d. Rachel took the wall down.	(VOR) Resultative

very likely be grouped together on the basis of overall meaning despite the fact that the argument structure patterns are distinct. Conversely, *Pat shot the elephant* and *Patricia stabbed a pachyderm* probably would be grouped together despite the fact that no exact words were shared. The stimuli were designed to minimize such contentful overlap contributed by anything other than the lexical verb. No other lexical items in the stimuli were identical or near-synonyms.

Use of the sorting paradigm is a particularly stringent test to demonstrate the role of constructions. Medin, Wattenmaker, and Hampson (1987) have shown that there is a strong, domain-independent bias toward sorting on the basis of a single dimension, even with categories that are designed to resist such one-dimensional sorts in favor of a sort based on a family resemblance structure (Rosch and Mervis 1975). One-dimensional sorting has been found even with large numbers of dimensions (Smith 1981), ternary values on each dimension (Anh and Medin 1992), holistic stimuli, and stimuli for which an obvious multidimensional descriptor was available (Regehr and Brooks 1995).

The stimuli used in Bencini and Goldberg (2000) presented subjects with an opportunity to sort according to a single dimension: the verb. Constructional sorts required subjects to note an abstract relational similarity that required recognition that several grammatical functions co-occur. Thus, we would expect verb sorts to have an inherent advantage over constructional sorts.

Nonetheless, six subjects produced entirely construction sorts. Seven other subjects produced entirely verb sorts, and four subjects provided mixed sorts. To include the mixed sorts in the analysis, the results were analyzed according to how many changes would be required from the subject's sort to produce a sort entirely by verb (VS) or a sort entirely by construction (CS). The average number of changes required for the sort to be entirely by verb was 5.5; the average number of changes required for the sort to be entirely by construction was 5.7. The difference between these scores does not approach significance. That is, subjects were just as likely to sort by construction as they were to sort according to the single dimension of the morphological form of the verb. If verbs provided equally good cues to overall sentence meaning, there would be no motivation to overcome the well-documented preference for one-dimensional sorts: Subjects would have no motivation to sort by construction instead of by verb. Bencini and Goldberg (2000) hypothesize that constructional sorts were able to overcome the one-dimensional sorting bias to this extent because constructions are better predictors of overall sentence meaning than the morphological form of the verb.

A question arises about why constructions should perform at least as well as predictors of overall sentence meaning as verbs. The answer, we believe, stems from the fact that in context, knowing the number and type of arguments conveys a great deal about the scene being conveyed. To the extent that verbs encode rich semantic frames that can be related to several different basic scenes, the complement configuration or construction will be as good a predictor of sentence meaning as the semantically richer but more flexible verb.

On the multiple-sense view, the reason instances of *throw*, for example, were put into separate piles was that each instance represented a distinct sense that was more similar in meaning to one of the senses of another verb than to the other senses of *throw*. The only way for subjects to discern which verb sense was involved, however, was to recognize the argument structure pattern and its associated meaning. That is, the proposed different verb senses all look the same; the only way to determine that a particular sense is involved is to note the particular argument structure pattern that is expressed and infer which verb sense must have produced such a pattern. Therefore, at least from a comprehension point of view, the pairing of argument structure pattern with meaning must be primary.

The most important contribution of the studies cited in this section are that they provide a sufficiency proof that types of complement configurations play a crucial role in sentence interpretation, independent of the contribution of the main verb. The results suggest that constructions are psychologically real linguistic categories that speakers use in comprehension.[3]

Evidence for Constructions in Language Production

In this section we provide experimental evidence that units of the type and kind of constructions are activated during the processes of language production. We present three studies. These three studies build on a large body of work conducted primarily by Bock and colleagues that employ a structural priming methodology (Bock 1986).

In structural priming, the basic finding is that people tend to reuse the syntactic structure of a sentence (the prime) they have previously produced (Bock 1986) or heard (Branigan et al. 2000). Participants are exposed to a long sequence of pictures and auditorily presented sentences. On each priming trial, participants first hear a priming sentence such as "The new graduate was hired by the software company." They repeat the sentence out loud and decide whether they have said this sentence before. They then see and describe a pictured event that can be described with either of the targeted structural alternatives. Their description might be something like "The mailman is being chased by an angry poodle." On the same priming trial, another group of participants hears and repeats the sentence "The new graduate left the software company." Structural priming occurs when participants match the overall structure of the sentence prime in their subsequent picture description.

Structural priming provides a powerful tool to investigate the mental representation of linguistic units at the level of the sentence (Branigan et al. 1995; Bencini 2002). The ecological validity of the structural priming paradigm is supported by the finding that a tendency toward structural repetition occurs in more naturalistic settings, such as written and spoken corpora (e.g., Tannen 1989; Weiner and Labov 1983) and dialogue (Levelt and Kelter 1982), suggesting that it is not a laboratory-induced phenomenon.

Bock and colleagues (e.g., Bock and Griffin 2000; Bock and Loebell 1990; Bock, Loebell, and Morey 1992) have shown in several studies that passives prime passives, ditransitives prime ditransitives, and datives prime datives (cf. also Abbott-Smith, Lieven, and Tomasello 2004; Branigan et al. 1995; Chang et al. 2000; Hare and Goldberg 1999; Potter and Lombardi 1998; Smith and Wheeldon 2001; Tomasello 2003; Yamashita, Chang, and Hirose 2003). Bock's original claim was that syntactic tree structures, not constructions with associated meanings, were involved in priming.

More recent work has investigated the question of whether constructional priming exists. That is, can abstract pairings of form with meaning be primed? Chang, Bock, and Goldberg (2003) conducted an experiment in which syntactic structure was controlled for, while two different constructions were used as primes. Sample prime and target sentences are given below:

Sample Primes

load with	She loaded the wagon with hay.
load onto	She loaded hay onto the wagon.

Sample Targets

He embroidered the shirt with flowers.

He embroidered flowers onto the shirt.

Subjects were asked to recall a sentence as it was presented after a short distractor task. Such rapid serial visual presentation (RSVP) tasks have been shown to allow priming effects (Potter and Lombardi 1998). If semantics matters in priming, we should see "load-with" structures priming other "load-with" structures more than "load-onto" structures. In fact, this is exactly what Chang, Bock, and Goldberg (2003) found. In our experiment with 80 subjects, "load-with" structures primed other "load-with" structures in 99 percent of cases, whereas "load-onto" structures primed "load-with" structures in 95 percent of the cases.

Likewise, Griffin and Weinstein-Tull (2003) have shown that object-raising sentences prime object-raising sentences more than object-control sentences. This finding also suggests constructional priming; the results would be unexpected if only surface form were taken into account because the two constructions arguably have the same surface form.

Given these results, it is worth returning to the original motivation for earlier claims that syntactic constituent structure, not constructions (form-meaning pairings), are primed. Bock and Loebell (1990) made perhaps the strongest case for this claim with a series of experiments. In one experiment, they showed that both datives and locatives primed dative descriptions of (unrelated) pictures equally well. Example primes are given below:

Primes:

A. The wealthy widow gave her Mercedes to the church. (dative)

B. The wealthy widow drove her Mercedes to the church. (locative)

The constructional interpretation of this result stems from the idea that "dative" and "locative" expressions are actually both instances of the same Caused-Motion construction (Goldberg 1995, 2002).

Caused-Motion Construction:
X causes Y to move Z
Subj V Obj Obl

Examples:
She drove the box to Missouri.
She drove the box to Mary.
She threw the box to Mary.
She gave the box to Mary.

Therefore, the findings are that caused-motion expressions prime caused-motion expressions—a result that is predicted by a constructionist account of priming. In fact, Bock and Loebell (1990) also acknowledge that locative and dative expressions are semantically similar. They therefore performed a second experiment in which they investigated whether intransitive locative expressions primed passives—a construction with the same syntax as locatives but with clearly distinct meaning (table 1.3).

Table 1.3.
Example of priming sentences in Bock and Loebell (1990)

Prime Type	Examples
Passive	The 747 was radioed by the airport control tower.
Intransitive locative	The 747 was landing by the airport control tower.
Active (control)	The 747 radioed the airport control tower.

Bock and Loebell (1990) found that, in fact, intransitive locatives did prime passives. This finding was the strongest evidence for purely syntactic, nonconstructional priming. Yet a close look at the stimuli used revealed that the preposition *by* and the auxiliary *be* appeared in every intransitive locative prime. A question naturally arises: Was it the shared morphemes, rather than the shared syntactic structure, that produced the priming? To address this question, Bencini, Bock, and Goldberg (n.d.) attempted to replicate the Bock and Loebell (1990) findings while adding a fourth condition in which intransitive locatives without shared morphology were used as primes. The four conditions are shown in table 1.4.

Bencini, Bock, and Goldberg (n.d.) replicated Bock and Loebell's (1990) results, demonstrating that locatives with shared morphology primed passives and, also as expected, passives prime passives. Bencini, Bock, and Goldberg (n.d.) also found a significant difference, however, between the passive condition and the locative condition without shared morphology; in contrast, the locative without shared morphology condition did not prime passives significantly more than the control group. This finding is intriguing because it may indicate that shared syntactic structure is not sufficient to induce priming.[4]

Hare and Goldberg (1999) designed a different test of the idea that pure syntactic tree structure rather than some sort of form-meaning pairing was involved in priming. Recall that it has been well established that ditransitives prime ditransitives and that instances of the caused-motion construction prime other instances of the caused-motion construction. Hare and Goldberg (1999) attempted to determine whether a third sort of prime—"provide-with" primes—would differentially prime either caused-motion expressions ("datives") or ditransitive descriptions of scenes of transfer. Examples of the "provide-with" sort of primes are given in table 1.5.

"Provide with" sentences arguably have the same syntactic form as caused-motion expressions—NP [V NP PP]—yet the order of rough semantic roles involved parallels the ditransitive: Agent Recipient Theme. Results demonstrated that "provide-with" expressions prime ditransitive descriptions of (unrelated) pictures as much as ditransitives do. There was no evidence of priming of caused-motion expressions, despite the shared syntactic form. Thus, when order of semantic roles is contrasted with constituent structure, only the order of semantic roles shows priming, with no apparent interaction with constituent structure.[5]

What do the structural priming facts mean? First, constructions can be primed, which means that the level of generalization involved in argument structure constructions is psychologically real. Furthermore, it is possible that priming of structure may

Table 1.4.
Example of priming sentences in Bencini, Bock, and Goldberg (n.d.)

Prime Type	Examples
Passives	The 747 was landed by the pilot.
Locatives w/ shared morphology	The 747 was landing by the airport control tower.
Locatives w/o shared morphology	The 747 might land near the airport control tower.
Active (control)	The 747 radioed the airport control tower.

Table 1.5.
Example of priming sentences in Hare and Goldberg (1999)

Sample primes in "provide-with" condition
The government provided the troops with arms.
His editor credited Bob with the hot story.
The father entrusted his daughter with the keys.

not be independent of meaning; thus, the priming mechanism may encourage speakers to categorize on the basis of form and meaning—exactly the sort of categorization that is required by construction-based approaches. We briefly discuss a very general processing advantage of CxG and other theories that assume a parallel representation of linguistic knowledge (e.g., Jackendoff 2002; Sag and Wasow 1999).

Recognition of the Incrementality of Language Processing

Like other parallel constraint-based models of grammar (e.g., head-driven phrase structure grammar), CxG assumes that syntactic, semantic, and phonological information is represented in parallel. Parallelism has some attractive features from the perspective of processing (Bencini 2002; Sag and Wasow 1999; Jackendoff 2002). These features are evident when one contrasts parallel grammars with the mainstream generative grammar architecture, in which syntax is the "engine" and semantics and phonology are interpretative levels (e.g., Chomsky 1981). Although mainstream generative grammar is a model of competence, it is possible to derive a certain general processing implication from its main organizational features (see Bock, Loebell, and Morey 1992 for a good example): Namely, it is presented as inherently directional. Derivations are always computed from the syntax (through various intermediate derivational steps) to meaning and sound.

This type of grammar clearly requires some sort of adjustment to be compatible with the disparate processes of language comprehension and production. In language production, the starting point is a meaning to be conveyed, and the goal is to convert this meaning into a motor program for speech. Along the way, syntactic information is used to produce a well-formed utterance (Bock 1995; Bock and Levelt 1994; Garrett 1980). In comprehension, the starting point is a phonetic representation derived from auditory or visual input, and the goal is to compute a meaning.

The parallel architecture, on the other hand, is not inherently directional and therefore is compatible in a transparent way with both comprehension and production. Parallelism allows for differential weighting and ordering of linguistic information in processing (e.g., Bencini 2002). For example, in comprehension one need not assume that a syntactic structure must be computed "first." A more rapid and incremental integration of different sources of information can be assumed to constrain the interpretation as information becomes available. This analysis is consistent with many findings from online comprehension studies (e.g., Just and Carpenter 1982; Garnsey et al. 1997).

Summary and Conclusions

In this essay we have reviewed several pieces of experimental evidence for argument structure constructions from adult language processing. Section 2 provides evidence from comprehension that sentence patterns such as the ditransitive, caused-motion, and resultative contribute to overall sentence interpretation independently of the specific contribution of the main verb. Section 3 shows that linguistic units of the kind posited by construction-based grammars are accessed in the normal processes of language production. Section 4 observes a basic advantage of parallel approaches such as CxG: They allow for a fairly transparent interface simultaneously with both comprehension and production.

Although there has been a large amount of fruitful research in language acquisition from a constructional perspective, research in language processing from this perspective is only beginning. We believe that continued research in this area may well aid in discovering new mechanisms at work in processing and ultimately may lead to our grounding of linguistic theory in a theory of performance.

NOTES

1. See Jackendoff (1997, 2002) or Goldberg (2003) for more comprehensive summaries and discussions of the differences between parallel constraint-based approaches to grammar (of which CxG is an exemplar) and classical generative accounts. See Bencini (2002) for a discussion of the advantages of parallel constraint-based grammars from a processing point of view.
2. The study by Bencini and Goldberg (2000) was inspired by a Healy and Miller (1970) sorting experiment, which had been titled "The Verb as the Main Determinant of Sentence Meaning." Healy and Miller (1970) created stimuli by crossing subject arguments with verbs because they assumed that the two best candidates for determining what the sentence was about were the verb and the subject argument.
3. See also work by McRae, Ferretti, and Amyote (1997) and Ahrens (2003), who demonstrate that the sorts of verb-specific participant roles posited by CxG (e.g., Goldberg 1995) are required to account for on-line sentence processing.
4. At the same time, the data are a bit ambiguous because there is a stepward trend such that passives prime passives and by-locatives prime passives (significantly), but more passives also were produced after non–by-locatives than after controls; the difference was nonsignificant, however, despite the running of 130 subjects.
5. One interpretation of the Hare and Goldberg (1999) findings is that order of animate participants, not the order of semantic roles, affected priming. This possibility is strengthened by the fact that animacy has been shown to induce priming, even when the overall construction is held constant (Bock, Loebell, and Morey 1992). In fact, it remains to be shown that ditransitive versus dative priming is not induced by differing order of animate participants as well (see Bencini 2002 for discussion).

   Yamashita, Chang, and Hirose (2003) have shown that dative sentences with the order AGENT-wa RECIPIENT-ni PATIENT-o (wa-ni-o) prime other wa-ni-o ordered productions, even though the animacy of recipients and patients was controlled for. Although these results suggest that structural priming can be sensitive to the order of syntactic functions, thematic roles, or morphology independently of animacy, the experiment does not tease apart these possible interpretations.

REFERENCES

Abbott-Smith, Kirsten, Elena Lieven, and Michael Tomasello. 2004. Training 2;6-year-olds to produce the transitive construction: The role of frequency, semantic similarity and shared syntactic distribution. *Developmental Science* 7, no. 1:48–55.

Ahrens, Kathleen. 1995. The mental representation of verbs. Ph.D. diss., University of California at San Diego.

———. 2003. Verbal Integration: The interaction of participant roles and sentential argument structure. *Journal of Psycholinguistic Research* 22:497–516.

Anderson, Steven. R. 1971. On the role of deep structure in semantic interpretation. *Foundations of Language* 6:197–219.

Anh, Woo-Kyong, and Douglas L. Medin. 1992. A two-stage model of category construction. *Cognitive Science* 16:81–121.

Bates, Elizabeth, and Judith Goodman. 1997. On the inseparability of grammar and the lexicon: Evidence from acquisition, aphasia, and real time processing. *Language and Cognitive Processes* 12, nos. 5–6:507–84.

Bencini, Giulia M. L. 2002. The representation and processing of argument structure constructions. Ph.D. diss., University of Illinois.

Bencini, Giulia, and Adele Goldberg. 2000. The contribution of argument structure constructions to sentence meaning. *Journal of Memory and Language* 43:640–51.

Bencini, Giulia, Katheryn J. Bock, and Adele E. Goldberg. n.d. How abstract is grammar? Unpublished manuscript.

Bock, Kathryn. 1986. Syntactic persistence in language production. *Cognitive Psychology* 18:355–87.

———. 1995. Sentence production: From mind to mouth. In *Handbook of perception and cognition: Speech, language and communication,* vol. 11, ed. Joanne L. Miller and Peter D. Eimas, 181–216. Orlando, Fla.: Academic Press.

Bock, Kathryn, and Zenzi M. Griffin. 2000. The persistence of structural priming: Transient activation or implicit learning? *Journal of Experimental Psychology-General* 129:177–92.

Bock, Kathryn, and Wilhelm Levelt. 1994. Language production: Grammatical encoding. In *Handbook of psycholinguistics,* ed. Morton Ann Gernsbacher, 945–84. San Diego: Academic Press.

Bock, Kathryn, and Helga Loebell. 1990. Framing sentences. *Cognition* 35:1–39.

Bock, Kathryn, Helga Loebell, and Randal Morey. 1992. From conceptual roles to structural relations: Bridging the syntactic cleft. *Psychological Review* 99:150–71.

Branigan, Holly P., Martin J. Pickering, Simon P. Liversedge, Andrew J. Stewart, and Thomas P. Urbach. 1995. Syntactic priming: Investigating the mental representation of language. *Journal of Psycholinguistic Research* 24:489–506.

Branigan, Holly P., Martin J. Pickering, Andrew J. Stewart, and Janet F. McLean. 2000. Syntactic priming in spoken production: Linguistic and temporal interference. *Memory and Cognition* 28, no. 8:1297–1302.

Chang, Franklin, Kathryn Bock, and Adele E. Goldberg. 2003. Do thematic roles leave traces in their places? *Cognition* 90, no. 1:29–49.

Chang, Franklin, Garry S. Dell, Kathryn Bock, and Zenzi M. Griffin. 2000. Structural priming as implicit learning: A comparison of models of sentence production. *Journal of Psycholinguistic Research* 29:217–29.

Chang, Nancy C., and Tiago V. Maia. 2001. Learning grammatical constructions. *Proceedings of the 24th Annual Cognitive Science Society.* Mahwah, N.J.: Lawrence Erlbaum Associates.

Childers, Jane B., and Michael Tomasello. 2001. The role of pronouns in young children's acquisition of the English transitive construction. *Developmental Psychology* 37:739–48.

Chomsky, Noam. 1981. *Lectures on government and binding.* Dordrecht, The Netherlands: Foris Publications.

Croft, William. 2001. *Radical construction grammar.* Oxford: Oxford University Press.

Diessel, Holger, and Michael Tomasello. 2001. The acquisition of finite complement clauses in English: A usage based approach to the development of grammatical constructions. *Cognitive Linguistics* 12:97–141.

Fillmore, Charles J. 1968. The case for case. In *Universals in linguistic theory,* ed. Emmon Bach and Robert T. Harms, 1–88. New York: Holt, Rinehart and Winston.

Garnsey, Susan, Neal J. Pearlmutter, Elizabeth Myers, and Melanie A. Lotocky. 1997. The contributions of verb bias and plausibility to the comprehension of temporarily ambiguous sentences. *Journal of Memory and Language* 37:58–93.

Garrett, Merril. F. 1980. Levels of processing in sentence production. In *Language production,* vol. 1, ed. Brian Butterworth. London: Academic Press.

Gleitman, Lila, Henry Gleitman, Carol Miller, and Ruth Ostrin. 1996. Similar and similar concepts. *Cognition* 3:21–76.

Goldberg, Adele. E. 1995. *Constructions: A construction grammar approach to argument structure.* Chicago: Chicago University Press.

———. 2002. Surface generalizations: An alternative to alternations. *Cognitive Linguistics* 13:327–56.

———. 2003. Constructions: A new theoretical approach to language. *Trends in Cognitive Sciences* 7:219–24.

———. In press. Constructions in context. Oxford: Oxford University Press.

Green, Georgia. 1974. *Semantics and syntactic regularity.* Bloomington: Indiana University Press.

Griffin, Zenzi M., and Justin Weinstein-Tull. 2003. Conceptual structure modulates structural priming in the production of complex sentences. *Journal of Memory and Language* 49:537–55.

Hare, Mary, and Adele E. Goldberg. 1999. Structural priming: Purely syntactic? *Proceedings of the 22nd Annual Cognitive Science Society.* Mahwah, N.J.: Lawrence Erlbaum Associates.

Healy, Alice F., and George A. Miller. 1970. The verb as the main determinant of sentence meaning. *Psychonomic Science* 20:372.

Jackendoff, Ray. 1997. Twistin' the night away. *Language* 73, no. 3:534–59.

———. 2002. *Foundations of language.* Oxford: Oxford University Press.

Just, Marcel, and Patricia Carpenter. 1982. A model of the time course and content of reading. *Cognitive Science* 6:157–203.

Kaschak, Michael P., and Arthur M. Glenberg. 2000. Constructing meaning: The role of affordances and grammatical constructions in sentence comprehension. *Journal of Memory and Language* 43:508–29.

Kay, Paul, and Fillmore, Charles J. 1999. Grammatical constructions and linguistic generalizations: The what's X doing Y? construction. *Language* 75:1–34.

Lakoff, George. 1970. *Irregularity in syntax.* New York: Holt Rinehart and Winston.

Lambrecht, Knud. 2001. A framework for the analysis of cleft constructions. *Linguistics* 39:463–516.

Langacker, Ronald W. 1988a. An overview of cognitive grammar. In *Topics in cognitive linguistics,* ed. Brygida Rudzka-Ostyn. Philadelphia: John Benjamins Publishing Co.

———. 1988b. A view of linguistic semantics. In *Topics in cognitive linguistics,* ed. Brygida Rudzka-Ostyn. Philadelphia: John Benjamins Publishing Co.

Levelt, Willem, and Kelter, Stephanie. 1982. Surface form and memory in question answering. *Cognitive Psychology* 14:78–106.

Levin, Beth. 1993. *English verb classes and alternations.* Chicago: University of Chicago Press.

McRae, Ken, Todd Ferretti, and Liane Amyote. 1997. Thematic roles as verb specific concepts. *Language and Cognitive Processes* 12:137–76.

Medin, Doug L., William D. Wattenmaker, and Sarah E. Hampson. 1987. Family resemblance conceptual cohesiveness, and category construction. *Cognitive Psychology*12:242–79.

Michaelis, Laura A. 2001. Exclamative constructions. In *Language universals and language typology: An international handbook,* ed. Martin Haspelmath, Ekkehard König, Wulf Österreicher, and Wolfgang Raible, 1038–50. Berlin: Walter de Gruyter.

Michaelis, Laura A., and Lambrecht, Knud. 1996. Toward a construction-based model of language function: The case of nominal extraposition. *Language* 72:215–47.

Partee, Barbara H. 1965. *Subject and object in modern English.* New York: Garland.

———. 1971. On the requirement that transformations preserve meaning. In *Studies in linguistic semantics,* ed. Charles J. Fillmore and D. Terence Langedoen, 1–21. New York: Holt, Rinehart and Winston.

Pinker, Stephen.1989. *Learnability and cognition: The acquisition of argument structure.* Cambridge, Mass.: MIT Press/Bradford Books.

———. 1994. How could a child use verb syntax to learn verb semantics? In *The acquisition of the lexicon,* ed. Lila Gleitman and Barbara Landau. Cambridge, Mass.: MIT Press.

Pollard, Carl, and Ivan Sag. 1994. *Head-driven phrase structure grammar.* Stanford, Calif., and Chicago: CSLI and University of Chicago Press.

Potter, Mary C., and Linda Lombardi. 1998. Syntactic priming in immediate recall of sentences. *Journal of Memory and Language* 38:265–82.

Rappaport-Hovav, Malka, and Beth Levin. 1996. Building verb meanings. In *The projection of arguments,* ed. M. Butt and W. Gerder. Stanford, Calif.: Center for the Study of Language and Information.

Regehr, Glenn and Lee R. Brooks. 1995. Category organization in free classification: The organizing effect of an array of stimuli. *Journal of Experimental Psychology: Learning, Memory and Cognition* 21:347–63.

Rosch, Eleanor, and Carolyn B Mervis. 1975. Family resemblances: Studies in the internal structure of categories. *Cognitive Psychology* 7:573–605.

Sag, Ivan, and Thomas Wasow. 1999. *Syntactic theory.* Stanford, Calif.: Center for the Study of Language and Information.

Smith, Linda B. 1981. Importance of overall similarity of objects for adults' and children's classifications. *Journal of Experimental Psychology: Human Perception and Performance* 7:811–24.

Smith, Mark, and Linda Wheeldon. 2001. Syntactic priming in spoken sentence production—An online study. *Cognition* 78:123–64.

Tannen, Deborah. 1989. *Talking voices: Repetition, dialogue and imagery in conversational discourse.* Cambridge: Cambridge University Press.

Tomasello, Michael. 2003. *Constructing a language: A usage-based theory of language acquisition.* Cambridge, Mass.: Harvard University Press.

Weiner, Judith, and William Labov. 1983. Constraints on the agentless passive. *Journal of Linguistics* 19:29–58.

Wierzbicka, Anna. 1988. *The semantics of grammar.* Amsterdam: John Benjamins.

Yamashita, Hiroko, Franklin Chang, and Yuki Hirose. 2002. Separating functions and positions: Evidence from structural priming in Japanese. Paper presented at 15th Annual Human Sentence Processing Conference, City University of New York (March).

Zwicky, Arnold. 1994. Dealing out meaning: Fundamentals of syntactic constructions. *Berkeley Linguistics Society* 20:611–25.

2

Homonyms and Functional Mappings in Language Acquisition

DEVIN M. CASENHISER
Princeton University

Mapping Form and Meaning

Because language is used for communication, we might expect it to exist in and evolve toward a state in which communication is optimally facilitated. Yet there are some aspects of language whose existence contradicts the communicative purpose of language. The case under consideration in this chapter involves mappings between form and meaning. One might expect that sounds and meanings should be mapped to each other with a one-to-one correspondence as in bi-uniqueness—each sound (or string of sounds) having a single meaning associated with it and vice versa. This sort of language would both minimize ambiguity and maximize the language's communicative potential. In fact, languages are not so perfectly composed. For example, there are cases in which the mapping between sounds (or strings of sounds) and meanings are many-to-one or one-to-many, as represented by examples B and C in figure 2.1.

The non–bi-unique mappings B and C create a potential problem for language and communication. Synonymy (represented by B in figure 2.1) should be less preferred for reasons of economy. In principle, a language that reserves more than a single word for a particular meaning creates the potential for redundancies that may overwhelm a speaker's memory. If two-to-one mappings are not dispreferred on grounds of economy, then three-, four-, or five-to-one mapping might also be created.

Where homophony (represented by example C in figure 2.1) is concerned, it is not economy that degrades the communicative potential of language but ambiguity resulting from the fact that there are too few forms to associate with each meaning. When a speaker is confronted with a homophonous word, the speaker cannot rely on the form of the word alone to determine its meaning. Instead, the speaker must interpret its meaning from the context in which the word is encountered. If the context does not effectively disambiguate the meaning of the homonym, the potential for misunderstanding arises, which may make it more difficult for speakers to communicate successfully.

If synonymy and homophony do degrade the communicative potential of language, and language exists for communication, then both synonymy and homophony should be dispreferred ways of mapping form to meaning. Scholars have long noted a

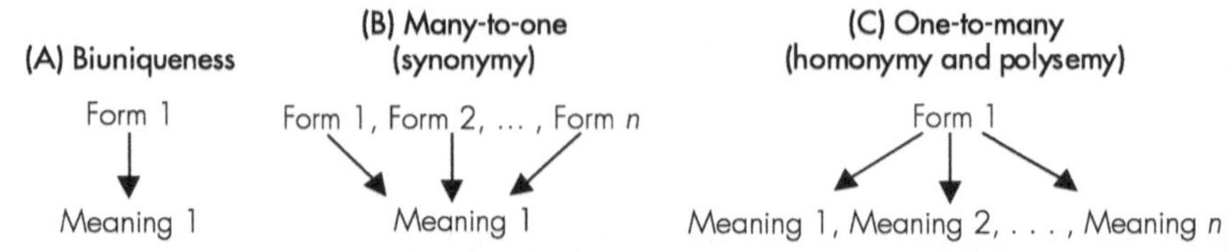

Figure 2.1. Three types of form-to-meaning mappings

tendency for languages to avoid synonymy. Bréal (1897), for example, proposes a law of differentiation in which several forms that are associated with a single meaning come to distinguish themselves so that their meanings are no longer synonymous. The law predicts, in other words, that however two words come to mean the same thing, the language will evolve so that eventually the two words will no longer be synonyms—thus preserving bi-uniqueness.

Once we have noted that languages seem to change to avoid synonymy, the next step is to attempt to determine if there is a psychological or cognitive explanation for this tendency. In the case of synonymy, language researchers have indeed discovered evidence for a psychological tendency that may account for the rarity of synonymy in language. The "disambiguation effect" (Merriman and Bowman 1989) occurs when children are asked to find the referent of an unfamiliar object in a set of objects that contains one familiar and one unfamiliar object. In such a situation, children normally choose an object whose name they do not know. To account for this effect (at least in part), researchers have proposed several principles—including the Mutual Exclusivity Principle (Markman 1992), Novel Name for Nameless Categories (Golinkoff et al. 1992), the principle of contrast (Clark 1983), and Grice's (1975) Cooperation Principle (Gathercole 1989). Although there is disagreement about the exact nature of the cognitive principle that is responsible for the disambiguation effect, what is important for the present discussion is that children assume by default that a many-to-one mapping between form and meaning is less likely than a one-to-one mapping. Given that children have such an assumption, to possibly learn a synonym they must first overcome their bias against many-to-one mappings.

Where a single form is mapped to many meanings, the case is not so clear. For one thing, homophony is not uncommon in languages—especially if one considers grammatical morphemes as well as words. Along these lines, Clark (1983, 70) points out that the English *–s* morpheme is used for possessives, marking plural forms on nouns and marking the third person singular form on present-tense verbs. Moreover, polysemy, which involves different but related senses, seems to be the norm for both lexical items and grammatical morphemes (Lakoff 1987; Taylor 1995). Nevertheless, there is some research that suggests that at least homonyms, though not impossible, may be dispreferred in lexical acquisition. Research on near-mergers, for example, indicates that words that seem to be converging phonetically over time often will change (or be changed) to make their differences more acoustically salient, or one of the pair will be lost entirely (Labov 1994, esp. Part C). Research into processes of phonological change has yielded similar conclusions. For example, Gurevich (2004) found that among nearly 300 processes of lenition in 170 different languages, only about 15 percent resulted in a change that *might potentially* cause a form in the language to become homophonous.[1] Accordingly, one might expect that there is a corresponding psychological constraint to account for this diachronic change, just as the disambiguation effect accounts for Bréal's Law of Differentiation. In other words, is there evidence that, as Slobin (1973, 1977, 1985) argues, children do have a one-to-one form-to-meaning assumption that extends to homophony as well as synonymy?

In this chapter I raise several methodological issues that indicate that previous research has not demonstrated this finding conclusively. I then describe an investigation that offers an empirical test that aims to eliminate previous confounds. Evidence from this study suggests that in fact homonyms are dispreferred in lexical acquisition.

Previous Research on Homophony

Campbell and Bowe-Macdonald (1977, 1983) conducted an experiment in which they read stories containing the less familiar meanings of homonyms to children (three- to five-year-olds). The experimenters then questioned the children about their understanding of the homonyms and asked them to illustrate their referents. For example, one story told about a wing of a castle:

> At the far side of the wood was a castle. "Look at this castle," said Jane's Daddy. "The oldest *wing* is over 500 years old."

The children's illustrations of this passage often depicted the castle's *wing* like that of a bird or airplane sticking out of a building. The results of the experiment indicated that 31 percent of the children in all age groups responded by giving the primary, more familiar meaning of the homonym in spite of the fact that clinging to the primary meaning of the homonym caused the story to seem bizarre or fanciful.[2]

The design of the experiment does not allow us to draw the conclusions we need, however. First, the experiment did not take into account children's previous experience with the homonyms used in the experiment. The number of children who correctly interpreted the homonyms may be related to individual children's familiarity with a particular homonym; on the other hand, children's failure to interpret homonyms correctly may result from a lack of previous experience with the secondary meaning of the word. Moreover, the children who failed to interpret the homonym correctly might not have been provided with enough context to fully disambiguate the two meanings (Donaldson 1978).

Furthermore, where homonym *acquisition* is concerned, the task requires that participants who are unfamiliar with the secondary meaning of the homonym be willing to override their present understanding of a word's meaning to accept the addition of some new understanding. Children simply may require more evidence to change the established meaning of a word than they need to map an entirely new word and its meaning (Keil 1991). In this case, children might not be receiving enough evidence (linguistic and/or extralinguistic) to necessitate a modification of their established mapping. Moreover, the fact that homonyms are used in the study without a baseline for lexical acquisition prevents us from determining if there was enough context for a child to map even a nonhomophonous word. The experiment demonstrates only that young children will sometimes make fanciful or bizarre interpretations of stories to try to make the context fit with what they already know.

To address these problems, Mazzocco (1997) conducted an experiment with "pseudohomonyms." A pseudohomonym is a word that is applied to an object other than the one commonly associated with the word. For example, labeling a clown with the word "door" makes "door" a pseudohomonym. In the study, participants (thirty-two preschoolers, thirty-two second graders, and sixteen college students) were read a story and then shown a page containing six illustrations. The story incorporated one of three word types: pseudohomonyms, nonsense words, and familiar words (used correctly). The context of the story was crafted to indicate a plausible meaning for the target word. One story, for example, takes place at a birthday party: "then James saw that a *door* was standing there making funny faces and doing tricks. James laughed, because the *door* looked so funny." After the participants listened to the story, each was shown a page containing six illustrations: the keyword's familiar meaning (i.e., a door); the keyword's meaning in the context (clown); something related to the context (e.g., cake); and three unrelated objects. The participant was then asked to "look at all of the pictures on this page, then show me the picture of the keyword in the story." The results are reproduced in table 2.1.

Because Mazzocco's (1997) study used nonsense words as well as pseudohomonyms, the results allow a point of comparison between the acquisition of homophonous and nonhomophonous words. The relatively high success with which preschool children were able to interpret the correct meaning of nonsense words from the context compared to the much lower rate of success for the same task with pseudohomonyms seems to indicate that a one-to-one mapping assumption may be at work in language acquisition with young children. Preschoolers in particular seem likely to base their interpretations of a homonym on their preexisting notions of what that word means rather than on the context in which the word is heard.

The design of the study, however, introduces the problem of synonymy into the acquisition task. The confusion lies in the fact that both the pseudohomonyms and their referents are words the children already know. Consider the situation of the task: The child hears a story in which what must be a clown, according to the context, is discussed, but the story is labeling the clown with a different name—in this case *door.* The child knows the meaning of both *clown* and *door* but is being asked to use both meanings interchangeably: *clown* means CLOWN; *door* means DOOR *and* CLOWN.

Table 2.1.
Mean number of correct responses from Mazzocco (1997)

	Type of key word		
Age Group	Accurately used	Nonsense	Pseudohomonym
Preschool	5.81 (0.40)	4.16 (1.61)	0.75 (0.98)

Note: N = 32; maximum correct = 6; standard deviation appears in parentheses.

Synonymy		and	Homonymy	
door	DOOR CLOWN	and	door clown	CLOWN

Figure 2.2. Comparison of many-to-one mapping with one-to-many mapping

It is true, however, that children do not seem to have the same difficulties when a nonsense word is used to refer to the object discussed in the story (twenty-three preschoolers got four or more nonsense word interpretations correct, compared with one preschooler who got four or more homonym interpretations correct). The existence of synonymy in the task leaves the interpretation of the processes involved somewhat uncertain, however. Consider that the nonsense word condition could be regarded as differing from the homonym condition in at least two ways that are relevant to lexical acquisition. First, although subjects know that the object being discussed is a clown, it is being given a new label in the nonsense condition; hence, the new label functions as a synonym for "clown." In the pseudohomonym condition, children must not only accept two labels for the same object (synonymy); they must accept a label that already refers to another object (homophony) as well. If we can simply subtract the effect of synonymy from both tasks, we are left with the conclusion that the difference in participants' performance is related to homophony alone. This conclusion, however, requires one to assume that the effect of violating these language constraints is additive. It may be, however, that concurrent violation of two constraints on language acquisition has an effect that is more or less than additive. This nonadditive effect may obtain especially if the difference between participants' performance on the accurately used words and the nonsense words did not differ significantly—an inference the reader is left to make because the comparison is not specifically reported by Mazzocco (1997). Moreover, the study also does not provide an accurate baseline we might use to quantify the relative difficulty in acquiring a novel word and meaning pair compared with the difficulty in mapping a familiar word to a second (i.e., homophonous) meaning.

The study I describe below seeks to address the foregoing questions and problems. An experiment was prepared to make a direct comparison between the acquisition of nonsense and homophonous words. The experiment also was designed to determine the extent to which the linguistic context and the visual context of a scene affect the acquisition of homonyms in comparison to nonhomonyms. The expected outcome is that children will be at least partially successful in mapping homonyms to new objects but that they will be significantly more successful in mapping nonsense words to new objects. The hypothesis is that differentiation provided by linguistic and visual context will aid children's acquisition of homophonous words.

Experiment One

Method

Participants The participants were sixteen four-year-olds (mean age = 4;6) from the Champaign-Urbana area of Illinois. All children were monolingual native speakers of English.

Materials A children's story was written in which the main character, Tommy, was searching for his baseball in each of five different scenes. Each of the five scenes had an accompanying illustration: a park, a pond, the front yard of a house, a kitchen, and a bathroom. Each scene included four landmarks (e.g., a pink tree, a boat, a bathtub, a stove); two novel creatures; two novel objects; and three known objects or animals, two of which were the same kind of object (e.g., two different kinds of dogs). All illustrations were in color and were similar in appearance to those in a children's picture book. An "answer" page reproduced the objects from the illustration out of context; children pointed to these illustrations to answer the experimenter's questions. A sketch of the illustrations used for Scene One of the story is included in figure 2.3.

The Stories Children heard a story about a little boy who was searching for his lost baseball. The landmarks in the scenes corresponded to each of the specific places where he looked for the baseball. In the course of his searching, the little boy encountered each of the target objects in the illustration. The target object is named in reference to the landmark with which it appears (e.g., "Tommy look under the slide, but all he saw there was a *snake*."), and the little boy engages in some activity specifically associated with the landmark so that the children's attention is unambiguously drawn to that place (e.g., "Tommy thought the slide looked like fun, so he climbed up and slid down it. 'Whee!' Tommy giggled."). The portion of the story immediately following the target word was approximately twenty-four words long (plus or minus two). The illustration of the story was then covered up and the answer page shown to the child. The child is reminded that "Tommy saw a *snake* under the slide, right?" and then asked, "Can you point to it?"

Target Words and Objects There were a total of twenty-five high-frequency, monosyllabic target words and twenty-five target objects in the experiment. The words and targets are divisible into five categories each, according to table 2.2.

Each of the seven objects noted in the last column of table 2.2 appear in the illustration of the story (see figure 2.3). These same seven objects, plus the object named by the noun-absent condition, appears on the answer sheet of illustrations—making a total of eight illustrations, arranged in a 2-by-4 configuration. With the exception of the vague condition, the objects to which the words referred were counterbalanced across participants so that a purple creature, for example, was called a *fidge* in the story for the first participant, a *pie* for the second participant, a *snake* for the third participant, and so on. The order of conditions for each scene was counterbalanced across trials.

Figure 2.3. Sketches of the illustrations used in experiment one

Table 2.2.
Target words and corresponding objects

Condition	Target word type	Word example	Target object type	Object example
Vague	Linguistically vague word	*dog*	Pair of objects of the same category	Two different dogs
Nonsense	Nonsense word	*fidge*	Unknown object or creature	Novel object or creature
Noun-Present	Noun homonym present in the scene	*pie*	Novel object or creature plus an object that corresponds to the meaning of the pseudohomonym	Novel object or creature plus an illustration of a pie
Noun-Absent	Noun homonym absent from scene	*snake*	Unknown object or creature	Novel object or creature
Verb	Verb homonym	*give*	Unknown object or creature	Novel object or creature

Explanation of Conditions Two baseline conditions were included in the experiment: the nonsense and vague conditions. The nonsense condition provides a baseline for comparison between acquiring homophonous and nonhomophonous words. The vague condition provides a way to gauge how well children are paying attention to the object named in the specific location. Failure in the vague condition might indicate that children were looking for *any* such object named by the experimenter—not necessarily the particular object associated with the location in the story. The vague condition is an especially appropriate comparison for the two noun homonym conditions. Both conditions require that the child attend to and remember the object referred to in the story and in the question, but the noun-present condition requires the additional task of creating a new form-to-meaning mapping. Differences between performance on these two tasks can be attributed to the additional task in the noun-present condition. A comparison of the noun-present and noun-absent conditions will illustrate the effect of context (in this case, visual context) on children's acquisition of homonyms. Finally, the verb condition was included to determine if linguistic context might play a role in homonym acquisition. The main comparison for the verb condition is the noun-absent condition because neither condition has a corresponding object that appears in the illustration. Children are expected to perform best on the vague and nonsense word conditions. The verb condition should be the next easiest task, followed by the noun-absent condition. The most difficult task is expected to be the noun-present condition. Table 2.3 lists words and landmarks in the five conditions in each of the five senses.

Procedure Children were tested individually and told that the experimenter was going to read a story to them while they looked at some pictures of the story. The instructions were as follows: "I've got some pictures for you to look at, and I'm going to read a story about the pictures. Once in a while I'm going to stop and ask you a

Table 2.3.
List of words and landmarks

Landmarks	Nonsense words	Nouns-Present	Nouns-Absent	Verbs	Vague words
Scene One: fountain slide (under) slide (on) (pink) tree flowers	fidge	pie	snake	give	dog
Scene Two: bridge boat island flowers water	goot	cake	owl	have	cat
Scene Three: wall roof car tree front door	snock	horse	bone	put	pig
Scene Four: refrigerator sink oven table chair	sarn	boat	leaf	get	fish
Scene Five: bathtub stool rug door toilet	mish	sheep	kite	sit	duck

question that only kids know the answer to—that's why I need your help—grown-ups don't know the answers, but I'll bet you do! Are you ready?" Children were shown a warm-up scene and read a short story in which they were asked to identify several objects in the picture that the character, Jan, saw in the park. Half of the word-object pairs were of the vague type, to reinforce the idea that children needed to pay attention to the location in which an object appeared.

After the warm-up scene, children listened to the story until the point at which the first landmark and target object were named:

> Next to the slide, Tommy saw a pink tree. Way up in the tree, Tommy saw a [keyword]. "Maybe my baseball is stuck up in the tree too," Tommy thought. Tommy climbed the tree and looked all around, but still didn't find his baseball.

At this point, the scene was covered up and the answer page was presented to the child. The experimenter then instructed the child as follows: "Tommy saw a [keyword] in the tree, right? Can you point to it?" The experimenter noted the child's answer, removed the answer page, uncovered the scene, and continued the story. A final, sixth scene was included at the end so that Tommy could finally find his baseball, but no questions were asked for this last scene.

Scoring The experimenter recorded participants' answers on a prepared answer form. Answers were scored as 'correct' if the participant indicated the object to which the story referred. 'Incorrect' answers were those in which the participant indicatedeither the familiar meaning of the homonym (in the case of the Noun-Present and Noun-Absent conditions) or the referent which appeared in a place in the scene other than where the story indicated (in the case of the Vague condition). Answers were scored as 'other' when participants indicated an object that did not fit either category.

Results

A repeated measures analysis of variance (ANOVA), with the dependent variable as the number of correctly mapped words, was performed for Experiment One. Significant differences were found between the two noun conditions and the other three conditions ($F(4, 15) = 33.32$, $p < .001$), but there were no significant difference between the noun-present and noun-absent conditions, nor among the three other conditions (see figure 2.4).

Scores support the main effect of homonyms anticipated by this study. Overall, participants mapped 77.5 percent of the vague words and 72.5 percent of the nonsense words to the correct referent. By comparison, only 11.25 percent and 17.5 percent of the homonyms in the noun-present and noun-absent conditions were mapped correctly. In the case of the noun homonym conditions, the majority of the incorrect responses (75 percent) indicated the familiar meaning of the homonym. The scores also support the assertion that verb homonyms are easier to map to object referents than are noun homonyms. Participants correctly mapped 76.25 percent of the verb homonyms, in contrast to the much lower scores on the noun homonym

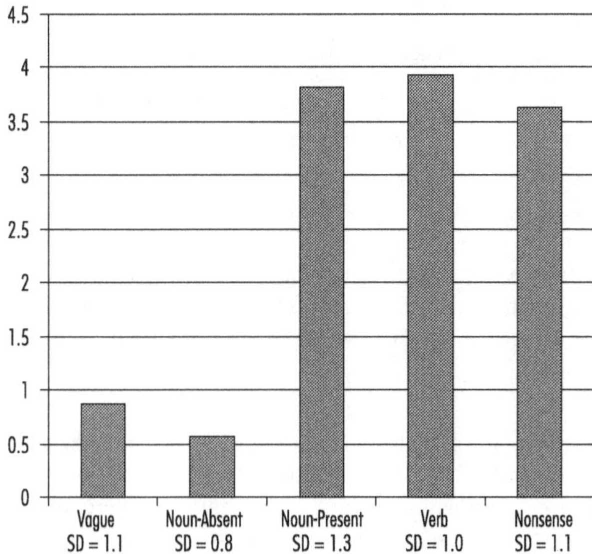

Figure 2.4. Mean number of correct responses

conditions. The difference between the verb and nonsense conditions is not significant, however. Likewise, there is only a slight, nonsignificant difference between the noun-present and noun-absent conditions. Complete numbers are reported in table 2.4.

Comparison to Chance Performance If performance were random, the probability that a participant would respond correctly to any single item is .125 because there are eight possibilities and only one correct answer. Because each participant was asked to answer five questions of each condition type, a score of three or better would indicate that the participant was performing significantly above chance (binomial $p = 0.015$). Results are reported in table 2.5.

Table 2.4.
Participant responses as a function of condition and response type[a]

Condition	Correct (%)	Distractor (%)	Other (%)
Nonsense	72.5 (58)		27.5 (22)
Vague	77.5 (62)	21.25 (17)	1.25 (1)
Verb	76.25 (61)		23.75 (19)
Noun-Present	17.5 (14)	81.25 (65)	1.25 (1)
Noun-Absent	11.25 (9)	86.25 (69)	2.5 (2)

[a] $N = 16$. There were five items for each condition. Raw numbers are given in parentheses; the maximum number for each cell is 80.

Table 2.5.
Participants performing significantly above chance ($N = 16$)

	Nonsense	Vague	Verb	Noun-Absent	Noun-Present
Number	15/16	15/16	15/16	1/16	1/16
% of Total	93.7	93.7	93.7	6.25	6.25

The scores from table 2.5 demonstrate that participants consistently failed to map noun homonyms to the novel objects they encountered, despite the fact that they were able to map nonsense words as well as verb homonyms to these same objects.

Discussion

The results concerning the learning of noun homonyms from Experiment One suggest that children disprefer homophony during lexical acquisition even when they are faced with evidence that a new meaning is appropriate. There also is evidence that the linguistic context—particularly part of speech—may play a prominent role in disambiguating the context for the child during acquisition. This conclusion is supported by the fact that children mapped verb homonyms as easily as they mapped nonsense words.

The design of Experiment One is biased, however, in favor of the verb homonym condition compared with the noun homonym conditions because a referent for the primary meaning of each noun homonym appeared on the answer sheet, whereas the verb homonyms did not have corresponding referents for the children to point to (e.g., there was no illustration for the verb *sit*). To attempt to correct this bias, a second study was designed in which an initial "go/no-go" decision was added to the existing story task. That is, children were first asked to determine if the object Tommy saw in the story appeared in the illustration they were looking at. If they saw the keyword in the illustration, they were to point it out on the answer sheet. Otherwise, they were to indicate that the keyword was not in the illustration. If the difference between the noun and verb homonym conditions was a result of the fact that an illustration for the verb referent was missing on the answer sheet (as in Experiment One), the number of no-go responses in the noun homonym and verb homonym conditions should be roughly the same. On the other hand, if the result was caused by part-of-speech differences, Experiment Two should show a significantly greater number of no-go responses for the noun homonyms than for the verb homonyms. Because the illustrations of the scenes contain neither pictures of the noun homonyms nor pictures of the verb homonyms, any difference that does exist between the number of no-go responses for the noun-homonym and verb-homonym conditions might be accounted for by part of speech.

Experiment Two

Method

Participants Participants were eighteen four-year-old subjects (mean age 4;5) from the Champaign-Urbana area. All subjects were native speakers of English.

Materials The illustrations and story from Experiment One were modified so that only four objects appeared in each illustration, and all four objects were named in the corresponding story. The answer sheets included eight objects, as in Experiment One.

Explanation of Conditions Experiment Two included noun, verb, and nonsense conditions that were identical to the noun-absent, verb, and nonsense conditions in Experiment One. In addition, there was a foil condition in which a noun was named that did not appear in the illustration of the story. Order of word type was counterbalanced across trials. The answer sheet included the three novel objects or creatures that were referred to in the first three conditions, an object representing the primary meaning of the noun homonym, the object named in the foil condition, and three novel objects that did not appear in the illustration.

Procedure The procedure was the same as with Experiment One except that children were instructed to first determine whether the object Tommy saw in the story appeared in the illustration. For example, children heard the following portion of the story:

> Next to the slide, Tommy saw a pink tree. Way up in the tree, Tommy saw a [keyword]. "Maybe my baseball is stuck up in the tree too," Tommy thought. Tommy climbed the tree and looked all around, but still didn't find his baseball.

The experimenter then covered the illustration of the story and said, "Now, Tommy saw a [keyword] in the story. Did you see one too?" If the child answered yes, the child was presented with the answer sheet and asked to point to it. If the child responded no, the experimenter marked the answer as a no-go and proceeded to the next part of the story.

Results

Statistics were first run to compare the number of no-go answers in each of the four conditions. Repeated measures ANOVA with post hoc comparisons were performed using word type (foil × noun × verb × nonsense) as the within-subjects factor. Tests show that all conditions differ significantly at or below the .01 level. In particular, a comparison between the noun (M = 2.89, SD = 1.23) and the verb (M = 1; SD = 0.69) conditions reveals a significant difference ($F(1,17) = 32.32$; $p < .001$), indicating that children rejected noun homonyms more readily than verb homonyms. The mean number of no-go answers for each condition is reported in figure 2.5.

Statistics also were run to compare participants' success at mapping each of the word types to their object referents. For the purposes of scoring, no-go responses as well as responses that indicated an object other than the intended referent of the story were considered incorrect. Again, repeated measures ANOVA with post hoc comparisons were performed, using word type (noun × verb × nonsense) as the within-subjects factor. The tests found that all conditions differed significantly at or below the $p < .001$ level. Results are reported in figure 2.6.

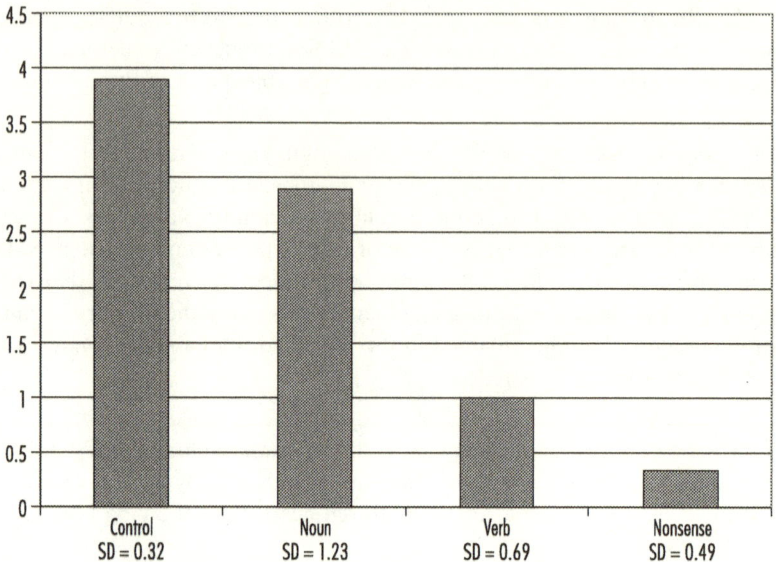

Figure 2.5. Mean number of no-go responses

The line graph in figure 2.6 shows the trend of increased difficulty in mapping each word type. As with Experiment One, children are significantly less willing to map a new meaning to a noun homonym than to a verb homonym. Unlike Experiment One, however, this experiment suggests that children do experience more difficulty mapping verb homonyms than nonsense words ($F(1,17) = 17, p < .001$).

Discussion

The primary goal of this investigation was to determine if children disprefer homophony during lexical acquisition. The results of Experiment Two indicate that when children encounter a lexical item for which they have an established meaning, they will prefer that meaning even when they are faced with evidence indicating that a different meaning is appropriate. The point is most obvious when one considers the data concerning the mapping of noun homonyms to new meanings, but Experiment Two indicates that even verb homonyms are significantly more difficult to map to new meanings compared with mapping nonsense words to those same meanings. This conclusion is further supported by children's comments during the experiment that indicated that they were resistant to accepting a second meaning for a word. To cite one of several examples: After hearing a sentence that said a snake was under the slide, B.S. remarked, "Where? I don't see a snake! [looks closely at the picture] Oh, I know! Maybe the snake is behind this thing! [points to the novel object under the slide]."

The results also support the hypothesis that it is easier to map new meanings onto verb homonyms than onto noun homonyms. Children's comments during the experiment indicate that they treated verb homonyms as novel words rather than as

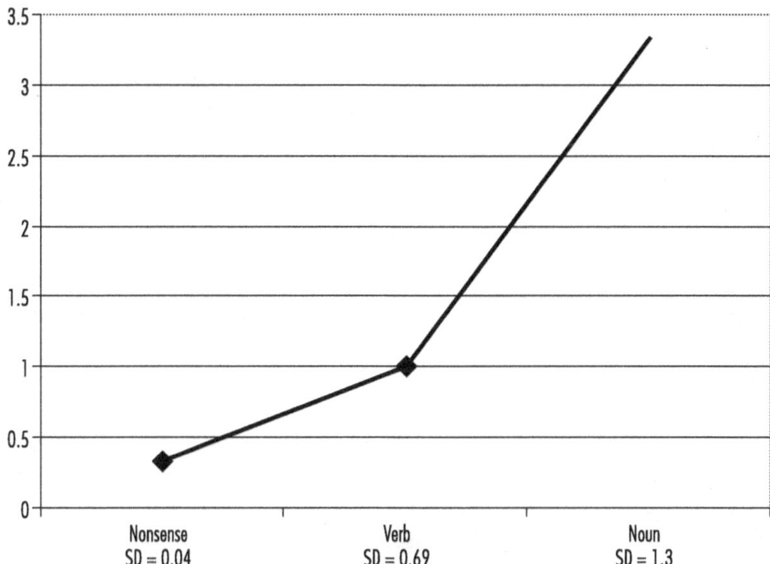

Figure 2.6. Mean number of incorrect responses

homonyms, sometimes asking questions such as, "*Sit*? What's a *sit*?" (O.J.). Because children's performance on the verb homonyms also is significantly better than their performance on noun homonyms, it may be that the linguistic context—specifically part of speech—plays a prominent role in disambiguating the context for the child during acquisition. Exactly what portion of this effect is related to the syntactic or semantic differences associated with different parts of speech must be determined by further study.

The third hypothesis in this investigation was that the presence or absence of a referent for the primary meaning of the homonym in the illustration accompanying the story would influence children's willingness to map a new meaning to the homonym. The results did not support this hypothesis. There was a slight but non-significant difference, however, between the noun-present and noun-absent conditions, which might indicate that the design of this experiment was not sensitive enough to illuminate the differing effects of these two conditions.

Finally, it should be noted that this experiment investigates only one type of one-to-many mapping—one in which meanings are unrelated. Another type of one-to-many mapping is polysemy, which involves two or more different but related meanings. This experiment does not manipulate the relatedness of the primary referents of the homonyms and the novel objects introduced because the experimenters consistently used two unrelated meanings. Therefore it is impossible to draw any conclusions about the acquisition of polysemes per se. Furthermore, polysemes represent a different situation, in which the primary meaning of the word may actually aid in learning extended meanings for the same word. This situation would obtain if theorists who believe that there are definite patterns for defining extended meanings of words are correct (Langacker 1987, 1991; Lakoff 1987). If such patterns exist and children do learn them, it may be possible to learn new meanings for words that have been defined by one of the learned patterns. Precious little research (Gropen, Epstein, and Schumacher 1997) has been done on the acquisition of polysemes, so any proposal about how polysemes are learned remains speculative. Nonetheless, this topic may shed a good deal of light on the way we learn the meanings of words and therefore is worthy of investigation.

Conclusion

The research described in this chapter supports the idea that communicative goals of language are reflected in learning biases. I have demonstrated that children disprefer learning a different, unrelated meaning for a known word when that word is used in a linguistic context that fails to bias strongly for a new meaning. Children appear to have much less difficulty in learning homonyms when the syntactic context clearly indicates that a new meaning is required (cf. the verb homonym condition verses the two noun homonym conditions). I do not suggest that children are incapable of learning homonyms; clearly that is not the case. Nonetheless, the experiment presented in this chapter does demonstrate a bias against homophony in the acquisition process.

Acknowledgments

I am very grateful for the advice and guidance of Adele Goldberg in the planning stages of this study as well as in the preparation of this chapter. I am also indebted to Dan Silverman, whose thought-provoking phonology courses planted the initial seeds for this research. Finally, I thank the teachers, students, and parents at Countryside and Next Generation schools for assisting with and participating in this study. This chapter is an abbreviated version of "Children's resistance to homonymy: An experimental study of pseudohomonyms," which appears in the *Journal of Child Language*, 32, no. 1 (2005), © Cambridge University Press.

NOTES

1. Gurevich (2004) did not verify that the changes did result in homophony of any kind.
2. Compare this result with the 25 percent of all participants who responded with the correct meaning of the homonym (the remaining 44 percent of participants invented answers, could not respond, or gave answers the experiments could not classify).

REFERENCES

Bréal, Michel. 1897. *Essai de sémantique.* Paris: Hachette.

Campbell, Robin N., and Theresa Bowe. 1977. Functional asymmetry in early language understanding. In *Salzberger Beitrage für Linguistik,* ed. Gaberell Drachman. Tubingen, Germany: Gunter Narr.

Campbell, Robin N., and Theresa Bowe-Macdonald. 1983. Text and context in early language comprehension. In *Early child development and education*, ed. Margaret Donaldson, Robert Grieve, and Chris Pratt, 115–26. Oxford: Blackwell.

Clark, Eve. 1983. Meanings and concepts. In *Handbook of child psychology,* 4th ed., vol. 3: *Cognitive development*, ed. John H. Flavell and Ellen M. Markman, 787–840. New York: John Wiley and Sons.

Donaldson, Margaret C. 1978. *Children's minds.* London: Fontana.

Gathercole, Virginia C. 1989. Contrast: A semantic constraint? *Journal of Child Language* 16:685–702.

Golinkoff, Roberta M., Kathy Hirsch-Pasek, Leslie M. Bailey, and Neill R. Wenger. 1992. Young children and adults use lexical principles to learn new nouns. *Developmental Psychology* 28:99–108.

Grice, H. Paul. 1975. Logic and Conversation. In *Syntax and Semantics 3: Speech Acts*, ed. Peter Cole and Jerry L. Morgan, 41–58. New York: Academic Press.

Gropen, Jess, Trina Epstein, and Lisa Schumacher. 1997. Context-sensitive verb learning: Children's ability to associate contextual information with the argument of a verb. *Cognitive Linguistics* 8, no. 2:137–82.

Gurevich, Naomi. 2004. *Lenition and contrast: The functional consequences of certain phonetic conditioned sound changes.* New York: Routledge.

Keil, Frank C. 1991. Theories, concepts, and the acquisition of word meaning. In *Perspectives on language and thought: Interrelations in development,* ed. Susan Gelman and James P. Byrnes. New York: Cambridge University Press.

Labov, William. 1994. *Principles of linguistic change: Internal factors*. Cambridge, Mass.: Blackwell.

Lakoff, George. 1987. *Women, fire, and dangerous things*. Chicago: University of Chicago Press.

Langacker, Ronald. 1987. *Foundations of cognitive grammar,* vol. 1. Stanford, Calif.: Stanford University Press.

———. 1991. *Foundations of cognitive grammar,* vol. 2. Stanford, Calif.: Stanford University Press.

Markman, Ellen. 1992. Constraints on word learning: Speculations about their nature, origins and domain specificity. In *Modularity and constraints in language and cognition. The Minnesota symposia on child psychology,* ed. Megan R. Gunnar and Michael P. Maratsos. Hillsdale, N.J.: Lawrence Erlbaum Associates.

Mazzocco, Michèle M. M. 1997. Children's interpretations of homonyms: A developmental study. *Journal of Child Language* 24:441–67.

Merriman, William E., and Laura L. Bowman. 1989. The mutual exclusivity bias in children's word learning. *Monographs of the Society of Research in Child Development* 54, nos. 3–4 (serial no. 220): 1–123.

Slobin, Dan. I. 1973. Cognitive prerequisites for the development of grammar. In *Studies of child language development,* ed. Dan. I. Slobin. New York: Springer.

———. 1977. Language change in childhood and in history. In *Language learning and thought*, ed. John T. Macnamara, 185–214. New York: Academic Press.

———. 1985. Crosslinguistic evidence for the language-making capacity. In *A Crosslinguistic study of language acquisition*, ed. D. I. Slobin, 1157–1256. Hillsdale, N.J.: Lawrence Erlbaum Associates.

Taylor, John R. 1995. *Linguistic categorization*. Oxford: Oxford University Press.

3

Little Persuaders: Japanese Children's Use of *Datte* (*but-because*) and Their Developing Theories of Mind

TOMOKO MATSUI, PETER McCAGG, AND TAEKO YAMAMOTO
International Christian University Japan

THE CONTRIBUTION OF LANGUAGE to the development of preschoolers' theory of mind has begun to attract a great deal of attention in developmental psychology and language acquisition circles. Roughly speaking, the research can be divided into two threads: one that investigates the contribution of language (typically syntax) toward developing representational capacity (Astington and Jenkins 1999; de Villiers and de Villiers 2000; Farrar and Maag 2002; Tager-Flusberg 2000) and one that focuses on the role of language in communication that continuously cultivates children's socio-communicative competency as they move through infancy to early and middle childhood (Astington 1998; Bartsch and Wellman 1995; Bretherton and Beeghly 1982; Dunn et al. 1991; Lalonde and Chandler 1995; Nelson 1996). The use of tests to assess children's ability to attribute false beliefs to others—an ability that presumably marks a significant change in their representational capabilities—has played a significant role in research in the first thread (Perner, Leekam, and Wimmer 1987). Researchers have pointed out, however, that false-belief test results can make only a limited contribution to research in the second thread because they cannot tap children's mental state understanding prior to the stage at which they succeed in false-belief attribution, which typically is observed around the age of four years. Researchers who are interested in early cognitive development have claimed that children's use of language itself is the prime indicator of their developing ability to understand mental states and have provided detailed analyses of children's use of language in daily conversation to argue for early precursors of a full-fledged theory of mind (Wellman and Woolley 1990). The investigation described in this chapter follows this line of research and provides further evidence regarding young children's continuous development of mental state understanding in the preschool period by examining children's use of language in a communicative setting that requires use of suasion.

The literature on children's use of mental terms and causal talk in naturalistic data is abundant with evidence suggesting that even two-year-olds are capable of justifying their desires, feelings, and behaviors in attempts to persuade others when they encounter opposition or disinterest (Eisenberg and Garvey 1981; Tesla and Dunn

1992). A series of studies on children's use of causal expressions by Bloom and colleagues supports this view. They found that children develop an understanding of causality and the ability to express causal relations using connectives such as "because" and "so" between the ages of two and three years (Bloom and Caspides 1987; Hood and Bloom 1979). They also found that children's early use of "because" is restricted primarily to the domain of psychological/motivational cause for actions, rather than physical causation. Bartsch and Wellman (1995) add that young children's explanations of action is desire based at first and that belief-based explanation of action appears later—around the age of three years. Dunn and Brown (1993) report that at thirty-three months, children's causal talk is mostly about behaviors or actions, but at forty months they talk more about the causal relations of internal states. In general, there is strong consensus that between the ages of two and four years, children begin to show rudimentary understanding of "belief" through their use of language.

Naturalistic data regarding young children's justifications suggest that being able to explain actions and behaviors is important in their social life. Existing analyses of naturalistic data have not yet shown, however, just when or how children start using their understanding of belief and causality to persuade others about their own beliefs. In particular, analyses of naturalistic data to date provide almost no information about when children start to offer justifications for their beliefs by referring to evidence to support them. One notable exception reveals that young children's justifications typically occur in disputes over a person's goals or actions but that they rarely provide justifications in disputes over the truth of a proposition or the nature of categorization (Dunn and Munn 1987). Given, however, that in adult discourse one of the most fundamental argumentative goals is to convince others that what you say is true—providing evidence to support your statement, if necessary—children's ability to defend their own beliefs should gradually develop as their understanding of suasion becomes more sophisticated. If the hypothesis that verbal communication continuously cultivates children's sociocommunicative competency throughout infancy and in the early childhood years is correct, children's preliminary understanding of other's mental states may also enable them to detect the need to justify their statements and beliefs and, moreover, enable them to offer adequate justifications for their beliefs, provided they have a communicative need to do so.

Thus, the present investigation addresses the questions of when and how preschoolers begin to provide adequate justifications for the veracity of their statements in naturalistic and experimental settings. To tap Japanese three- and four-year-olds' willingness and ability to justify the truth of their own statements, we created a task in which children first make guesses about the identity of familiar pictorial objects shown only partially and then find those guesses constantly challenged by an adult. We focused on their use of the Japanese discourse connective *datte* (*but-because*)—a frequent conversational justification marker. Our analysis of *datte* suggests that use of the marker presupposes sensing opposition in one's interlocutor. If Japanese three-year-olds are competent users of the connective in a context in which they need to defend their beliefs, this finding points to an ability to understand the mental states of others as evidenced in a verbal challenge.

We first discuss the adult meanings and uses of *datte*. Second, we present the rationale for our research design and articulate our hypotheses about Japanese preschoolers' use of the connective. We then lay out the results of our two studies, and we conclude with some observations and comments about the implications of our findings.

Meanings of *Datte*

Several Japanese linguists have analyzed *datte*. Maynard (1993), for example, describes the functions of this connective in terms of "position," "dispute," and "support," following categories suggested by Schiffrin (1987). Position refers to a speaker's commitment to an idea; dispute to opposition to the expressed position; and support to utterances categorized as providing explanation, justification, or defense of a disputed position. Maynard argues that *datte* is used with the intent to support a position uttered in a context in which that position is in dispute (Maynard 1993, 107). Hasunuma (1995) suggests that *datte* occurs in contexts in which the speaker believes that the hearer, or some indefinite third person, may hold a different opinion from the speaker's. Mori (1999) considers use of *datte* in three contexts: delivering agreement, delivering disagreement, and pursuing agreement. In the cases of delivering and pursuing agreement, however, the speaker perceives an external, third-party challenge or opposing position, and the agreement the speaker seeks or offers is to build solidarity with the speaker's interlocutor against the perceived or potential third-party challenge.

We suggest that all of the insights gleaned by these previous considerations of *datte* can be encapsulated as follows: Speakers use *datte* when they believe they need to justify their own positions against opposition explicitly expressed, implicitly conveyed, or presumed to be commonly held by others (Yamamoto, Matsui, and McCagg, in press). We further claim that *datte* semantically encodes (as opposed to pragmatically implicates) the speaker's attitude that the information contained in the utterance immediately following the connective strengthens the speaker's position and weakens the position held by the hearer or some indefinite third person. The English causal connective *because* and the Japanese equivalent *kara* encode a causal relation only, although they may pragmatically implicate the speaker's attitude when they are used in a context in which the hearer's attitude clearly stands in opposition to that of the speaker. The following examples illustrate typical adult uses of *datte*. The "but" sense of *datte* may be seen most clearly in (1), where A explicitly states disapproval of B's action:

(1) A: I think you've been spending too much on your shoes recently.
B: *Datte* (*But-because*) these were half price.

Often, *datte* appears at the onset of answers to why-questions when disapproval is detected, as in (2):

(2) A: Why did you buy another pair of shoes?
B: *Datte* (*But-because*) they were half price.

Here B's use of *datte* suggests an interpretation of A's utterance in which implicit disapproval of B's action is conveyed by the why-question. Note that why-questions, in general, do not necessarily communicate implicit challenges. In (2), however, *datte* is followed by a justification, which further indicates that B has detected a challenge. When no challenge is sensed in a why-question, one need only provide the genuine causal marker *kara* (*because*), as in (3):

(3) A: Why did you buy another pair of shoes?
B: They were half price *kara (because)*.

Datte also is used when there is no ostensive challenge in the immediate communicative context but the speaker still senses one, as in (4):

(4) I bought another pair of shoes yesterday. *datte* (*but-because*) they were half price.

Unlike the uses of *datte* illustrated in (1) and (2), this use requires speaker ability to infer what the hearer likely believes without any help from verbal clues.

Rationale and Hypotheses

Our sketch of the semantics of *datte* suggests that full, adult-like understanding of the connective rests on an ability to understand others' mental states—in this case, perceiving doubt about or denial of the validity of one's stated proposition. Moreover, to be able to provide an adequate justification in the utterance that follows *datte*, one must have some sense of what consists of good evidence to support one's position. With fully developed adult meta-representational abilities, inferring others' attitude toward one's own beliefs usually is not difficult, and we can safely assume that adults who use *datte* are fully competent to do that.

When we talk about young children's use of newly acquired words—*datte* included—however, we cannot assume that they understand the meaning of the word in the same way adults do. Nelson (1996), for example, points out that although English children begin to use causal expressions such as "because" and "so" early in the preschool period, full understanding of their logical implications can be achieved only much later. An important question arises when we try to determine what young preschoolers are cognitively capable of on the basis of their use of language. If doubt is cast on using the semantics of words such as "because" or *datte* as an index of development, what rationale do we have for basing our assessment of children's understanding of causality or others' mental states on their use of the words?

The answer to the question, we believe, lies in how children come to understand and use new words. Something happens between the time a child first uses an expression with limited understanding of its meaning and the time the child achieves full understanding of it—but what? In an emerging view, learning the meaning of a new word requires a child to continuously extract important features of the discourse contexts in which adults use the word, until the child acquires the adult-like semantics of the word (Nelson 1996). Nelson provides numerous examples that support the claim, including that English children's use of the causal expressions mentioned above greatly improves between ages two and three years, as does their grasp of the format of psychological justification. In Nelson's view, such an improvement is a result of children's successful inferences about appropriate uses of the causal expressions, which ultimately lead them to achieve full grasp of the expressions' logical implications.

Nelson's claim that "use before meaning" proceeds and develops into "meaning from use" is independently supported by numerous studies that show that young children are sensitive to discourse contexts in which a novel word is used and are able to use these contexts to hypothesize the meaning of the word in the context (Baldwin 1993; Bloom 2000; Clark 1997; Tomasello and Akhtar 1995). Crucially, children's ability to pick up appropriate contextual clues to learn the meaning of a novel word may be a by-product of their developing theory of mind ability (Sperber 2000; Sperber and Wilson 2002). We endorse this constructive, inferential view of meaning acquisition and further assume that the ability to extract important contextual features relevant to a novel word is most vital when a child has to learn lexical items that do not have perceptible real-world counterparts—prime examples of which include discourse connectives, particles, pronouns, and other function words.

This view of meaning acquisition assumes that long before children achieve full understanding of the meaning of *datte*, they need to be able to extract relevant features of the context in which the connective is used by adults. The key feature to be noticed by children in the context of *datte*-use is that of the speaker's opinion having been challenged. In this dynamic view of meaning acquisition, we hypothesize that if children's use of *datte* reflects their grasp of this particular contextual feature, there is an indication that children correctly understood that their opinion has been challenged in the communicative context.

This fundamental assumption, in turn, leads us to investigate exactly how young Japanese children use the connective during the preschool period. The findings of our studies should show increased sophistication over time in their understanding of others' challenging attitudes toward their own beliefs. Our hypotheses are as follows:

(a) If children are capable of using *datte* in any of its appropriate ways, prior to passing the standard false-belief test, it strongly supports the view that there are intermediate stages of mind-reading that require more finely tuned instruments to capture.

(b) If Japanese children can use *datte* as in examples (1) and (2) above, it strongly suggests that they can understand the mental states of others—at least to the extent that they can understand challenges expressed in others' utterances.

(c) The level of mind-reading ability required to use *datte* in the absence of an immediate challenge, as in (4), is greater than that required to produce a *datte* utterance in response to a challenge indicated in the immediately preceding communicative context, as in (1) and (2).

(d) The quality of utterances immediately following occurrences of *datte* will gradually come to approximate adult-like *datte* justifications over time.

Study 1: Analysis of Longitudinal Data

To begin to see when and how children start to use *datte*, we examined the longitudinal data available in J-CHAT, a Japanese children's speech corpus (Miyata 2000). Reliable data are available only for a single child called Tai. Generalizations on the basis of a single case study are unwise, but the patterns of use discernable in the Tai corpus fit the picture of acquisition outlined above. Tai's utterances were collected between ages 1;5 and 3;2 and were gathered during once-a-week recording sessions that lasted for about forty minutes each. A total of seventy-five sessions make up the Tai corpus.

Table 3.1 shows the number of utterances containing *datte* spoken by Tai. His first use of *datte* appeared three days before his second birthday (1;11.28). Near the end of his second year, use of the connective seems to jump: Twenty-five of the thirty-two total uses of *datte* by Tai occur in the last six months of the record.

All thirty-two instances of *datte* produced by Tai were in response to his mother's verbal challenges. Although these challenges were expressed in various forms, Tai appears focused on his mother's intent. Table 3.2 shows the kinds of challenges to which Tai responded with *datte* before age three years.

Tai's *datte*-utterances reveal a clear pattern of use. His initial uses of *datte* were all prompted by explicit opinion assertions, rather than why-questions. By the age of three years, Tai had acquired the use of the connective as a part of his responses to why-questions. It is worthy of note that in his early responses to why-questions, Tai began to use the pragmatically simpler causal marker *kara*, well before he started using *datte.* Given that why-questions encode a speaker's desire for the hearer to respond with a reason, and given the causal meaning of *kara,* we expected this finding. We also anticipated that later, when Tai was able to understand the implicit challenge pragmatically communicated by some why-questions, his use of *datte* in the same context would follow. The data support our expectations. Finally, our inspection of Tai's utterances revealed an interesting characteristic in his later use of *datte*: Tai frequently and legitimately used causal markers such as *kara*, or *mon* together with *datte,* in utterances such as (5):

(5) Tai's age: 2;10.20
Mother: *Konnichiwa*. Hello.
Tai: *Demo, hairenaiyo*. But, you cannot enter this.

Table 3.1.
Number of utterances containing *datte* spoken by Tai

Age range	1;09–1;11	2;00–2;02	2;03–2;05	2;06–2;08	2;09–2;11	3;00–3;01
No. of sessions	12	13	12	11	11	5
MLU[a]	2.44	3.1	3.17	3.65	4.17	4.43
Frequency of *datte*	1	3	2	1	11	14

[a]MLU = mean length of utterance

Table 3.2.
Number of Tai's *datte*-responses by adult challenge types

	Age of Tai					
Challenge types	1;09–1;11	2;00–2;02	2;03–2;05	2;06–2;08	2;09–2;11	3;00–3;01
Assertion					3	2
Suggestion		2				4
Request for confirmation	1		1		3	1
Why-question					2	7
Request for action			1		2	
Accusation				1		
Uncategorizable		1			1	
Total	1	3	2	1	11	14

Mother: *Doshite?* Why?
Tai: *Datte, ookii kara.* But-because, because it is too big.

Such use clearly shows that Tai assigned *datte* a distinct function from that of genuine causal markers such as *kara*.

The corpus of this single child strongly suggests that children can develop command of the discourse connective sometime between ages two and three years. As expected, however, the naturalistic data did not contain any examples of *datte*-utterances used to justify beliefs or statements. To elicit children's justification of their own beliefs, we presented children with a very specific communicative setting in Study 2.

Study 2: Collection and Analysis of Elicited Data

Participants

Sixteen 3-year-olds (seven males and nine females) and twenty 4-year-olds (ten males and ten females) participated in this study. Data were collected at the Chokyuuji Nursery School in suburban Tokyo over a six-week period during May and June 2002.

Methods

Method 1: False-Belief Test To investigate children's development of theory of mind, we conducted a Japanese version of the "Smarties" test—a standard false-belief task—using a "Pocky" package to conceal the unexpected contents (in this case, small batteries). Passing this test is thought to indicate that a child is capable of attributing to others beliefs that differ from the child's own.

Method 2: "Hidden Picture" Game We devised an activity that would engage children in making difficult guesses; guesses they might well have doubts about; and guesses that, in the course of the activity, were challenged by the adult experimenters. Four "hidden pictures" were prepared for use in the study. Each picture was concealed by a cover sheet that had four windows cut to reveal a different—and potentially misleading—portion of the picture underneath. After greetings were exchanged and the children indicated that they understood the nature of the game, the first window was opened, and the children were encouraged to make a guess about the picture beneath. Once a guess was offered, the adult researcher probed for reasons or explanations for why the children thought the picture was what they had guessed. The adult portions of each interaction were scripted so that the children would be presented with the same set of explicit and implicit verbal challenges in the form of why-questions, counter-assertions, alternative suggestions, and requests for clarification.

The interactions with the children were recorded on videotape and audiotape for later transcription and coding.

Results

In this section we lay out the principal results of our analysis of elicited data. We begin with the results of the false belief tests for three- and four-year olds, which we present in table 3.3. As expected—based on many studies that employ the false-belief test as a measure of cognitive development—the test proved to be almost impossible for the three-year-olds in our study, and results with the four-year-olds were mixed. Table 3.3 also shows the numbers of three- and four-year-olds who used *datte* in the hidden picture game and the number of those three- and four-year-olds who failed the false-belief test but used *datte* in communicatively appropriate ways. As suggested by the numbers presented in table 3.3, at least some of the three- and four-year-olds who do not pass the false-belief test do use *datte* in certain contexts. We discuss the implications of the results—showing use of *datte* by children who did not pass the false-belief test—in the discussion section below.

Table 3.4 shows the numbers of challenges of each type that were addressed to the children in the study. Imbalances in these numbers are a consequence of trying to maintain naturalistic conversation with the children.

Table 3.3.
False-belief test results and *datte* use

	Result of false-belief test		Number of children	Failed FB test
Age	Pass	Fail	who used *datte*	but used *datte*
Three-year-olds (n = 16)	1	15	10	10
Four-year-olds (n = 20)	6	14	13	9

Table 3.4.
Number of challenge types addressed to participants

Challenge type	Three-year-olds	Four-year-olds
Counter-assertion	40	51
Alternative suggestion	124	129
Request for confirmation	248	312
Why-question	230	219
Request for action	10	14
Total	652	725

We coded children's responses to verbal challenges made by the experimenter into six categories. Table 3.5 shows those six categories and an illustrative example for each.

Table 3.6 shows the types of child responses to the total number of adult challenges. The *datte* responses and explanations arguably require greater communicative skill and more sophisticated cognitive ability than do reiterations of previous utterances or simple yes/no responses—which, in turn, typically are more appropriate

Table 3.5.
Types of children's responses to adult challenges

Response type	Coded example
Datte	A: *Kujira-san no shippo kana?* "Could it be whale's tail?"
	C: *Datte, kujirasan ne shippo wa haato ni natteru no.* "But/because a whale's tail is heart-shaped."
Explanation	A: *Kore sa kirin-san janai?* "Isn't this a giraffe?"
	C: *Chiaguyo. Kirinsan wa butsubutsu ni natteru.* "No. Giraffes have a spotted pattern."
Reiteration	C: *Sakkaa booru.* "Its's a soccer ball."
	A: *Doushite korega sakkaa booru nano?* "Why is it a soccer ball?"
	C: *Sakaa booru.* "It's a soccer ball."
Yes/no	C: *Zousan no ohana.* "It's an elephant's trunk."
	A: *Honto?* "Really?"
	C: *Un.* "Yeah."
Revision	C: *Jitensha.* "It's a bike."
	A: *Jitensha? Honto?* "A bike? Really?"
	C: *Baiku.* "It's a motorcycle."
Other	A: *Doushite kore kumasan?* "Why is this a bear?"
	C: . . .

Table 3.6.
Number of response types addressed to challenges

Response type	Three-year-olds	Four-year-olds
Datte	55	79
Explanation	129	181
Reiteration	105	97
Yes/no	154	233
Revision	58	62
Other	151	73
Total	652	725

than "other" types of responses when some defense of a position presumably is called for. Some evidence for this claim is presented in table 3.6, which indicates that more four-year-olds than three-year-olds offer explanations in the face of challenges.

Table 3.7 shows the number of *datte* utterances produced by the children, according to the types of challenges to which they were responding. Most of the *datte* utterances produced by the children came in response to why-questions. Requests for confirmation also elicited a small number of *datte* utterances, whereas counter-assertions and alternative suggestions elicited almost no *datte* utterances.

To address the possible objection that the children were only providing *datte* in a nonthinking, formulaic way, and to address our fourth hypothesis, we looked at what kinds of information the children provided after their *datte* utterances. We coded this information into five categories: appropriate explanation; repetition; *datte*-alone; inappropriate explanation; and unclear. Table 3.8 shows examples of these categories (except the last one).

Table 3.9 presents the coded results of this analysis. Although there is a clear increase in the ratio of appropriate explanations following *datte* use from the three-year-old group to the four-year-old group, even the three-year-olds provided appropriate explanations following their uses of *datte* about 64 percent of the time—

Table 3.7.
Number of *datte*-utterances produced according to types of challenges

Challenge type	Three-year-olds	Four-year-olds
Counter-assertion	1	2
Alternative suggestion	2	5
Request for confirmation	9	12
Why-question	43	59
Request for action	0	1
Total	55	79

Table 3.8.
Types of child utterances that followed their use of *datte*

Response type	Coded example
Appropriate explanation	C: *Zousan.* "(It's) an elephant." A: *Houtou? Kore, kirin-san dayo.* "Really? This is a giraffe." C: *Chigauyo. Datte, kirin-san tte mizutamato chairo damon.* "No, it's not. But-because, a giraffe has spots and a brown (pattern)."
Repetition	C: *Minamino shima.* "(It's) a southern island." A: *Doushite kore ga minamino shima nano?* "Why is this a southern island?" C: *Datte, kireina minami no shima nanda mon ne.* "But-because, because it's a beautiful southern island."
Datte alone	A: *Kore wa jitensha no taiya kana*? "These might be bicycle tires." C: *Chigau.* "It is not." A: *Nande?* "Why?" C: *Datte.* "But-because."
Inappropriate explanation	A: *Doushite kore okao ja naino?* "Why isn't this a face (of a car)?" C: *Wakannai.* "I don't know." A: *Okao aru yone.* "(A car) has a face, doesn't it?" C: *Datte, yoru demo kuruma wa hashitteru mon.* "But-because, because a car runs even at night."

suggesting that they were aware that some justification of their previous statements was called for.

Discussion

Only one of the sixteen three-year-olds passed the false-belief test, yet ten of them used *datte* in response to a variety of explicit and implicit verbal challenges. More of the four-year-olds passed the false-belief test, but nine of the four-year-olds who failed this test used *datte* in fully appropriate ways. These results suggest that children who are unable to make the appropriate inference of false belief in the "Smarties" test nevertheless are able to understand when an interlocutor holds a belief or an opinion that does not match their own; moreover, when verbally queried, they can

Table 3.9.
Number of utterance types that followed *datte*

Age	Total no. of *datte* used	Appropriate explanation	Repetition	*Datte* alone	Inappropriate explanation	Unclear
Three-year-olds	55	35 (64%)	4 (7%)	5 (9%)	4 (7%)	7 (13%)
Four-year-olds	79	70 (89%)	0 (0%)	5 (6%)	4 (5%)	0 (0%)

mark their utterances with an expression that indicates that they recognize the need to defend their own belief.

Although we did not observe large differences in the verbal behavior of three-year-olds and four-year-olds, the older children tended to use *datte* slightly more often, and they provided explanations for their responses more frequently than the younger children did. The older children also produced far fewer responses that were difficult to categorize.

In terms of what preceded *datte* utterances, both age groups used the discourse connective nearly 80 percent of the time to respond to why-questions. Responses to confirmation requests accounted for most of the rest of the occurrences of *datte.* In contrast with counter-assertions and alternative suggestions, these adult utterance types only implicitly carry challenging intent. This finding suggests to us that even three-year-olds can notice implicit challenges in their adult interlocutor's utterances.

Finally, the information provided by children after their *datte* utterances further suggests that they are not mindlessly responding without recognizing the implicit challenges; instead, it suggests that in many cases they do recognize the need to provide support for their own assertions.

Conclusion and Implications

We believe that the findings of this study are consistent with the hypotheses we set forth. Three- and four-year-old children apparently do not use *datte* in the absence of a perceived verbal challenge. That is, they do not appear to be able yet to mark their speech with a discourse device that indicates awareness of another's potential objection in the absence of immediate verbal clues. When a challenge is verbally manifested, however—either explicitly (as in being told that the other person has a different opinion) or implicitly (as in being asked why one thinks something is true)—even three-year-olds can, and sometimes do, mark their utterances with *datte.*

According to de Villiers et al. (2002), children become fully capable of providing adequate explanation only when they are equipped with theory of mind capabilities. The fact that some children can use a discourse connective such as *datte* prior to being able to pass the standard false-belief test, however, suggests that development of pragmatic inferencing capabilities precedes—and to some extent may be independent of—full-fledged development of theory of mind capabilities (as measured by the standard false-belief test). Our study participants' use of *datte* strongly indicates that they know when they need to provide good evidence for their beliefs, even though they do not always appear capable of providing it. We would argue that by having their beliefs challenged in the immediate communicative context, children come to understand that others can and do have different thoughts than they do, and this understanding at some point can extend to situations in which there are no verbal clues to indicate that others hold beliefs that differ from one's own. To see more precisely how and when this shift begins to happen, however, a more sensitive test of mind-reading abilities in children seems necessary. We are working on developing a false-belief test that gets at young children's mind-reading abilities of speaker intentions. Similar work is being conducted by Happe and Loth (2002) within a word-learning paradigm.

Our study also provides strong support for the dynamic view of meaning acquisition. In a study described in Yamamoto, Matsui, and McCagg (in press), we found that five-year-old children are able to use *datte* when no objection was explicitly expressed in the same experimental setting as Study 2. This finding suggests that these five-year-olds sensed potential objections to the guesses they had made and tried to defend themselves beforehand by presenting counterevidence to overrule the inferred objection. No such uses were observed with the three- and four-year-olds in Study 2. This finding combined with our findings about the difference between three- and four-year-olds' use of the connective strongly suggest a gradual developmental pattern in children's ability to use *datte* appropriately. Children's increasing knowledge about the world and their developing cognitive abilities, including meta-representational ability, surely contribute to their mastery of language use. The most important implications of our study, however, are that such mastery is gradual and continuous and begins well before children can talk about false beliefs and that children's use of language provides an ideal platform for such an investigation. Inasmuch as many precursors of theory of mind seem to be required to enable children to learn the meanings of new words, much more effort should be made to investigate the cognitive development of this period. It is no secret that young children are superbly good at learning word meanings from a very young age, yet we still lack full cognitive explanation for that ability.

REFERENCES

Astington, Janet W. 1998. The language of intention: Three ways of doing it. In *Developing Theories of intention: Social understanding and self-control,* ed. Philip D. Zelazo, Janet W. Astington, and David R. Olson, 295–315. Mahwah, N.J.: Erlbaum.

Astington, Janet W., and Jennifer M. Jenkins. 1999. A longitudinal study of the relation between language and theory-of-mind development. *Developmental Psychology* 35, no. 5:1311–20.

Baldwin, Dare A. 1993. Infants' ability to consult the speaker for clues to word reference. *Journal of Child Language* 20:395–418.

Bartsch, Karen, and Henry M. Wellman. 1995. *Children talk about the mind.* Oxford: Oxford University Press.

Bloom, Lois, and Joanne B. Caspides. 1987. Sources of meaning in the acquisition of complex syntax: The example case of causality. *Journal of Experimental Child Psychology* 43:112–28.

Bloom, Paul. 2000. *How children learn the meanings of words.* Cambridge, Mass.: MIT Press.

Bretherton, Inge, and Marjorie Beeghly. 1982. Talking about internal states: The acquisition of an explicit theory of mind. *Developmental Psychology* 18:906–21.

Clark, Eve. V. 1997. Conceptual perspective and lexical choice in acquisition. *Cognition* 64:1–37.

de Villiers, Jill G., and Peter A. de Villiers. 2000. Linguistic determinism and the understanding of false-beliefs. In *Children's Reasoning and the Mind*, ed. Peter Mitchell and Kevin J. Riggs, 191–228. Hove, U.K.: Psychology Press.

de Villiers, Jill G., Nicole Eddy, Kimberley Broderick, and Jennie Pyers. 2002. A longitudinal study of explanation action. Paper presented at Joint Conference of 9th International Congress for the Study of Child Language and the Symposium on Research in Child Language Disorders, Madison, Wisconsin.

Dunn, Judy, and Jane R. Brown. 1993. Early conversations about causality: Content, pragmatics and developmental change. *British Journal of Developmental Psychology* 11:107–23.

Dunn, Judy, and Penny Munn. 1987. Development of justification in disputes with mother and sibling. *Developmental Psychology* 23, no. 6:791–98.

Dunn, Judy, Jane Brown, Cheryl Slomkowski, Caroline Tesla, and Lise Youngblade. 1991. Young children's understanding of other people's feelings and beliefs: Individual differences and their antecedents. *Child Development* 62:1352–66.

Eisenberg, Ann R., and Catherine Garvey. 1981. Children's use of verbal strategies in resolving conflicts. *Discourse Processes* 4:149–70.

Farrar, Jeffery M., and Lisa Maag. 2002. Early language development and the emergence of a theory of mind. *First Language* 22:197–213.

Happe, Francesca, and Eva Loth. 2002. Theory of mind and tracking speaker's intentions. *Mind and Language* 17, nos. 1–2:24–36.

Hasunuma, Akiko. 1995. Danwa setsuzokugo *datte* ni tsuite (On the discourse connective *datte*). *Himejidokkyo Daigaku Gaikokugogakubu Kiyou* 8:265–81.

Hood, Lois, and Lois Bloom. 1979. What, when and how and why: A longitudinal study of early expression of causality. *Monographs of the Society for Research in Child Development* 44, no. 6 (serial no.181).

Lalonde, Chris E., and Michael J. Chandler. 1995. False belief understanding goes to school: On the social-emotional consequences of coming early or late to a first theory of mind. *Cognition and Emotion* 9:167–85.

Maynard, Senko. 1993. *Discourse modality: Subjectivity, emotion and voice in the Japanese language.* Amsterdam: John Benjamins.

Miyata, Susanne. 2000. The Tai corpus: Longitudinal speech data of a Japanese boy age 1;5.20–3;1.1. *Bulletin of Syukutoku Junior College* 39:77–85.

Mori, Junko. 1999. *Negotiating agreement and disagreement in Japanese: Connective expressions and turn construction*. Amsterdam: John Benjamins.

Nelson, Katherine. 1996. *Language in cognitive development: The emergence of the mediated mind.* Cambridge: Cambridge University Press.

Perner, Josef., Susan R. Leekam, and Heinz Wimmer. 1987. Three-year-olds' difficulty with false belief: The case for a conceptual deficit. *British Journal of Developmental Psychology* 5:125–37.

Schiffrin, Deborah. 1987. *Discourse markers.* Cambridge: Cambridge University Press.

Sperber, Dan. 2000. Metarepresentations in an evolutionary perspective. In *Metarepresentations: A multidisciplinary perspective*, ed. Dan Sperber, 117–37. Oxford: Oxford University Press.

Sperber, Dan, and Deirdre Wilson. 2002. Pragmatics, modularity and mind-reading. *Mind and Language* 17, nos. 1–2:3–23.

Tager-Flusberg, Helen. 2000. Language and understanding minds: Connections in autism. In *Understanding other minds: Perspectives from developmental cognitive neuroscience*, ed. Simon Baron-Cohen, Helen Tager-Flusberg, and Donald J. Cohen, 124–49. Oxford: Oxford University Press.

Tesla, Caroline, and Judy Dunn. 1992. Getting along or getting your own way: The development of young children's use of argument in conflicts with mother and sibling. *Social Development* 1:107–21.

Tomasello, Michael, and Nameera Akhtar. 1995. Two-year-olds use pragmatic cues to differentiate reference to objects and actions. *Cognitive Development* 10:201–24.

Wellman, Henry M., and Jacqueline D Woolley. 1990. From simple desires to ordinary beliefs: The early development of everyday psychology. *Cognition* 35:245–75.

Yamamoto, Taeko, Tomoko Matsui, and Peter McCagg. In press. Use of the connective *datte* and development of theory of mind. *Studies in Language Sciences* 4.

4

"Because" as a Marker of Collaborative Stance in Preschool Children's Peer Interactions

AMY KYRATZIS
University of California, Santa Barbara

IN HER DEFINITIVE BOOK on discourse markers, Deborah Schiffrin (1987) documented that particles such as "so," "because," "now," and so forth function at many levels of discourse beyond the level of the sentence and have more than a semantic meaning. With regard to the specific discourse marker "because," Schiffrin argues that the marker can function at the action level of the talk, at the level of participation frameworks, and at the ideational level. In terms of the action level, "because" is used to mark causal relationships between speech acts such as directives, questions, and claims and the reasons these speech acts are committed. At the level of participation frameworks, at a turn boundary use of "because" in sentence-initial position by a speaker can signal continuity with the previous speaker's topic, thereby indexing support of that previous speaker. Actually, Schiffrin found that only "so" but not "because" worked in this way in her texts, but Schleppegrell (1991), using Schiffrin's (1987) model, found "because" to operate at the level of participation frameworks to signal continuity of a partner idea across speaker turns. Finally, discourse markers can function at the textual level to create larger, thematic ideational structures, creating cohesion through the talk.

Andersen et al. (1999) argue that one function of discourse markers that has not been well studied is "their use as markers of the social relationships between interlocutors in any speech event" (1340)—that is, their use at the level of participation frameworks. Andersen et al. extrapolated from the finding that markers such as "well," "so," and "now" function as boundary markers to the implications for social relationships, arguing that among a group of speakers, the asymmetrical privilege to mark new topics or topic transitions would index greater power in the talk and an authoritative stance. They found that preschoolers taking on authoritative roles such as doctors, teachers, and fathers in puppet role play were more likely to use these forms than the same children enacting less authoritative roles such as nurse, student, and mother. This finding is noteworthy because it suggests that speakers index their social relationships to one another through their use of discourse markers. By studying the comparative use of discourse markers—who uses them and who does not—we can hope to discern the stances toward one another that speakers are seeking to construct in their talk in different settings.

The study I describe in this chapter took just such a comparative approach to the study of discourse markers. By comparing contexts in which "because" is used to those in which it is not used, the study investigates what aspects of social relationship speakers seek to index with "because." In this study of talk in preschool children's same-sex friendship groups, "because" was used more in girls' friendship groups than in boys' friendship groups. The main research question of the analysis was to discover why. Girls' talk was characterized by collaborative narratives of pretense (Cook-Gumperz 1995) and boys' by arguments, in which speakers opposed one another and spoke authoritatively ("No, you can't do that, two people are in there!"). By analyzing features of the social contexts in which "because" was and was not produced, the study was designed to answer the following questions: Could use of "because" have to do with the establishment of a collaborative stance? Could omitting the marker have to do with the establishment of an authoritative, threatening demeanor?

This study undertook a qualitative analysis of the use of "because." The analysis reported here examines whether children were using "because" to establish a collaborative participation framework, in the sense of continuing the partner's turn, as described by Schleppegrell (1991). The analysis was also designed to look at whether "because" was used to establish a collaborative participation framework in other ways. The study also examined how "because" was used at the level of action structures and ideational structures.

The Study

Children in two preschool classrooms in California participated in an ethnographic study of talk in friendship groups. The children were from middle-class families. Ten four-year-old girls and eleven four-year-old boys, who participated in friendship groups of three or more children in the classroom, were counted in the analysis. Two-thirds were European American, and one-third were of other ethnicities. The children were followed and videotaped in their friendship groups in each classroom over one year.

Interactions were transcribed, and transcripts were analyzed for justifications—defined as explanations of states and events in the world or as reasons for the commission of speech acts and claims. (A second coder analyzed one-quarter of the transcripts, and there was an agreement of 83 percent between the two coders in identifying justifications in the texts.) Then we examined whether these justifications contained a "because" marker between the head act and justification. Qualitative analysis of how "because" was used for marking participation frameworks and other uses was conducted. Some of these factors were then entered into quantitative analyses.

Results

"Because" at the Action and Ideational Levels of the Talk

The comparative feature that the analysis was designed to explain was why girls' groups used higher rates of marking of justifications with "because" than boys' groups. Of the justifications produced, girls' groups marked 23–45 percent with "because." Boys' groups marked only 7–9 percent of their justifications.

One feature that was considered to explain the difference in "because" marking between girls' and boys' friendship group talk was the types of causal relationships that occurred in the justifications (Sweetser 1990). Whereas boys justified mostly at the speech act level, producing justifications mainly for why they were committing specific speech acts—particularly requests and prohibitions—girls justified at the speech act, content, and epistemic levels of the talk. That is, girls specified reasons for why events in the real world occurred (Content-Level Causals) and for beliefs (Epistemic Causals), as well as for speech acts. The following set of eight justifications comes from a text produced by a friendship group of girls that was analyzed for these uses. As the selected examples show, the justifications produced operate at both the ideational level (content level) and action levels (speech act level and epistemic level) of the talk.

1. I'm sure glad we're both handsome and pretty, because if I married Raggedy Ann, I would have a really dumb life (content level)
2. Raggedy Ann made a sound/she wanted to kill him/ (content level)
3. Get out of here! I'm mad! (speech act level, content level)
4. Have you healed your back yet? Cause I really need to take you to the midnight ball. (speech act level)
5. And tonight it's cold// 'cause it's the first day of winter// (epistemic, content level)
6. No she can't (steal one of your pods)/ I have the strongest horns (epistemic, content level)
7. C1: I hate being poor

   C2: Well *her house (which I've just given you) is warm

   C1: Because I'm a summer dinosaur (speech act level)
8. When it's warm in the night *I go out/ 'cause last night it was warm (speech act level)

In the boys' groups, justifications were mostly of the speech act–level variety ("No, you can't go in, two people are in there.").

Sweetser (1990) argues that speech act–level and epistemic causals—those with requests and claims in the main clause, in which the causal clause explains the reason for committing the speech act or claim—would have more discontinuous marking between the two clauses of "because" constructions (i.e., they would be more likely to have comma intonation than continuous intonation). This discontinuous marking comes about because the main clauses entail commission of the speech act or claim; hence, there is less presupposition than in a content-level causal, which does not commit a speech act. If boys produce more speech act–level causal constructions than content-level causals relative to girls, and if speech act–level causals have more discontinuous syntax and prosody between the clauses, these factors might explain the difference between unmarked and marked constructions that were observed between boys' and girls' groups.

In the specialized discourse context of children conducting pretend play and arguments in this study, this explanation did not account for more "because" marking in girls' groups. (This explanation might hold up in other discourse contexts—for example, with adults engaged in more reflective forms of talk.) Speech act–level causals did not have less "because" marking than content-level causals or any other type. For all four types of causal relationship, the rate of "because" marking was the same: 50–60 percent. Therefore, the high incidence of speech act–level causals produced in boys' friendship group talk, and the lack of production of causal constructions in other domains, do not explain why boys' groups produced less "because" marking. Because the action-level versus content-level uses did not explain the difference between girls' and boys' talk in "because" marking, the analysis next looked at how "because" was operating in the marking of participation frameworks.

"Because" in Participation Frameworks

The most salient aspect of use of "because" in these girls' groups' narratives seemed to be in terms of its use in marking a participation framework of solidarity or collaboration. Schleppegrell (1991) describes a use of "because" as a discourse marker for indexing a positive stance toward the partner. Namely, the speaker would use "because" to continue a partner's idea across speaker turns. In this study, "because" was used in this way, as when one child made a proposal (e.g., "[it would be] so ugly and gross") and the other provided a reason the proposal was a good idea ("because inside of me looks uglier than outside"). In addition to this use, we observed two further, related ways that justifications could continue or validate a partner's idea across speaker turns; we termed all three of these uses "validating." The first of the two additional uses was when "because" marked a justification that followed the speaker's own agreement with a partner proposal (indicated through "yeah"). For example, if child 1 said, "and I say, let *you be in Raggedy Ann's home," and child 2 said, "Yeah// because I *hate being poor," we considered this use a validating use of a justification because the justification provides a reason for agreeing with the partner. The second of the two additional uses was when a justification followed a speaker's own elaboration of a partner proposal in the speaker's own turn. For example, in one instance, child 1 proposed that the prince and the princess were in love. Child 2 elaborated this idea ("I'm sure glad that we're both handsome and pretty"), then provided a reason why this elaboration was a good idea ("because if *I married Raggedy A::nn/ *I would have a really dumb life"). These three types of "because" use all involve the use of a justification to affirm a partner proposal (either by providing a justification for it or by providing a justification for agreement to or elaboration of it). "Because" seemed to occur with just such validating uses of justifications. In these ways, "because" seemed to be used to mark support of the partner.

Figures 4.1 and 4.2, considered together, demonstrate that the use of "because" to mark validation is a good explanation of the gender difference in use of "because." Girls used more validating justifications. Moreover—for girls and for boys—the context of validation was the one that favored use of "because." Figure 4.1 shows the overall rate of validating, oppositional, and neutral justifications produced by the girls' and boys' friendship groups. The three girls' groups are shown on the left; the two boys' groups are shown on the right. As figure 4.1 shows, the three girls' groups used justification for validation more frequently than the two boys' groups in this

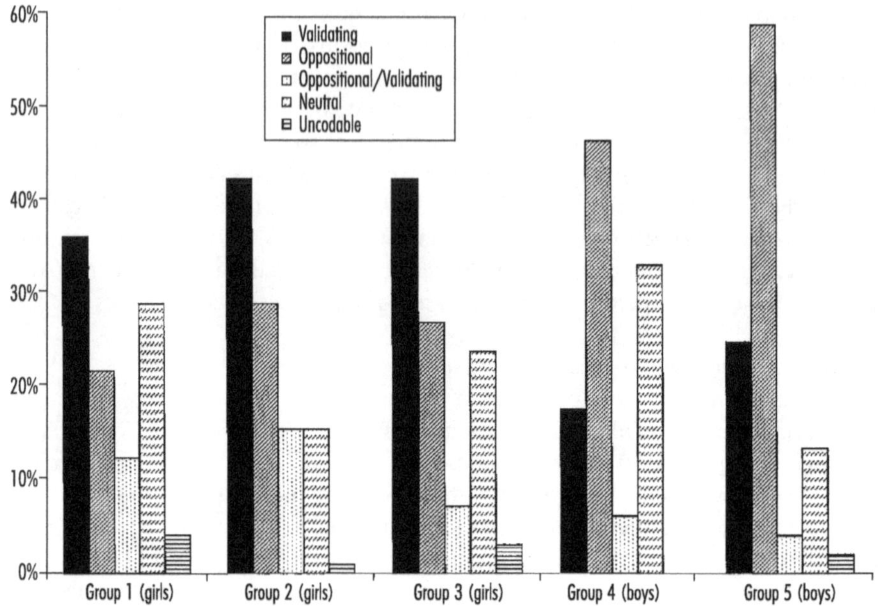

Figure 4.1. Motivation of justifications by group

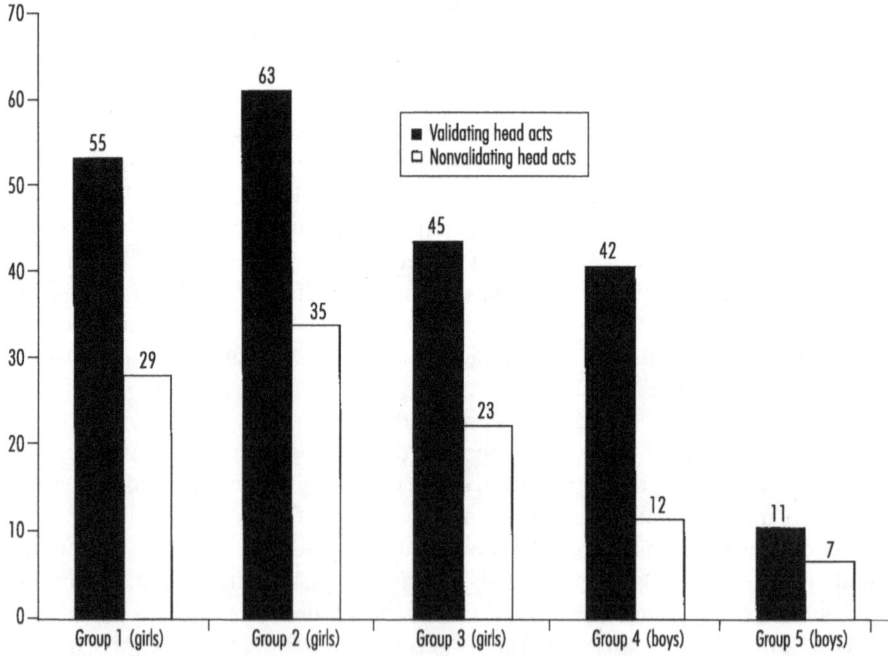

Figure 4.2. Allocation of validating and nonvalidating justifications to "because"

study, whereas the boys' groups used justification for opposition—that is, for disagreeing with the partner ("no, you can't go in, two people are in there")—more frequently than the girls' groups did.

We compared the proportion of validating justifications that received "because" to the proportion of oppositional and neutral justifications that received "because." Figure 4.2 shows the result of this analysis. For both girls' and boys' groups, validating justifications received considerably more "because" marking (at least 22 percent more and as much as 30 percent more—about twice as much as with other types of justifications).

These findings suggest that "because" goes to validating justifications and hence that speakers may use "because" strategically and indexically to mark the fact that they are confirming the partner in their talk—that is, to mark a collaborative floor. "Because" may be used as a discourse marker to mark the continuation of a partner idea across speaker turns and hence, in a collaborative way, to mark a certain type of participation framework and stance toward the partner in the talk—namely, a supportive stance. Girls' groups, which use more validating justifications, rely on "because" more.

Validating discourse marker uses are exemplified in excerpts from a transcript of talk produced within a girls' friendship group. The group had three members: Gwen, Barb, and Dee—although Gwen and Barb often played together without Dee. In the transcript, Gwen and Barb are enacting a script that—based on the thematic content of the play—was titled "Dating Dinosaurs." They are playing with Barney-like plastic dinosaur figures on a table, animating the voices of characters. The main protagonists of their scenario are "Gabriella," a princess; "the Prince"; and a contender for the Prince's affections, called "Raggedy Ann." In Example 1, Barb is enacting the Prince's role and Gwen is enacting Gabriella's role. The example shows use of a causal clause to provide support of a proposal made by the partner in the immediately preceding turn (i.e., a validating use of a justification), and that "because" is used to mark this partner continuation. (Justification constructions are indicated with arrows extending from the justification to the head act or source statement being modified.)

Example 1

1.	Barb	(as Prince) I *never would dream of biting off *your head/
2.	Gwen	(as Princess Gabriella) Ewww, right? It would be bloody/
3.	Barb	I would *never dream of biting off my wife's head/my wife's head/
4.	Gwen	I know/ and I never dream of *biting you with my tail/ my husband/ it
5.		would be so bloody/
6.	Barb	Yeah/
7.	Gwen	↗So ugly/ and gross/
8.	Barb	'Cause ["because"] inside of me it looks *uglier than the *outside/
9.	Gwen	Yes/ I know/

In line 8, Barb continues the idea Gwen introduced in the previous turn that biting off her husband's (the Prince's) tail would be "so ugly and gross." Barb supports this idea by saying that biting off her husband's tail would be ugly and gross "'cause inside of me it looks uglier than outside" (line 8). Note that prior to this line, Gwen had supported Barb's idea about the undesirability of biting off the head of a wife for several turns, with "right" and "I know" and the justification "it would be bloody" (first introduced in line 2 without the "because" marker). Barb, in turn, justifies the justification that Gwen had made of her proposal in line 2. The girls continually pick up and justify one another's ideas. This collaborative context both supports the use of "because" and is supported and constituted by the marker.

In example 2, supportive uses of causal clauses and discourse markers can be seen. Validating uses of justifications can be seen in lines 4, 5, 7, 8, 9, and 11. Four of these supportive justifications are rendered with "because."

Example 2

1.	Gwen	(as Princess Gabriella) Bye, bye, you guy/
2.		Can I go to my-can I live in her home?
3.	Barb	(as Prince) Sure/
4.	Gwen	Because *I don't have a home/
5.	Barb	After all *i'm the king/ and I say/
6.		let *you be in Raggedy Ann's home/
7.	Gwen	Yeah/ because I *hate being poor/
8.	Barb	Well *her home is really warm/ (xx)
9.	Gwen	Because *i'm a summer dinosaur/ *and a night dinosaur/
10.		a summer night dinosaur/ when it's *warm in the night
11.		time *I go out/ 'cause last night it was warm/
12.	Barb	But tonight it's cold/ 'cause it's the first day of winter/

The first validating justification occurs in line 4 ("because *I don't have a home"). Here Gwen supports her own request from line 1. Because Barb had already agreed to grant the request, however, in line 4 Gwen is supporting both her own request and Gwen's compliance to it with her justification; hence she also is supporting Gwen. The "because" seems to mark the fact that Gwen's utterance is support of support. Another justification that is support of support occurs in line 5, where Barb justifies why she complied with Gwen's request in line 2 and supported her ("after all, *i'm the king"). This justification receives a discourse marker ("after all") rather than "because," but it suggests that validating uses of justifications tend to get marked. In line 7, Gwen agrees with Barb's granting of the request (she says "yeah"). She then supports her agreement with Barb by giving a reason for it marked with "because" ("because I *hate being poor"). Barb's justification, in line 8, of Gwen's move (it's a good idea to pretend that the princess is really poor [and homeless] because Raggedy Ann's house is really warm) also is a supportive move; it gives a reason that Gwen had nothing to fear with respect to her stated fear in the previous line of "being poor." This move is marked with "well" rather than "because" but despite the marker of dispreference indexes a positive participation framework. The construction might be rephrased as "it is valid to hate being poor, but *her home (the confiscated home) is really warm" ("so it's okay or good that we pretended that you hate being poor"). In line 9, Gwen gives a reason that provides support for why Barb's proposal, stated in the previous turn, is a good idea—it's a good idea to pretend that the house that Gwen is getting is really warm because Gwen is a summer dinosaur. "Because" is repeatedly used either to justify the partner or to justify an agreement with the partner. These constructions are not comprehensible without interpreting them across several turns of talk.

In the last line, line 12, Barb seems to use "because" to introduce a justification of a pretend proposal that does not seem very supportive of Gwen. Gwen had stated that she is a summer dinosaur and likes to go out when it's warm. In line 12, Barb is suggesting that the night is cold, which seems to be a state of affairs that would harm Gwen. However, pretending that the night is cold might be a good idea from the perspective of the joint script being created. If the night is cold, it creates a state of affairs that renders the act made earlier in the example of the Prince (Barb) giving over the house confiscated from Raggedy Ann to Gwen's character, the Princess, even more meaningful or supportive. By supporting the idea of the coldness of the night, Barb is supporting the goodness of fit of the Prince's gesture, referenced earlier in the discourse (lines 3 and 5), to a current state of affairs (that it's cold). Barb's justification is supporting and validating the idea that had collaboratively emerged in the script. The "because" marks the fact that this justification is supportive of and validates the joint script: It refers back to the earlier move made by Barb (lines 3 and 5) and supports it.

Example 3 shows use of "because" as a discourse marker to build ideational units across utterances *within the speaker's own turn*. Though this use reinforces the speaker's own proposal, it also affirms the joint script in showing, through a series of proposals, how bad the protagonist Raggedy Ann was to the Princess. By using "because," Gwen shows that she is affirming their joint problem—the treachery of Raggedy Ann. By doing so, Gwen also is affirming the joint script that the children are building together, which has as its main idea the happiness of the Prince and Princess and the threat to their happiness posed by Raggedy Ann.

Example 3

1.	Barb	{I don't think so either/ oh/ no Gabriella's hurtful, so *now what do I do/
2.		the midnight ball is our *honeymoo::n/ [ac, f]}
3.	Gwen	Maybe you can take Raggedy Ann?
4.	Barb	No/ she's =(x)=
5.	Gwen	=Why= don't you just look over the (pry) tonight?
6.		because since Gabriella is hurt, I
7.		I don't think she can *dance, because she hurt her foot/

8. and she broke her ba::ck/
9. because *she pushed her off the ledge/
10. Barb Around the ledge/
11. Gwen Really she did/
12. Barb I *don't care about *that/ {just get out of here/ I'm ma::d![ff]}
13. [talking to the Raggedy Ann figure]

In line 5, Gwen proposes that because the Princess is indisposed, Barb, as the Prince, forget the ball. This idea in line 5 has been built up collaboratively over several turns (lines 1–5). In line 5 Gwen uses "because" to relate this proposal back to a main idea of the story: the bad nature of Raggedy Ann. Therefore, the justification ("because since Gabriella is hurt") justifies an elaborative— hence supportive—move and is in keeping with other uses of "because." Gwen does not stop there, however. She goes through several further justifications (lines 5–9): "since Gabriella is hurt, I don't think she can *dance, because she hurt her foot/and she broke her ba::ck/because *she pushed her off the ledge!" Gwen uses "because" to build an ideational unit across several utterances within her own turn. However, the complex idea that she is building is itself supportive or validating of what they have been doing together all along—building a case against Raggedy Ann. The sequence justifies just how bad Raggedy Ann is.

To summarize example 3, "because" marks the fact that the justifications are validating both the partner and the joint script. Moreover, this example shows that, by encouraging the relating of current proposals to the joint script and by encouraging "because" marking that serves as a cohesive device linking utterances together, a participation framework of collaboration supports the building of complex ideational units through the talk.

Note the use of a causal construction in line 12 that lacks "because" ("just get out of here/I'm mad! (Barb could have said, "just get out of here! Because I'm mad!") The next example suggests that omitting "because" in causal justification constructions where it can occur may convey anger, urgency, and a threatening demeanor. Barb, voicing the Prince, omits the marker in line 12. She is in the process of conveying an angry stance toward Raggedy Ann, who has committed the heinous offense of having hurt the Princess so badly that she had to miss the Ball. In trying to echo a voice of a particular sort, she uses the forms associated with that voice.

Omitting the "Because" Marker—Echoing Voices with an Urgent or Threatening Demeanor

The foregoing three examples demonstrate use of "because" for validation of several types: justifications of partner ideas presented in a previous turn; justifications of agreements with partner proposals; justifications of elaborations of partner proposals; and relating back of new proposals to the joint script.

If "because" marks validation, what does omission of "because" mark? Omission of the marker is used for justifications that oppose the speaker (e.g., "no, you can't go in, two people are in there"). Whereas validating justification constructions received "because" 42–63 percent of the time, refusals or oppositional justifications received "because" between zero and 25 percent of the time.

Given the findings of Chafe (1984), this result is not surprising. A syntactic construction that allows less incorporation of the reason within the main clause (i.e., a less embedded construction, which a construction without "because" represents) allows stronger assertion of the main clause. A speaker would want to have strong assertion of information that was new or under dispute. Proposals that are in the form of refusals are under dispute and therefore require strong assertion.

Justifications that omit the marker sound authoritative or threatening. This claim is evident when the collaborative examples of text produced by Barb and Gwen in examples 1–3 are compared to example 4. Gwen is joined by Dee and another girl, Vera. The justifications are spoken by Gwen, voicing the role of the Mom, speaking both to the Father (played by Vera) and to Big Sister (i.e., the child, who is played by Dee). Gwen omits "because" and does not mark these justifications. The markers seem to be omitted because she is constituting or echoing an authoritative stance in her role as mother and is conveying either an urgent tone (to Father) or a no-nonsense tone (to Dee, in the child role).

Example 4

1. Gwen: *Fa::ther, i'm gonna watch the baby if *y::ou get um -um go get -um –um *big *sister/
2. Vera: Sorry Gwen, but i-
3. Gwen: ==She's at *jumping *jack class! and that's the *wrong *class/ she'll get *beaten up! it's *high school, she's in *col::lege!
4. [Vera walks over to far side of yard, gets Dee, and brings her back to play area]
5. Gwen: [To Dee who comes back] you're grounded for a *week!
6. Dee: I'm going to my *room/
7. Gwen: Okay, *stay there!
8. Dee: Okay, I'm just going to ride my bike there.
9. Gwen: Okay, *do that! but don't be too long! dinner is *soon! [shaking her finger at Dee]

In line 1, Gwen makes an urgent request to Father, which he begins to refuse in line 2 ("sorry Gwen, but i-"). To dispute this refusal, Gwen produces a series of justifications in line 3 ("she's at jumping jack class! And that's the wrong class! she'll get *beaten up! It's *high school, she's in college!"). She could have used "because" here ("you gotta go, because she's at jumping jack class! And that's the wrong class! she'll get *beaten up! Because it's *high school, and she's in college!").

Gwen may omit these "becauses" in an effort to speak in ways appropriate to the character whose role she has selected to take on in the play. When adults whom she has heard are issuing urgent commands, they probably use certain forms of speech. For reasons described by Chafe (1984), adults in these situations omit the marker.

Gwen, echoing the way adults speak in these situations, herself takes on this feature of omission.

Similar urgency is needed in Gwen's speech to Dee in line 9. Mom does not want the child to "be too long." Gwen wants to accomplish her request and convey her disagreement with Dee, rather than showing solidarity with her at this point, and she speaks as she has observed adults speak in these situations. Therefore, Gwen says "but don't be too long! Dinner is soon!" rather than "don't be too long, because dinner is soon." If she had used "because," it would have conveyed continuation of a proposal of Dee's or validation of what Dee was doing. Gwen probably is not explicitly aware of this form-function relationship but is echoing the ways an adult would speak in such a situation.

Discussion

In conclusion, "because" seems to be used in these children's texts to show validation of the partner, and its absence is used to convey disagreement with the partner, as well as urgency. Schleppegrell (1991) had suggested that "because" could operate to create a supportive participation framework by continuing a partner turn. This study has shown that "because" can create a supportive participation framework in three additional ways: by supporting agreement with the partner within the speaker's own turn; by supporting elaboration of the partner within the speaker's turn; and by relating a new proposal to a joint theme being constructed collaboratively in the talk (even when the new proposals and reasons are related consecutively within the speaker's own turn), which in turn validates that theme.

Children seem to actively manipulate features of language to indexically create particular stances (collaborative or authoritative/threatening floors), or at least to use forms to echo the ways different characters speak in particular situations. Children are not passive acquirers of language forms; they are reflexive language users. Discourse markers can be regarded as a type of contextualization cue that is used to create given character voices or stances (Cook-Gumperz and Gumperz 1978; Gumperz 1994).

A final important implication concerns the ways in which the different levels of talk implicated by discourse marker theory interact with one another. In these data we see girls discussing a range of causal relationships, at both the action and ideational levels. To some extent, marking seems to be independent of the domain being accessed. However, a positive, collaborative participation framework, as well as influencing marking, seems to interact with these other levels of talk. A collaborative stance toward the partner may lead a set of speakers to look for more validation of one another's individual proposals, as well as of their shared script—thereby leading them to access more ideational and action-level causal relationships, as well as more complex ones (as we saw Gwen building a complex ideational unit through her turn to validate the treachery of Raggedy Ann). Participation frameworks and speaker goals may affect not only the degree of marking but also the richness and range of causal relationships that are accessed in the talk, as well as their thematic linkage into broader, more complex units.

Acknowledgments

The author is indebted to Eve Sweetser for helpful discussions on content, speech act–level, and epistemic causals in this transcript. Any errors are the author's.

NOTE

Pseudonyms were assigned to children in the study and are used here to indicate whose talk is featured in examples.

Transcription Conventions

/	Final fall
?	Final rise
,	Slight rise as in listing intonation (e.g., more is expected)
::	Lengthened segments
-	Truncation
=	single = before and after the appropriate portions of text to indicate overlap
[]	Latching (simultaneous or overlapping speech)
*	Asterisk appears to left of accented syllable.
( )	(word or phrase in parentheses) description of nonspeech activity

REFERENCES

Andersen, Elaine, Maquela Brizuela, Beatrice DuPuy, and Laura Gonnerman. 1999. Cross-linguistic evidence for the early acquisition of discourse markers as register variables. *Journal of Pragmatics* 31:1339–51.

Chafe, Wallace. 1984. How people use adverbial clauses. *Berkeley Linguistics Society* 10:437–50.

Cook-Gumperz, Jenny. 1995. Reproducing the discourse of mothering: How gendered talk makes gendered lives. In *Gender articulated: Language and the socially constructed self*, ed. Kira Hall and Mary Bucholz, 401–19. London: Routledge.

Cook-Gumperz, Jenny, and John Gumperz. 1978. Context in children's speech. In *The development of communication*, ed. Catherine Snow and Natalie Waterson, 3–25. New York: Wiley.

Gumperz, John. 1994. Contextualization and understanding. In *Rethinking context: Language as an interactive phenomenon,* vol. 11 of *Studies in the Social and Cultural Foundations of Language*, ed. Alessandro Duranti and Charles Goodwin, 229–52. Cambridge: Cambridge University Press.

Schiffrin, Deborah. 1987. *Discourse markers: Studies in interactional sociolinguistics, 5.* Cambridge: Cambridge University Press.

Schleppegrell, Mary. 1991. Paratactic because. *Journal of Pragmatics* 16:323–37.

Sweetser, Eve. 1990. *From etymology to pragmatics: Metaphorical and cultural aspects of semantic structure.* Cambridge Studies in Linguistics, 54. Cambridge: Cambridge University Press.

II

Issues in Second-Language Learning

5

Contextualizing Interlanguage Pragmatics

KATHLEEN BARDOVI-HARLIG
Indiana University

IN THIS CHAPTER I consider what we can learn about interlanguage pragmatics by placing it in the broader context of communicative competence. What concerns me is not the theoretical positioning of interlanguage pragmatics vis-à-vis communicative competence—that topic has already been explored by others (e.g., Bachman 1990; Canale 1983; Kasper 1997)—but a practical positioning that influences research design, data collection, and analysis. I begin with the claim that, in general, in interlanguage pragmatics the theoretical understanding of the complex interaction of components of linguistic, social, interactional, and strategic knowledge (as demonstrated in introductions and reviews of the literature as well as in survey articles) far outstrips implementation of such frameworks in research questions or research design.

My goal in this essay, therefore, is not to convince readers that communicative competence is an appropriate theoretical framework but to demonstrate the benefit to interlanguage pragmatics research of using communicative competence to map out additional areas of inquiry. Orienting research in interlanguage pragmatics to communication and communicative competence enriches the questions that we can ask about how second-language (L2) pragmatic competence is acquired, as well as our interpretation of the answers; in addition, it also suggests appropriate means of investigation of those areas.

I begin with a section of definitions that are crucial to this endeavor, reviewing the terms *pragmatics*, *interlanguage pragmatics*, *communication*, and *communicative competence.* The succeeding section provides a brief sketch of Schmidt's (1983) study as a model for current and future work in this area. After laying the groundwork, I devote the bulk of the chapter to showing what we can learn about interlanguage pragmatics through an investigation of the intersection of pragmatic competence with the other components of Canale's (1983) construct of communicative competence—namely, grammatical, discourse, and strategic competence.

Definitions

Pragmatics

Traditionally, the study of pragmatics is considered to encompass at least five main areas: deixis, conversational implicature, presupposition, speech acts, and conversational structure (Levinson 1983). In addition, L2 pragmatics traditionally investigates areas considered to be in the realm of sociolinguistics, such as choice of address forms (Kasper and Dahl 1991; Stalnaker 1972; Serra et al. 2000). An even greater move toward sociolinguistics is evident in the introduction to Rose and Kasper (2001), who characterize pragmatics "as interpersonal rhetoric—the way speakers and writers accomplish goals as social actors who do not just need to get things done but must attend to their interpersonal relationships with other participants at the same time" (Rose and Kasper 2001, 2). In the intersection of second-language studies and pragmatics, research is best characterized by Stalnaker's definition (1972, 383) of pragmatics as "the study of linguistic acts and the contexts in which they are performed" (where "contexts" often have been interpreted as scenarios created by researchers). Within this intersection, the most-studied areas (in order of decreasing attention) are speech acts, conversational management, and conversational implicature.

Within L2 studies, definitions of pragmatics reflect the dominance of speech acts as an area of inquiry. Pragmatic competence generally is partitioned into social and linguistic knowledge, although the boundaries vary with the definitions. Blum-Kulka (1982) posits a three-way division between social acceptability (which determines when to perform a speech act, sequencing and appropriateness, and degree of directness), linguistic acceptability (deviations from which result in utterances that are "perfectly grammatical but fail to conform to the target language in terms of what is considered an 'idiomatic' speech act realization" [1982, 52]), and pragmatic acceptability (that an utterance has the intended illocutionary force). Blum-Kulka (1982) identifies unintended shifts in illocutionary force as the most serious consequence of nonnative speech act realization. Such shifts can occur with both linguistically acceptable and unacceptable utterances. Thomas (1983) identifies sociopragmatic failure (inappropriate utterances resulting from a misunderstanding of social standards) and pragmalinguistic failure (utterances that convey unintended illocutionary force). A more recent formulation of these concepts in terms of knowledge rather than failure comes from Kasper (2001):

> Pragmalinguistic knowledge requires mappings of form, meaning, force, and context. . . . Sociopragmatics refers to the link between action-relevant context factors and communicative action (e.g., deciding whether to request an extension, complain about the neighbor's barking dog) and does not necessarily require any links to specific forms at all (Kasper 2001, 51).

Cohen (1996) suggests a third division—between sociocultural and sociolinguistic ability. Sociocultural ability refers to a speaker's ability "to determine whether it is acceptable to perform the speech act at all in the given situation and, if so, to select one or more semantic formulas that would be appropriate in the realization of the given speech act" (1996, 254). In contrast, sociolinguistic ability consists of speakers' control over their selection of language forms used to realize a speech act. Cohen's introduction of *control* is particularly compatible with an acquisitional perspective: Do the forms exist in the learners' grammars and lexicons, and can they be accessed?

The Acquisitional Component of Interlanguage Pragmatics

Kasper and Dahl (1991, 216) define interlanguage pragmatics as referring to nonnative speakers' comprehension and production of pragmatics and how that L2-related knowledge is acquired. Although the number of studies that focus on the development of interlanguage pragmatic competence is steadily growing, far more studies have compared the production of advanced nonnative speakers to native speakers. This imbalance was first observed by Kasper (1992) and has been addressed more recently by others (e.g., Bardovi-Harlig 1999; Kasper and Rose 1999). The study of the acquisition of L2 pragmatic knowledge addresses questions concerning measurement (e.g., How can approximation to target language norms be measured?), development (e.g., What are the stages of L2 pragmatic development? Is there a natural route of development as evidenced by difficulty, accuracy, or acquisition orders or discrete stages of development?), L1A and L2A comparisons (e.g., Is the development of L2 pragmatics similar to learning a first language? Are there universals of pragmatics, and do they play a role in interlanguage pragmatics?), variables (e.g., Do children enjoy an advantage over adults in learning a second language? Does environment make a difference?), and mechanisms of change (e.g., How do learners move from one pragmatic stage to another? What mechanisms drive development from stage to stage?) (see Kasper and Schmidt 1996).

Communication

Whether one continues to focus on speech acts or goes beyond them, it is important to see pragmatics in the larger framework of communication. I adopt Canale's (1983) definition of communication because of its familiarity to both researchers and teachers and because its formulation speaks directly to the investigation of L2 pragmatics. Canale (1983, 3–4) writes:

> Communication is understood here to have the following characteristics: it (a) is a form of social interaction, and is therefore normally acquired and used in social interaction; (b) involves a high degree of unpredictability and creativity in form and message; (c) takes place in discourse and sociocultural contexts which provide constraints on appropriate language use and also clues as to correct interpretation of utterances; (d) is carried out under limiting psychological and other conditions such as memory constraints, fatigue and distractions; (e) always has a purpose (for example, to establish social relations, to persuade, or to promise); (f) involves authentic, as opposed to textbook-contrived, language; (g) is judged as successful or not on the basis of actual outcomes.

Several points of Canale's definition act as guideposts for (re)contextualization of the study of L2 pragmatics: The emphasis on social interaction, context, on-line limitations, and communicative outcomes emphasizes the need to study pragmatics in conversation. Even allowing that experimental controls, such as production questionnaires, are sometimes desirable in L2 acquisition, Canale's (1983) definition of communication warns us away from the exclusively experimental.

Communicative Competence

Along with the study of communication by learners comes study of the knowledge that drives successful communication—namely, communicative competence. I adopt Canale's (1983) definition of communicative competence. Communicative competence can be regarded as the underlying systems of knowledge and skill required for communication (Canale and Swain 1980). Canale (1983) describes communicative competence as having four parts: grammatical competence, sociolinguistic competence, discourse competence, and strategic competence.[1] Grammatical competence refers to knowledge of the language in all areas of grammar, including the lexicon, phonology, morphology, syntax, and semantics. In L2 acquisition research proper, grammatical competence is the most researched area of development.

Sociolinguistic competence addresses the extent to which utterances are produced and understood appropriately in different sociolinguistic contexts, depending on contextual factors such as status of participants, purposes of the interaction, and norms or conventions of interaction. Appropriateness of meaning includes what one does in particular situations and what communicative functions or acts may be expressed. For example, as Schmidt (1983) notes, in English one does not normally ask strangers their age, marital status, or salary on first meeting, although these inquiries may be acceptable first questions in other cultures. The reader will recognize an extensive overlap in the definitions of pragmatic competence discussed earlier and Canale's (1983) sociolinguistic competence. For that reason, I refer to sociolinguistic competence as pragmatic competence to tie it into the investigation of interlanguage pragmatics, although I acknowledge that they may not be identical in detail.

Discourse competence is the knowledge required to combine grammatical forms and meanings into coherent and cohesive oral and written texts. Discourse competence includes the ability to distinguish among types of texts. In this essay I focus only on spoken discourse. Because spoken discourse typically is dyadic and cooperative, Schmidt (1983) calls this aspect of discourse *conversational* or *interactional* competence.

Strategic competence is composed of mastery of verbal and nonverbal communication strategies. Learners use communication strategies to overcome inadequacies of their interlanguage resources (Ellis 1994) or to make up for insufficient competence in one or more of the other components of communicative competence (Canale 1983). Typical examples are the use of paraphrase, requests for repetition, clarification or slower speech, and the use of reference sources.[2]

Pragmatics, Communication, and Communicative Competence: An Early Study

I begin this call for the recontextualization of interlanguage pragmatic inquiry with a brief review of Schmidt's (1983) study. Schmidt reports on the development of an adult Japanese learner of English named Wes, a successful artist who has relocated to Hawaii. The case study follows the learner's development over the course of three years. At the end of the three-year period Schmidt summarized Wes's progress in the four areas of communicative competence outlined by Canale (1983). Schmidt's (1983) study is cited for many reasons throughout the L2 acquisition literature. I cite it here as a model of integration of pragmatic competence in the larger setting of developing communicative competence.

Grammatical and Sociolinguistic/Pragmatic Competence

In grammatical competence Schmidt (1983) details the learner's development in morphology and syntax, as well as his use of formulaic expressions. Wes apparently made very little progress in grammatical competence, whereas he had developed a certain repertoire of formulaic expressions. Schmidt concludes that Wes's development in the acquisition of productive grammatical rules was "minimal and almost insignificant" (1983, 151)

In contrast, Wes showed development in pragmatic competence. Schmidt reports that Wes's earliest directives were innovative, as in (1), as well as formulaic, as in (2). In addition, Wes also used indirect requests, as shown in (3).

(1) a. Please, never thinking ("don't think about it")
    b. Maybe curtain ("maybe you should open the curtain")
(2) a. Shall we go?
    b. Ah, I have a Big Mac, n I have a French fries, small and Coke, that's all
(3) a. This is all garbage ("put it out")
    b. Ah, I have two shirt upstairs ("please get them while you're there")

Wes exhibited development in his use of directives. Schmidt (1983) notes that by the end of the observation period, gross errors in the performance of directives had largely been eliminated. Progressive forms such as "Sitting?" dropped out of Wes's directives, and the use of imperatives increased (*please next month send orders more quick*). Patterns such as "Shall we?" and "let's" were used productively for a range of different requests. In addition, directives showed more elaboration (*shall we maybe go out coffee now, or you want later? Ok, if you have time please send two handbag, but if you're too busy, forget it*).

An example of an early complaint made at a restaurant in (4) shows that Wes received help from both his native-speaker companion and the waitress. In contrast, three years later in a restaurant Wes delivered the complaint in (5) without assistance.

(4) *Early complaint at restaurant*
    Wes: Ah, Miss (looks at cup; waitress looks puzzled)
    NS: Could ya warm up his hot chocolate a little bit?
    Waitress: Oh, is it cold, love? Sure!
    Wes: Sorry. (softly)
(5) *Three years later in restaurant*
    Excuse me, this milk is no good, sour I think

Discourse Competence

At the end of the observation period, Schmidt (1983) notes that Wes showed a good sense of discourse components and the order in which they occur. Schmidt surveyed a wide range of oral texts produced by Wes, including narratives, descriptions, and conversations. Over the three year period of observation, Wes produced more elaborated discourse. To keep to the type of features typically examined in interlanguage pragmatics, Wes developed frequent use of back-channel signals such as *uh huh, I see, really?, yeah, I know what you mean,* and *my goodness*, as well as the ability to repeat fragments of an interlocutor's turn. In addition, Wes was a good conversationalist and could engage in small talk.

Strategic Competence

Schmidt (1983) also investigated Wes's development of communication strategies. Wes employed several strategies, perhaps as a result of his relatively undeveloped grammar. Although most of Wes's strategies compensate for deficiencies in other areas of his development, Schmidt does isolate communicative strategies that directly address pragmatics. A relevant example is the use of disambiguators such as *please* to clarify the illocutionary force of an utterance, as in (6). Similarly, Wes's use of *Can I getting some more coffee?* could be ambiguous in illocutionary force between a request (Can you get me some more coffee?) and an offer (Can I get you some more coffee?). The use of *please* could disambiguate the illocutionary force, as shown in the constructed example in (7b).

(6) Pragmatic strategies: use of *please* to disambiguate illocutionary force
  a. Please n you taking this suitcase
  b. Please, never thinking ("don't think about it")

(7) Extrapolated from the data:
  a. Can I getting some more coffee? (at home intended as a request, ambiguous request/offer)
  b. Can I getting some more coffee, please? (constructed)

Schmidt's outline of Wes's development shows how a learner's L2 pragmatic development is related to his L2 development more generally. We see how far-reaching and intertwined pragmatics is with other areas of language and language use. We see how the study of interlanguage pragmatics could be contextualized both in acquisition and in the other components of communicative competence.

Pragmatics and Communicative Competence

In this section I examine how research in each of the other components can inform research in pragmatic competence. This examination represents a slightly different approach from that of Schmidt (1983), who examined each area of development independently, although I am indebted to Schmidt's work for my approach. This section examines the intersection of pragmatic competence with grammatical, discourse, and strategic competence in turn for what we can learn about pragmatic development.

Pragmatic Competence and Grammatical Competence

Although still not very common, the best-represented area of inquiry among inquiries investigating the relation of pragmatic competence to the other developing competences that make up communicative competence is the relation of pragmatics to grammar. As Olshtain and Blum-Kulka (1985) and Bardovi-Harlig and Hartford (1990) argue, grammatical competence, however implicated in pragmatic development, does not constitute pragmatic development. What are the logical possibilities for the relationship between L2 grammatical and pragmatic development? There are at least four: Learners don't have grammatical resources and therefore cannot use them; learners have grammatical resources and use them appropriately; learners have grammatical resources but don't use them; and learners have linguistic resources but use them innovatively. The study of grammatical development as it relates to the study of speech acts has to do with the control of resources (Cohen 1996). This resource control impinges most directly on the forms in which speech acts are realized.

No Resources, No Use Consider the first possibility, in which learners don't have grammatical resources and therefore cannot use them. One area of grammatical development includes the lexicon. Effects of development in the lexicon were noted by Blum-Kulka and Levenston (1987); learners of Hebrew use the equivalent of *have* in requests such as "Can I have your notes?" rather than more specific terms such as *borrow* or *lend*—which, according to Blum-Kulka and Levenston, are less scary to the addressee. Cohen and Olshtain (1993) also identify development in the lexicon as the culprit behind the awkward request "I want to drive with you" in a context in which "Could you give me a lift?" would be appropriate. In a retrospective task, the learner reported not knowing how to use the word *lift,* which had appeared in the role-play scenario.

Rose (2000) and Ellis (1992) provide examples that illustrate the simultaneous development of conventional realization of speech acts and grammar in the interlanguage of children acquiring a second language. Ellis (1992) investigated the classroom requests of two boys, ages ten and eleven, who were enrolled in an English as a second language (ESL) language unit designed to help primary-school children learn enough communicative English to join appropriate content classes. As (8) shows, the use of nominal utterances—an early stage of language development—corresponds to the pragmatic request strategy of naming the desired item. The "give me" strategy in (9) and the "want" strategy (softened with "Miss") in (10) emerge before the learner produces a direct object.

(8) Big circle (R needed a cutout of a big circle) Term 1
(9) Give me (R wanted a ruler from another student) Term 2
(10) Miss I want [the stapler] Term 3 (addressed to teacher)
(11) Tasleem, have you got glue? Term 4 (addressed to classmate)
(12) Can I take my book with me?/ Can you pass me my pencil? Term 5

Data from adult learners of ESL engaged in conversation show a slightly different picture from that in the child data above. The adults show general fluency and multiword utterances, as well as knowledge that mitigation is required, but may exhibit lack of development in a particular area of grammar. Consider an example from a longitudinal study of the development of modality. In the acquisition of L2 English, the earliest expressions of modality are *I think* and *maybe* followed by *can* and *will* and only much later *could* and *would* (Salsbury 2000). Comparing learners' modal inventories in a longitudinal study to their production of speech acts allows a comparison of grammatical resources and pragmatic practice. A learner who productively uses only the lexical markers of modality does not use modals to mitigate her disagreements (Salsbury and Bardovi-Harlig 2000), as (13) shows. This same learner begins to use *would* and *could* tentatively two months after this example.

(13) Interviewer: Oh, but you'd be such a good mom!
Marta: I *think*
Interviewer: Oh, you would!
Marta: Yeah, I don't like because *maybe* I change my think, my think (Month 7)

The final examples in this section come from a longitudinal study of the acquisition of future expression (Bardovi-Harlig 2004). Aggregate-use inventories for the written and oral production of sixteen learners during a nine- to eighteen-month observation period show that *will* emerges early and dominates grammatical forms of future expression, constituting 79 percent of the oral corpus for future expression. In contrast, *going to* emerges much later and captures only 9 percent of future expression. Pragmatically, this finding means that in the initial stages of future expression, learners lack the grammatical means to produce pragmatically targetlike utterances involving future expression; in other words, at the early stages, learners were unable to accommodate to the language of the interlocutor.

(14) Interviewer: What are you going to do for Christmas Break?
Carlos: I will go back to my country on December 8. [L1 Spanish, month 3.0]

(15) Interviewer: Are you planning a vacation during, um . . . Spring Break?
Guillermo: I will go to Mexico in spring break with a friend of mine
[four turns]
Interviewer: *What are you going to do?*
Guillermo: Well, *I will go* with that, with, that one group from, from the /cher/ [church] and:: we'll *we'll go about thirty-five people*, and *we will go to see* the . . . [L1 Spanish, month 6.0]

In these examples the learners use *will* to answer the interviewer's *going to;* because of the apparent contrast, the learner responses seem much more determined or insistent about their plans than the situation warrants. Because the learners use their only productive future marker, this discourse does not represent an actual contrast, however. Without a choice between *will* and *going to*, the use of *will* conveys no more than the future. As a result, what may sound insistent to the outside observer (e.g., the analyst or the reader) very likely has neutral pragmatic value within the learner's interlanguage.

Grammatical Resources, Used Appropriately

In this scenario, learners have grammatical resources and use them appropriately (in ways that approximate native speakers). Because these examples are very likely to be in the target range, they are largely unremarkable. They could be missed unless one is looking for them. Because appropriate grammatical sentences fall in this category, there are virtually an unlimited number of possible examples in the literature. I offer some that are taken from the two longitudinal studies I have already introduced, where examples are in direct contrast to the ones I have just presented.

In contrast to Marta, who showed later development of modal expressions around the tenth month of her stay in the United States and her study in the Intensive English Program, Mousa began to use *would* in month 3 and *could* in month 5. As a result, Mousa's disagreements exhibit the use of *could* in (16), giving a quite different feeling from Marta's disagreement.

(16) Interviewer: The most important thing is just relax [when taking the Test of English as a Foreign Language (TOEFL)]
Mousa: *Relax, relax, yeah, but I think I could* do at least, like, 500, because I didn't finish, the problem, you know [L1 Bambara/French, month 10.0]

In the area of future expression, a learner who can use the *going to* future is able to match the interviewer's use of *be going to;* the result is a neutral report of his plans, as (17) shows.

(17) Interviewer: *What are you going to do?*
Hamad: *We're gonna go to, Daytona Beach.*
Interviewer: To Daytona? Ah! When are you going?
Hamad: [ ] spring break, on the first I think.
Interviewer: On the first of March?
Hamad: Yeah
Interviewer: Uh huh. So, what [I], *how long are you gonna stay*?
Hamad: *If we enjoy there we gonna stay*, one week ten days. [L1 Arabic, month 1.5]

Resources That Are Not Used

In the third scenario, learners may have certain grammatical resources but do not use them. Such examples are found in the spontaneous talk of advanced nonnative speakers of English who are enrolled as graduate students in linguistics at an American university (Bardovi-Harlig and Hartford 1990). Whereas native speakers often replied to the question in (18) by using the past progressive (*was* Verb+*ing*) to mitigate their turns, nonnative speakers often used the unmitigated future, *will*.

(18) Professor: OK, let's talk about next semester.
Native English-speaking student: I *was thinking of* taking syntax.
Nonnative English-speaking student: I *will* take syntax.

Although there was no grammatical inventory (that was not undertaken until several years later, by Salsbury and Bardovi-Harlig 2000), I argue that on the basis of the high level of grammatical competence, TOEFL scores, admission to a graduate linguistics program, and the fact that the speaker aspired to be an English teacher, one could assume that she had acquired (or at least learned) the past progressive, although not this pragmatic use.

Resources with Interlanguage Use

In this scenario learners may have linguistic resources but use them in ways or situations that native speakers do not. Pinto (2002) reports that learners of L2 Spanish overgeneralize the limited use of the formal past subjunctive, which is found with *quisiera* "I would like" to other verbs and to informal contexts. Learners apparently have acquired the morphology for past subjunctive but not its rules of use.

This brief review shows that pragmatic competence is related to grammatical development. On one hand, learners such as Marta and Wes suggest that the social side of pragmatic competence can develop apart from grammar, to some degree. Marta, for example, shows that she knows that certain contributions should be mitigated, and she accomplishes this mitigation with the lexical markers of modality that she controls productively. On the other hand, targetlike pragmatic competence, which shows an integration of the linguistic and the social, seems to require the development of grammatical resources (although as the examples also show, this is not the same as the requirement that utterances be grammatical). This observation speaks to Cohen's (1996) notion of sociolinguistic ability, which consists of speakers' control over their selection of language forms used to realize a speech act.

Pragmatic Competence and Discourse Competence

Although some studies in interlanguage pragmatics have investigated discourse competence, these studies have focused largely on conversational management, including greetings, closings, and turn-taking. Within speech act investigations, however, much less attention is paid to discourse competence. One of the reasons that discourse competence has been underrepresented in L2 speech act research is the prevalence of the production questionnaire, or discourse completion questionnaire (DCT). Whether the DCT takes the form of the more predominant written questionnaire or the more innovative oral questionnaire, it asks respondents to provide a single turn in response to a scenario provided by the researcher. In the absence of turn-taking and negotiation, there is no opportunity to study discourse competence. Research on speech acts that utilize role play or conversational data shows that speech acts can—and should—be investigated in light of interactive competence, not only for what it reveals about turns and sequencing of turns as turns but for what it reveals about sequencing and the use of strategies within the performance of speech acts. Moreover, negotiation is inherent to certain speech acts, including refusals and disagreements (Edmondson 1981; Gass and Houck 1999, 35); I examine those two cases in this section.[3]

Gass and Houck (1999) argue that in addition to helping us learn about sequential organization, studying discourse reveals the types of responses that certain speech act realizations evoke (not just on a global level but on a turn-by-turn basis). This line of inquiry relates to Canale's (1983) definition in which communication is judged as successful or not on the basis of actual outcome. It also provides an important way of measuring success that frees interlanguage pragmatic research and analysis from dependence on native-speaker speech act realization, shifting instead to a communicative value for success. Very simply, the interactional success of a learner's contribution may be more important than how it compares to a native speaker's production of the same utterance.

In addition, Kobayashi and Rinnert (2003) found that the level of imposition affected the amount of negotiation undertaken by high-intermediate learners. High-intermediate learners had more turns in high-imposition scenarios and took longer turns, as measured by words per turn. Lower-proficiency learners did not make this distinction.

In this section I consider an illustrative example as much for what it shows as for the fact that interlanguage pragmatics speech act studies rarely contain such stretches of talk; I hope that readers not only get used to seeing them but come to expect them. The example comes from Gass and Houck's (1999) role-play study of interlanguage refusals (native speakers of American English engaged in refusal role plays with young Japanese adults).[4] The learners were described as having low to intermediate proficiency in English. They had been in the United States for less than a month at the time of the role plays and intended to return to Japan within a few weeks of data collection. In the excerpt from a role play a learner responds to the following scenario:

> You are at your host family's home. Your host family, the Quentins, has gone to a neighbor's house to discuss a business matter. They have left you at home with specific instructions not to let anyone into the house, no matter what they say. It could be dangerous. About 5 minutes after they leave, the doorbell rings. It is a woman who says that she is Mr. Quentin's cousin from Detroit. She is just passing through Lansing and says, "Can I come in and wait?" (Gass and Houck 1999, 207).

(19) The "cousin" scenario

REQUEST 1	NS: . . . would you mind if I come in and wait for a minute or so an a till he comes back
Direct "no"	NNS: ah no wait wait
Reason a	I'm a guest in this home the-
Reason b	I can't uh I don't uh uh um I can't I don't know what uh I do this situation then eh
Request for Clarification	NS: I'm sorry?
Clar. for Reason b	NNS: uh he he don't tell me uh
	NS: ah
	NNS: if another person come in his home
Rejection of	NS: yeah yeah but I I I'm his cousin
Reason b	I'm sure it's going to be ok=
Repetition of	NNS: [
Rejection b/	But

Begin Reason c	= ((laughs)) I don't know=
Rejection of Reason b	NS: =I I know it'll be alright=
Reason c	NNS: =my first time to meet you (.) I don't know you
Response to Reason c	NS: y'know actually this is the first time I've met you too how do=
	NNS: [wait wait
	NS: =you do nice to meet you
Reason for alternative	NNS: [I think uh I think uh he come back not so late uh huh yeh uh
Alternative 1	Please wait in your car
Reaction to alt (rejects alt 1)	NS: ((gasps))

(Gass and Houck 1999, 73–74)

This example is excerpted from a much longer role play in which five separate reasons are given (and repeated) for why the cousin cannot wait inside the house. The example represents approximately 20 percent of the role play. In this example, the learner uses three reasons to deflect the reiterations of the original requests by the cousin to enter the house. The learner follows this reiteration with an alternative (*please wait in your car*), which also is unsuccessful. The role play extends for many turns, through five full request episodes. Finally the situation is resolved when the NS cousin leaves.

Gass and Houck (1999) observe that, as in advising session refusals (Bardovi-Harlig and Hartford 1990), learners in the role plays adjust the semantic formulas (or strategies) and the content as the interaction unfolds.[5] The presence of such adjustments within individual interactions strongly suggests that learners may be making the same adjustments across interactions, leading to learning of the L2 pragmatics—reflected by an increase of semantic formulas and content with the range of options used by native speakers. This view of interaction leads Gass and Houck to regard learners as active participants in the acquisition process: "Thus, we have evidence of a learner who is not simply transferring formulas from the first language, but who is actively searching for successful linguistic and attitudinal resources, and in so doing reveals a wide range of such resources applied in a reasonable problem-solving approach" (Gass and Houck 1999, 80).

Acquisition of Disagreement Turn Structure Like refusals, disagreements are speech acts that are always negotiated. Part of acquiring the speech act is acquiring the turn structure. In English, disagreements often include an agreement component (Pomerantz 1984). Disagreement components tend to be postponed in favor of agreement components within a single turn and if possible even postponed across turns. Learners of English must learn this order, in addition to learning the content and the language in which to express it.

Using Pomerantz's (1984) analysis to study the emerging turn structure of L2 disagreements in a longitudinal study, Bardovi-Harlig and Salsbury (2004) reveal the following sequence of development:

1. Strong disagreements, characterized chiefly by the occurrence of *no.*
2. Inclusion of agreement components with disagreement components. (At this stage a learner may use both the disagree-before-agree and the agree-before-disagree orders on different disagreements.)
3. Postponement of disagreement components within a turn.
4. Postponement of disagreement turns within a sequence of turns.

It is important to note that direct disagreements, although acquired early, are never abandoned as a strategy either by learners or by native speakers, who retain them in their repertoire. Instead, they become less frequent as learners gain other options. The first stage is characterized by strong disagreements, dominated by the use of *no.*

(20) Bob: So your intention is to go back to Mali to study . . .

Mousa: *No, no, here, yeah* . . . is depend on university, they need some TOEFL score [month 5]

(21) Bob: He'll have two wives too.

Mousa: No, he won't have two wives [month 6]

The second stage is characterized by the emergence of agreement components in the disagreements. At this stage, a learner may use either a disagree-before-agree order or an agree-before-disagree order. The former is more typical.

(22) Tom: . . . It's called test anxiety . . .

Mousa: *I don't have quite like this, but I have a little, but not quite like this,* [month 10]

(23) Donna: So, how does that affect your life now?

Marta: Now, mm, now, sometimes, yes, sometimes, I feel now, even now I am very shy, the people say I am not shy, but

Donna: *You're shy! Oh, honey, you're not shy!* [direct disagreement by interlocutor]

Marta: *Yes, yes, sometimes, I am very very shy, yes, and I say, Marta, go ahead, go! Talk! Oh! Yes* [direct disagreement by learner]

Donna: *If I were to describe you, to somebody, shy would not come up, I would not say shy*

Marta: Really, I am very very shy. [reiterated disagreement] No, ok, how can I say, maybe when I had good relationship with somebody, for example, you, Tom, I'm very open [agreement], but when I don't know somebody, and I feel no comfortable, I very very shy [disagreement]

Donna: . . . *That's natural* . . . [Marta, L2 Spanish, month 11]

Marta's disagreement takes a positive form—*yes, I am shy*—and is repeated twice before she finally concedes to agree with Donna: *maybe when I had good relationship with somebody, for example, you, Tom, I'm very open*. Marta then repeats her disagreement with an intensifier: *but when I don't know somebody, and I feel no comfortable, I very very shy.*

The third stage is characterized by postponement of disagreement components within a turn. Learners move from an unordered turn structure in which they use agreement-before-disagreement and disagreement-before-agreement to a turn structure in which agreement precedes disagreement. In the following examples, the learner first uses an unconventional marker of agreement—*I know your mean*[*ing*]—and the following month adopts the conventional *yeah but* strategy (LoCastro 1986).

(24) Tom: But if you don't take any IEP classes, then you have no connection to the university, cause IU has to accept you first as a student, do you see what I mean?

Eun Hui: *I know your mean, but I don't think so*

Tom: No? ok. [L1 Korean, month 10]

(25) Tom: It's a cultural difference, do you think . . . but I know in Asia, you can agree or disagree, it's more of a written culture . . .

Eun Hui: *Yeah, but, in Korea, in Korea culture,* during our class, we don't say many things, but even though I know about that, just we have to polite attitude during class, [month 11]

The fourth and last stage seems to be postponement of the disagreement across turns. Only one of the learners, Mousa, reaches that stage. Mousa utilizes the turns that have been identified in native-speaker realization of dispreferred turns. He requests clarification, he warns his interlocutor of the impending disagreement, and finally he disagrees directly.

(26) Tom: Would you marry more than one woman?

Mousa: Ah, I don't think, I don't know, I haven't decide yet.

Tom: I think he'd be more honest with me if you weren't here!

Takako: Yea! Because I don't know, like, first, I, first I heard about like more than one wife, like I thought, why is that, but now, like, I mean, I don't want to my husband to have more than one wife, but, honestly, I mean, I don't care . . .

(two turns)

Mousa: *You said like, if your, you don't care if your, your, your husband has other wife?* [clarification]

Takako: I don't know.

Mousa: *You don't care about that?* [clarification]

Takako: Like, now, I'm a little bit thinking, before I didn't like it, but now

Mousa: If you say that, I will say no, no [warning of impending disagreement]

Takako: *I don't care*

Mousa: *No, no, no, you care*! [direct disagreement] [month 11]

Although Mousa has interlanguage characteristics in his speech, his turn development fits the expected turn sequencing for dispreferred turns. Knowing how to disagree in English is not only a matter of knowing the component parts; it entails being able to sequence them during interaction, responding to the contributions of interlocutors.

As this section shows, there is no substitute for investigating disagreements or refusals in the context of discourse competence. The semantic formulas that are used by all speakers—not just learners—are dependent on the turns taken by the interlocutors. This information is important not only for studying turn organization and sequencing of turns but for understanding speech act realization—the most dominant investigation in interlanguage pragmatics.

Pragmatic Competence and Strategic Competence

In this section I examine the potential for research at the intersection of pragmatic and strategic competence. The component of strategic competence is composed of mastery of verbal and nonverbal communication strategies. Learners use communication strategies to overcome inadequacies of their interlanguage resources (Ellis 1994) or to make up for insufficient competence in one or more of the other components of communicative competence (Canale 1983). Communication strategies typically share three main attributes: problematicity, consciousness, and intentionality (Bialystok 1990; Dörnyei and Scott 1997; Gass and Houck 1999). Canale observes that a learner might have to handle the problem of addressing strangers when he or she is unsure of their social status. Such a problem might be solved through a pragmatic communication strategy that entails using the most sociolinguistically neutral form when the learner is uncertain about the appropriateness of other forms in a given communicative situation, such as the use of *Comment ça va*? instead of *Comment allez-vous*? or *Comment vas-tu*? to greet a stranger (Canale 1983, 24). As mentioned earlier, Schmidt (1983) identifies the use of disambiguators such as *please* to clarify the illocutionary force of an utterance as another strategy.

Kasper (1997) and Gass and Houck (1999) offer definitions of pragmatic communication strategies. Kasper (1997) identifies a speaker's goal as twofold: balancing effective performance of an act (such as clarifying the illocutionary force as identified by Schmidt 1983) with establishing or maintaining a positive relationship. Kasper observes that "if we define pragmatics as 'interpersonal rhetoric' (Leech 1983) and maintain problematicity as critical to the notion of CS [communication strategies], then problems in pragmatics are communicative events which fall short of participants' actional (illocutionary and perlocutionary) and relational goals" (1997, 346). Gass and Houck report that the "criteria for identifying a behavior as a pragmatic communication strategy include linguistic deviation from both L1 and L2 norms and explicit or implicit indications of awareness of his/her status as a non-native speaker by the non-native speaker" (Gass and Houck 1999, 136–37).

Although the intersection of pragmatics and communication strategies was identified as early as 1983, it did not result in widespread investigations. Gass and Houck (1999, 132) observe that in spite of the significant research in pragmatic competence and communication strategies in the past fifteen years and "despite the large body of emerging literature, pragmatic communication strategies have only begun to receive attention." In a chapter devoted entirely to pragmatic communication strategies, Gass and Houck (1999, 143–44) identify five communication strategies that are relevant to pragmatics and present in their corpus of refusals by low- and high-intermediate Japanese speakers of English.[6]

1. Bluntness (or directness)
2. Indications of linguistic or sociocultural inadequacy (cf. Aston 1993)
   a. explicit reference to lack of (sociocultural) knowledge
   b. explicit reference to lack of linguistic ability
   c. request for explanation of known term
   d. nonverbal demonstration of production difficulty
3. Use of the L1
4. Sequential shifts (in attention to goal, choice of semantic formula, and choice of content excuses or alternatives)
5. Nonverbal expression of affect.

Gass and Houck (1999) provide a full account of each of these strategies in their data. In this section I review only two: explicit reference to lack of knowledge and nonverbal expression of affect. One example of an explicit reference to lack of sociocultural knowledge appears in the cousin scenario in example (19) as the second reason for denying the cousin admission to the house, repeated here as (27).

(27) I can't uh I don't uh uh um I can't *I don't know what uh I do this situation the eh* . . . uh he he don't tell me uh if another person come in his home. (Cousin scenario, Gass and Houck 1999)

A similar appeal to lack of knowledge—this time linguistic rather than sociocultural—is used by Marta in a disagreement with her native English-speaking interlocutor (Salsbury and Bardovi-Harlig 2001). In a particularly thorny discussion of her feelings about gays on an American university campus, Marta works hard to balance her good relationship with Donna, who is offended by Marta's stand (her relational goal) and her expression of her beliefs (her actional goals). Because Marta lacks a range of expressions of modality that would allow her to mitigate her contributions (see foregoing discussion of grammatical competence), she performs frequent repairs that cite her lack of linguistic knowledge, such as that in (28).

(28) Marta: *No, no, excuse me, this is no my, I express, express bad,* (month 5)

Among the five communication strategies identified by Gass and Houck (1999) for the resolution of pragmatic difficulties are nonverbal demonstration of production difficulty and nonverbal expression of affect. Gass and Houck (1999) report a learner's reaction to the role play in which the learner's host family suggests that she get her ears pierced and offers to call a friend to do it.

(29) Pierced ears invitation
NNS: ah I don't want to be pierced (.) my ears
HAND TO EAR————————————
JERKY MOTION STOMP

Gass and Houck (1999) observe that it is not clear whether nonverbal behaviors qualify as communicative strategies, although they appear to be employed as communicative strategies in many cases. One such case may be the nonverbal strategy employed by one of the learners in the longitudinal study of modality and disagreements (Salsbury and Bardovi-Harlig 2000). One of the learners tried to get a drunk American friend to apologize for touching his girlfriend. When the learner's verbal attempts at securing the apology failed, he supplemented his speech acts by hitting his friend. Although this action is admittedly high risk for a communication strategy—and it caused other problems—it does, in fact, constitute an example of nonverbal expression of affect.

The intersection of the development of pragmatic competence and communication strategies is an area that warrants more investigation in conversational as well as role-play interactions. Gass and Houck (1999) offer an intriguing interpretation of communicative strategies—namely, that they may be instrumental in the acquisition of pragmatic competence.

Conclusion

What I hope to have shown in this review is how interlanguage pragmatics research can benefit from investigating L2 pragmatics in light of one or more components of communicative competence. Studying pragmatic and grammatical competence provides a picture of the linguistic resources available to learners for pragmatic expression. Investigating pragmatic and discourse competence encourages more conversational research. This line of research not only contributes to our understanding of turns, turn development, and general conversational management, it also enriches our understanding of speech act realization. Semantic formulas are distributed across turns strategically, and learners may use different strategies in response to the turns of interlocutors. Finally, investigating strategic competence in pragmatics, although it is potentially difficult to distinguish from general strategy use, shows how learners compensate for lack of knowledge. The very presence of communication strategies may signal a learner's perception of lack of competence, which may in turn inform the research. By expanding interlanguage pragmatics data to include online conversation, interlanguage pragmatics research gains by having two sources of online evaluation: interlocutors who provide immediate evaluation of the success of learners' turns and the learners themselves—who, through their use of communication strategies, indicate where they feel their own problems may lie. There is much to gain and nothing to lose by expanding the investigation of L2 pragmatic competence to include the areas shared by pragmatic competence and grammatical, discourse, and strategic competence.

NOTES

1. There are alternatives to Canale's (1983) communicative competence that also focus on learners, such as those proposed by Bachman (Bachman 1990; Bachman and Palmer 1996), and definitions of communicative competence that focus on native speakers (Hymes 1971). As Kasper (1997) points out, the crucial difference among the native speaker and nonnative speaker formulations is the addition of strategic competence.
2. Canale (1983, 10–11) suggests that communicative strategies also may have an enhancing function—serving "to enhance the effectiveness of communication (e.g., deliberately slow and soft speech for rhetorical effect)"—which Dörnyei and Scott (1997) point out was not adopted by later researchers; for that reason I do not discuss it further.
3. It seems that most, if not all, speech acts might be open to negotiation. At a lecture, Nessa Wolfson once gave an example of a compliment on a co-worker's performance that took twenty minutes to negotiate because the addressee was so adamant that she did not possess the positive qualities that had been attributed to her.
4. Gass and Houck (1999) examine two of the three areas of Canale's (1983) communicative competence. In addition to the negotiation of turns discussed in discourse competence in this chapter, they also examine learners' use of back channels. In addition, they investigate strategy use as discussed as part of strategic competence in the succeeding section.
5. Many recent studies use the term "strategy" to replace the older use of "semantic formula" to refer to parts of a speech act such as explanations, alternatives, apologies, and statements of philosophy that occur in refusals. I have tried to use "semantic formulas" to avoid confusion with communication strategies considered in the succeeding section. Both terms are potentially ambiguous, however. Semantic formulas could be mistaken for formulaic utterances in second-language acquisition, whereas semantic formulas need not be formulaic speech.
6. Verbosity—one of the pragmatic communication strategies identified by Kasper (1997)—was not used by the Japanese informants in the refusal role plays and thus was not included in this summative list.

REFERENCES

Aston, G. 1993. Notes on interlanguage comity. In *InterLanguage pragmatics,* ed. G. Kasper and S. Blum-Kulka, 224–50. Oxford: Oxford University Press.

Bachman, L. F. 1990. *Fundamental considerations in language testing.* Oxford: Oxford University Press.

Bachman, L. F., and A. S. Palmer. 1996. *Language testing in practice: Designing and developing useful tests.* Oxford: Oxford University Press.

Bardovi-Harlig, K. 2004. The emergence of grammaticalized future expression in longitudinal production data. In *Form and meaning in second language acquisition,* ed. M. Overstreet, S. Rott, B. VanPatten, and J. Williams, 115–37. Mahwah, N.J.: Erlbaum.

———.1999. The interlanguage of interlanguage pragmatics: A research agenda for acquisitional pragmatics. *Language Learning* 49:677–713.

Bardovi-Harlig, K., and B. S. Hartford. 1990. Congruence in native and nonnative conversations: Status balance in the academic advising session. *Language Learning* 40:467–501.

Bardovi-Harlig, K., and T. Salsbury. 2004. The organization of turns in the disagreements of L2 learners: A longitudinal perspective. In *Studying speaking to inform second language learning,* ed. D. Boxer and A. D. Cohen, 199–227. Clevedon, England: Multilingual Matters.

Bialystok, E. 1990. *Communication strategies: A psychological analysis of second-language use.* Oxford: Blackwell.

Blum-Kulka, S. 1982. Learning to say what you mean in a second language: A study of speech act performance of learners of Hebrew as a second language. *Applied Linguistics* 3:29–59.

Blum-Kulka, S., and W. A. Levenston. 1987. Lexico-grammatical pragmatic indicators. *Studies in Second Language Acquisition* 9:155–70.

Canale, M. 1983. From communicative competence to language pedagogy. In *Language and communication*, ed. J. Richards and R. Schmidt, 2–27. London: Longman.

Canale, M., and M. Swain. 1980. Theoretical bases of communicative approaches to second language teaching and testing. *Applied Linguistics* 1:1–47.

Cohen, A. D. 1996. Developing the ability to perform speech acts. *Studies in Second Language Acquisition* 18:253–67.

Cohen, A. D., and E. Olshtain. 1993. The production of speech acts by EFL Learners. *TESOL Quarterly* 27:33–56.

Dörnyei, Z., and M. Scott. 1997. Communication strategies in a second language. *Language Learning* 47:173–210.

Edmondson, W. 1981. *Spoken discourse: A model for analysis*. London: Longman.

Ellis, R. 1992. Learning to communicate in the classroom: A study of two language learners' requests. *Studies in Second Language Acquisition* 14:1–23.

———. 1994. *The study of second language acquisition.* Oxford: Oxford University Press.

Gass, S. M., and N. Houck. 1999. *Interlanguage refusals.* Berlin: de Gruyter.

Hymes, D. 1971. *On communicative competence.* Philadelphia: University of Pennsylvania Press.

Kasper, G. 1992. Pragmatic transfer. *Second Language Research* 8:203–31.

———. 1997. Beyond reference. In *Communication strategies: Psycholinguistic and sociolinguistic perspectives*, ed. G. Kasper and E. Kellerman. New York: Addison-Wesley.

———. 2001. Classroom research on interlanguage pragmatics. In *Pragmatics in language teaching*, ed. K. Rose and G. Kasper, 33–60. Cambridge: Cambridge University Press.

Kasper, G., and M. Dahl. 1991. Research methods in interlanguage pragmatics. *Studies in Second Language Acquisition* 13:215–47.

Kasper, G., and K. Rose. 1999. Pragmatics and SLA. *Annual Review of Applied Linguistics* 19:81–104.

Kasper, G., and R. Schmidt. 1996. Developmental issues in interlanguage pragmatics. *Studies in Second Language Acquisition* 18:149–69.

Kobayashi, H., and C. Rinnert. 2003. Coping with high imposition requests: High vs. low proficiency EFL students in Japan. In *Pragmatic competence and foreign language teaching,* ed. A. Martínez, E. Usó, and A. Fernández, 161–84. Castellon, Spain: Servei de Publicacions de la Univerisitat Jaume I.

Leech, G. 1983. *The principles of pragmatics.* London: Longman.

Levinson, S. C. 1983. *Pragmatics*. Cambridge: Cambridge University Press.

LoCastro, V. 1986. Yes, I agree with you, but . . . : Agreement and disagreement in Japanese and American English. Paper presented at Japanese Association for Language Teaching conference, Hamamatsu, Japan, November.

Olshtain, E., and S. Blum-Kulka. 1985. Degree of approximation: Nonnative reactions to native speech act behavior. In *Input in second language acquisition,* ed. S. M. Gass and C. Madden, 303–25. Rowley, Mass.: Newbury House.

Pinto, D. 2002. *Perdóname ¿llevas mucho esperando?* Conventionalized language in L1 and L2 Spanish. Ph.D. diss., University of California, Davis.

Pomerantz, A. 1984. Agreeing and disagreeing with assessments: Some features of preferred/dispreferred turn shapes. In *Structures of social action: Studies in conversation analysis,* ed. J. M. Atkinson and J. Heritage, 57–101. Cambridge: Cambridge University Press.

Rose, K. R. 2000. An exploratory cross-sectional study of interlanguage pragmatic development. *Studies in Second Language Acquisition* 22:27–67.

Rose, K., and G. Kaspar, eds. 2001. *Pragmatics in language teaching.* Cambridge: Cambridge University Press.

Salsbury, T. 2000. *The grammaticalization of unreal conditionals: A longitudinal study of L2 English.* Ph.D. diss., Indiana University.

Salsbury, T., and K. Bardovi-Harlig. 2001. "I know your mean, but I don't think so." Disagreements in L2 English. In *Pragmatics and language learning,* vol. 10, ed. L. Bouton, 131–51. Urbana-Champaign: University of Illinois, Division of English as an International Language.

———. 2000. Oppositional talk and the acquisition of modality in L2 English. In *Social and cognitive factors in second language acquisition: Selected proceedings of the 1999 second language research forum*, ed. B. Swierzbin, F. Morris, M. E. Anderson, C. A. Klee, and E. Tarone, 57–76. Somerville, Mass.: Cascadilla Press.

Schmidt, R. 1983. Interaction, acculturation, and the acquisition of communicative competence: A case study of an adult. In *Sociolinguistics and language acquisition*, ed. E. Judd and N. Wolfson, 137–74. Rowley, Mass.: Newbury House.

Serra, M., E. Serrat, R. Solé, A. Bel, and M. Aparici. 2000. *La adquisición del lenguaje.* Barcelona, Spain: Editorial Ariel, S. A.

Stalnaker, R. C. 1972. *Pragmatics*. In *Semantics of natural language*, ed. D. Davidson and G. Harman, 380–97. Dordrecht, The Netherlands: Reidel.

Thomas, J. 1983. Cross-cultural pragmatics. *Applied Linguistics* 4:91–112.

6

Learning the Discourse of Friendship

CATHERINE EVANS DAVIES
University of Alabama

THIS STUDY TAKES a discourse perspective on language learning to offer a window into a natural process of language socialization that classroom teachers typically never see, with an unexpected focus—by the participants themselves—on cognitive dimensions of a speech activity. This contextualized discourse analysis is part of a case study on the development of a cross-cultural friendship on a university campus in the United States. The participants—Steve from the American South and Roshan from India—are native speakers of two different varieties of English. This friendship, with accompanying openness and trust, allowed conditions to develop in which a form of pragmatic coaching could take place. In general terms, the Indian English speaker had grammatical and "strategic" competence but lacked some aspects of sociolinguistic and discourse competence, and in relation to this particular speech activity he lacked "interactional competence" (Hall 1995; Kramsch 1986). Attempts to describe what interactional competence would entail include subtle shifts toward a cognitive orientation that is more than "attention" as it is currently treated in the second-language acquisition literature. The shift I address here is from a focus on shared background knowledge and shared orientation within a particular context to a focus that includes these dimensions but emphasizes an immediate shared cognitive dimension in the form of a collaboratively constructed intersubjectivity. The data in this study suggest not only the difficulty of trying to separate different aspects of competence as currently defined (Canale and Swain 1980; Celce-Murcia 1995) but also some of the cognitive dimensions of discourse that the expanded notion of "interactional competence" may need to take into account.

Participants

The participants are a male Indian graduate student and a male Southern American undergraduate. The Indian student had set about cultivating a friendship with the American student in his French conversation class, who also happened to work at the information desk in the student center. Recognizing the availability for interaction that the American's job entailed, the Indian student initiated their first conversation at the information desk. The friendship developed from there, and a year later they both chose to share living space in the "French House" on campus, which had been created for students who were interested in practicing their French. As they became friends, they talked about cultural differences in conversation, leading to the American coaching the Indian on how to do the American speech activity known as "shooting the shit." They agreed to do a demonstration on videotape in my kitchen, with commentary on this process of socializing the Indian student into a typical American male speech activity. At the time of taping they had been friends for two years—talking daily, working out together, and considering each other as one of their best friends.

They both still remember their first awkward conversation. Steve (the American) was at work at the student union, and Roshan (the Indian) came by intentionally to strike up a conversation with Steve. Steve asked Roshan a question about Sikhs in relation to current world events, inviting a form of "casual conversation"; Roshan's response was what Steve experienced as a lecture, whereas Steve said that he was expecting something like "CNN Headline News." Roshan remembers that Steve was fidgety, but he didn't know why. Roshan clearly had an expectation that conversations should be about substantive issues, whereas Steve was expecting a form of small talk in this context.

Coaching Interaction

The ethnographic data presented below are transcriptions of a videotaped representation, with commentary by the friends in the presence of the researcher, of a typical pragmatic coaching session by the American of the Indian. I discuss the relationship between the ethnographic approach and the interactional sociolinguistic analysis following presentation of the data. It is important to note that what the participants are creating in this data is a "prototype" of the speech activity, in the form of an example of what had emerged spontaneously in the course of their friendship. The perceptions of some people who have seen the data that Roshan seems to be "making it up" are consistent with this performance dimension of the data; he is trying to demonstrate spontaneity on cue. The transcription begins with an "introduction" by the participants, followed by a "wrong" version to show Roshan's starting point in his attempts to master the speech activity. This introduction is followed by the participants' commentary, a "better" version, and some final commentary on the better version. The pragmatic coaching here is toward the learning of a typical male speech activity—a form of casual conversation referred to colloquially as "shooting the shit." "Coaching" seems to be a particularly applicable term (rather than "giving feedback") because it is a form of "practice" in relation to a jointly played game—a proceduralizing of knowledge. In the transcription R represents Roshan, the Indian; S represents Steve, the American; and C represents the researcher.

"Introduction"

(1) R: I always thought in this country it's important to be able to joke or at least understand the sense of humor to be able to build a rapport. They sometimes use an expression "shoot the shit" . . . you probably heard of that expression, right?

(2) S: Yeah, I have, ahm and there's an art to that and it's ah . . . you see it and hear it every single day.

(3) R: Yeah I guess to you it's just natural.

(4) S: It is natural. And ahm you know it's hard to say that it's something you have to . . . you have to work on, but ahm I guess like anything else . . . it takes practice.

(5) R: Yeah it's true. Do you remember the day ahm we talked about it in the kitchen?

(6) S: Um hm

(7) R: Sort of similar to this, I guess. A little bit bigger, though. And you actually told me how to do it. You said you hadn't thought of it until then but . . .

(8) S: No.

(9) R: But you actually came up with a fairly clinical analysis, man.

(10) S: Ha ha. It just slipped out. Yeah we even did a little role play.

(11) R: Yeah we did a role play then, you know?

(12) C: You did? (uh huh) Can you recreate it?

"Wrong" Version

(1) R: Hi, Steve. What's up, man?

(2) S: Ah not a whole helluva lot.

(3) R: No?

(4) S: Trying to do too many things at one time, I think.

(5) R: Yeah? How are your classes going?

(6) S: Well . . . I don't know. Slowly but surely. I don't know [unclear]

(7) R: Yeah?

(8) S: Trying, you know. Watched movies last night . . . should have been studying. Ah . . .

(9) R: ha

(10) S: just ah . . . couple of professors are rubbing me the wrong way, you know. I can't really put my finger on it yet, but ah. . . . Do you mind? [helps himself to food]

(11) R: No . . . go ahead, please.

(12) S: But ah, yeah, I think I'll make it. Get in a groove, you know.

Commentary on "Wrong" Version

(1) S: We had to start over.

(2) R: You see what had happened because . . . after I while I didn't know what to say. I was just asking him questions.

(3) S: He got quiet.

(4) R: And that's when he told me—do you remember what you told me?—he said you have to talk about yourself.

(5) S: Hm. Um hm.

(6) R: It's not an analysis that I'm listening to what you say. You're not even thinking about what you're saying. So . . . that's where the problem arose because . . . I don't know what to say. I'm just trying [to get in]. I want to talk to him because to me it's important, so . . . I'm just trying to ask him questions all the time like "how was your class?" or "what are you doing?" and after a while he's like . . . you know, he's uncomfortable: why doesn't this guy talk about himself? He's just analyzing me or something.

(7) S: Yeah there's a . . . yeah you feel like you're being drilled [grilled] after a couple of questions. But you don't know where to . . . you know . . . it just started to feel forced. And ah . . . I don't know if we tried it again?

(8) R: Yeah, I know we did.

"Better" Version [overlaps indicated by brackets]

(1) R: Hi, Steve. What's up, man?

(2) S: Oh, not much. I'm trying to get something in me.

(3) R: Yeah?

(4) S: I'm starving to death. What you been doin'?

(5) R: Yeah, me too. God I had this class today in math. You won't believe it. . . . I didn't understand a word of what he was saying. He was just, you know, way out there, man. And nobody else did, too. You won't believe this, I mean, some of those people in [that class are smart.

(6) S: [what math?

(7) R: This is Math 101 or or something like that.

(8) S: Yeah

(9) R: It was funny. So what are you doing tonight? Are you going out somewhere or what are you doing?

(10) S: I don't know I haven't really thought about it. I've got uh heh I've got so much to do.

(11) R: Yeah?

(12) S: Yeah. But ahm . . . I think ah I think Jill wants to do something.

(13) R: Really?

(14) S: Yeah.

(15) R: Well that's cool. [Like what?

(16) S: [Have you met her yet?

(17) R: No, I haven't, but this other girl I was telling you in class?

(18) S: uh huh

(19) R: I actually asked her out today.

(20) S: No way.
(21) R: And she said yes, [too.
(22) S: [TSSSSS
(23) R: So that's really cool. I'm excited about it, you know [(unclear)
(24) S: [Well I'll tell you one thing; we're not gonna double date.
(25) R: Hah.
(26) S: You know.
(27) R: All right, Steve, you just broke my heart and I was planning for that, you know.
(28) S: Well.
(29) R: And this other French assignment I gotta work on. That's . . . I don't know, I mean, you know I asked this girl out without thinking about my assignment and now . . . I don't know what I'm gonna do about the assignment.
(30) S: Is that Lautrec?
(31) R: Yeah, it's Lautrec. Do you know her?
(32) S: Um. I had her.
(33) R: Yeah. How is she? Would she mind if I don't turn in an assignment? Would she give [me (unclear)
(34) S: [Well she's . . . she gets a little moody
(35) R: Does she really?
(36) S: sometimes.
(37) R: Oh, man!
(38) S: But. . .
(39) R: Well, hey, what's another B. I might as well go out with this girl (unclear)
(40) S: Yeah, right. Uh heh heh.
(41) R: I'd hate to call her up and say . . . you know . . . because there's a million and one guys who want to go out with her. I mean, I hate to turn the opportunity down. I know it's a tough call . . . a grade and a girl.
(42) S: Yeah
(43) R: I don't know what I'm going to do. Did you see the NBA finals are on tonight, too. Are you gonna watch it?
(44) S: [yeah, I'm following. Three one right now, right?
(45) R: Yeah. It's really cool, man.
(46) S: I'm so sick of the fuckin' Lakers.
(47) R: Really? Ah heh
(48) S: [Yeah, it's about time.
(49) R: Me, man, I'm a Jordan man, too. God (unclear)
(50) S: [I didn't say I was a Jordan man

(51) R: You're not?
(52) S: No. I just . . . I'm just
(53) R: [you're kiddin', man
(54) S: an anti-Magic
(55) R: Heh heh
(56) S: That's all, you know.
(57) R: I can't believe you don't like Michael Jordan, man. Don't you think he's like God's gift to basketball?
(58) S: Why?
(59) R: The things he does in the air, man. It's just . . . it's just incredible. I mean it's not humanly possible, you know? It's just not possible.
(60) S: Are you wearing Nikes?
(61) R: Well, I wish I did.
(62) S: Hah hah
(63) R: The kind of money you make as a graduate teaching assistant at the University of (name of the university)
(64) S: hahahahaha
(65) R: [you know, heh
(66) S: Yeah
(67) R: That's funny, you know, you mention these shoes. People kill in these. Well, I mean it sounds (unclear)
(68) S&C: laughter
(69) R: That's it.

Commentary on "Better" Version

(1) S: Now give us about two or three more hours and we'll have it down.
(2) PAUSE WHILE THEY GET BEERS AND WE REPOSITION OURSELVES
(3) C: Let's see now . . . there was a balanced give and take there?
(4) S: Yeah, I think it was kinda rocky at first but we started . . . we hit a groove there for a minute and it was pretty balanced, I think. Do you agree?
(5) R: Yeah, but . . . do you think ah sometimes, you know, to me it's a conscious effort because I still haven't gotten the groove where I'm totally comfortable. I have to make an attempt not to let um . . . not ask questions and you know to have something to say all the time. So I don't know if . . . ah . . . I don't know how it appears to you. Does it seem to you like I'm making a conscious effort to talk or do I seem. . . .
(6) S: Yeah, but you . . . you're starting to trim the rough edges a little bit.
(7) R: Really?

(8) S: Yeah. I think ah . . . it's not nearly as forced as it used to be. You know it's coming across . . . it's like for a minute there while I was talking, behind a little voice was saying "oh, thank god his attention span is shortening up a little bit."

(9) R&C: laughter

(10) C: Oh this is fascinating.

(11) R: Well, see, that's true. That's a good point. . . . I mean, that's it. Attention span. You know in a casual conversation, which is to use the expression again, "shoot the shit," you don't expect a big attention span. You just . . . you don't even expect the other guy to listen to you, you know. You're just saying something.

(12) S: Hah hah. Yeah, you're just passing minutes, basically.

Analysis

The discourse analysis triangulates data from several sources as part of an interactional sociolinguistic approach. One source is the ethnographic data of the videotaped interaction, which itself includes commentary and analysis by the participants. Another is playback commentary by the participants, who viewed the videotape afterwards, making comments and responding to questions posed by the researcher. Another source is ethnographic interviews that allowed contextualization of the data in relation to the ongoing friendship.

Research on male sociability is limited. In a classic article, Philipsen (1975,15) comments about the working-class American men in his study that "when the social identity of the participants in a situation is symmetrical, the situation can appropriately realize a great amount of talking." Thus, male sociability among peers can involve much conversation, although we have very little research that documents the nature of that conversation. Recent work by Coates focuses on narratives within men's conversation and notes men's "seeming preference for friendships with other men which stress sociability rather than intimacy" (Coates 2003, 200). Drawing on Tannen's (1996) work on gender and language, we see that the speech activity represented in the data conforms to certain principles of gender socialization: talking for solidarity rather than intimacy—on safe topics, with a light touch; disclosing self, but not too much, and not asking too many questions that might feel like "grilling" the other; playing a game together. It seems very significant that these young men comment that "you don't even expect the other guy to listen to you" ("Commentary on 'Better' Version," turn 11)—in contrast with more typical women's conversations, in which "listening to the other" is a crucial aspect of the interaction.

Clearly both participants consider this speech activity to be very important for interaction among American men. Roshan's comments in the "introduction" also reveal that he conceptualizes the speech activity as related to joking interaction, which he regards as important in establishing rapport with Americans (Davies 2004). In fact, a particular form of joking is an embedded subactivity. The analysis reveals that important dimensions of "shooting the shit" as a speech activity seem to be keeping up the flow; talking about oneself but keeping it light; shifting topics rapidly; and maintaining balanced, rapid alternation of turns. A key idea of balanced participation is based in a collaborative discourse structure, which differs substantially from an "interview" in which one person asks questions and the other responds (cf. Johnson and Tyler 1998).

It is important to note some cross-cultural caveats. One is that American men clearly do engage in conversations on serious topics. Roshan has had intense conversations of this sort with his American friend. In fact, as they have become friends the proportion of "shooting the shit" has become smaller in relation to the "serious" conversations. The other caveat is that there may well be a comparable speech activity of the sort analyzed here in Roshan's home culture. What I claim is that Roshan wasn't aware of a comparable speech activity in his cultural repertoire that he could simply transfer over or adapt. We cannot be sure whether this difference is cultural, in the sense that there is no comparable speech activity, or individual in that the speech activity may exist but Roshan hadn't had a chance to learn it; the reality was that Roshan did not have interactional competence in this area.

The unexpected focus—by the participants themselves—on the cognitive dimensions of the speech activity that emerged during the commentary on the pragmatic coaching is framed partly in terms of "shortening up his [Roshan's] attention span." The shortening involves the joint timing of the activity, with the idea of hitting a "groove." Steve's criticism is tactful: "Now give us two or three more hours and we'll have it down" ("Commentary on 'Better' Version," turn 1). Roshan asks directly for feedback when he says, "Does it seem to you like I'm making a conscious effort to talk or do I seem . . . " ("Commentary on 'Better' Version," turn 5). This comment suggests that Roshan is aware that the "conscious effort" is still coming across, that he has not yet mastered the effortless flow of a natural speech activity. Steve responds in tactful but encouraging ways: "Yeah, but you . . . you're starting to trim the rough edges a little bit"; "it's not nearly as forced as it used to be"; "you know it's coming across" ("Commentary on 'Better' Version," turn 6).

Using only the data from the "better" version because of the space constraints of this chapter, I illustrate not only how difficult it is to separate aspects of "communicative competence" as currently defined, and I suggest some dimensions of the discourse that an expanded notion of "interactional competence" may need to take into account.

Dimensions of "Competence"

The notion of "communicative competence in most current communicative language teaching is that of Canale and Swain (1980), which is based on Hymes (1972). Canale and Swain (1980) emphasize that both knowledge and skill are incorporated in communicative competence. They offer four components of communicative competence: grammatical, referring to mastery of the language code; strategic, referring to mastery of techniques for dealing with breakdowns in communication; sociolinguistic, referring to appropriate use of language in context; and discourse, referring to the production of unified spoken or written text in different genres.

Grammatical Competence

The Indian English speaker clearly had grammatical competence, although a few minor breakdowns did occur. Some of these breakdowns are apparent only in relation to discourse as a dimension of cohesion. For example, at the beginning of the "better" version, in responding to Steve's "Oh, not much. I'm trying to get something in me. [as he eats chips and salsa] I'm starving to death. What you been doin'?" (S: 2–4), Roshan's "Yeah, me too" in utterance 5 doesn't seem to fit with the appropriate ellipsis ("I'm trying to get something in me. . . . I'm starving to death"—"Yeah, me too"). This apparent breakdown is largely a matter of timing; the ellipsis was accurate—Roshan just didn't get his response in fast enough before Steve had produced another question ("What you been doin'?"). A second instance occurs in the same turn at talk, when Roshan uses the wrong word in another elliptical structure: "I didn't understand a word of what he was saying . . . and nobody else did, too." This grammatical error was a product of the stress Roshan was feeling to keep the conversation going; he knew the correct form (according to later playback comments). This breakdown is more clearly a "grammatical" error with a polarity item. These breakdowns did not appear to cause confusion, but they might mark Roshan's speech as nonnative.

Strategic Competence

Roshan seems to be able to deal with the misunderstanding about whether Steve is a Michael Jordan fan in utterances 43 to 61. Clearly, this strategic competence also requires discourse and sociolinguistic competence. The discourse competence reveals itself in Roshan's ability to create appropriate cohesion, not only between his interlocutor's statements and his own questions and statements (as in lines 50–53, when Roshan responds with "you're not?" and "You're kiddin', man"). Sociolinguistic competence is demonstrated, for example, in Roshan's ability to infer that Steve's statement at 46, "I'm so sick of the fuckin' Lakers," probably means that he is a fan of the star player on the opposing team. When Roshan then identifies himself as a "Jordan fan" in solidarity (utterance 49) and discovers that Steve means something different, Roshan is able to carry on with a jocular challenge as an appropriate part of the speech activity (utterances 51–59).

Sociolinguistic Competence

Mastery of speech activities and knowledge of their appropriate use would seem to fit within "sociolinguistic" competence. In this case, there appears to be one aspect of the data that clearly fits under this rubric: lexical choices. Roshan has picked up "man" as a way of addressing his male friend and "cool" as a term of approval, but he seems to overuse them in this interaction, given that Steve never uses them at all. Is this a problem of sociolinguistic competence or discourse competence?

Choice of speech acts might seem to fit under sociolinguistic competence. Roshan has trouble using the appropriate speech acts: He asks too many questions rather than producing statements. The perception of "too many questions" creates the feeling that the addressee is being "drilled"; a shift in proportion of a certain type of speech act has the potential to transform the speech activity into an extreme form of interview known as interrogation.

Choice of topic might be another dimension of sociolinguistic competence—which Roshan seems to have mastered in that he sticks to school, social life, and sports and seems to know enough to hold up his end of the conversation. But how should we classify the apparent requirement within the speech activity of rapid shifts of topic? Roshan seems to know that this rapid shifting is required, but he doesn't always achieve it in a smooth way. Are rough transitions (as in utterance 43 of the "better" version: "I don't know what I'm going to do [in relation to the "a grade or a girl" dilemma]. Did you see the NBA finals are on tonight, too. Are you gonna watch it?") failures of sociolinguistic competence or of discourse competence?

Discourse Competence

Discourse competence is traditionally conceptualized as related most closely to matters of cohesion. The important dimension of "balanced participation" in this speech activity is based in a particular kind of collaborative discourse structure. Unlike in a prototypical interview, in which one person asks questions and the other responds, the challenge of "shooting the shit" for Roshan was to resist asking questions and to come up with his own volunteered contributions in balance with his American interlocutor. Roshan has trouble getting the balance of participation right so that it is relatively equal. Is this a failure of discourse or sociolinguistic competence?

Toward Interactional Competence

The analysis of this data set has yielded other important aspects of competence that suggest what might need to be included in the notion of "interactional competence."

Several aspects of competence in this data set relate to understanding the boundaries of application of certain principles in the interaction. The first has to do with "degree of seriousness": A basic principle of this sociable male interaction is that it should be kept "light." It is important to note that "seriousness" is not necessarily the opposite of "jocularity." Whereas Roshan has the right topic (sports), he violates a degree of seriousness norm for the activity when he shifts to an allusion to current events related to violent crime in the United States—that people would kill for Nike sport shoes. The second facet has to do with what might be called "degree of hyperbole." Roshan picks up on Steve's initial hyperbole ("I'm starving to death" in utterance 4 of the "better" version) but then generalizes it too much throughout the interaction (at utterance 5 in relation to math class: "I didn't understand a word of what he was saying"; at 41 in relation to a date: "there's a million and one guys who want to go out with her"; and at 57: "Don't you think he's like God's gift to basketball?" and 59: "I mean it's not humanly possible, you know" in relation to sports), whereas Steve does not. The third could be termed "degree of self-disclosure" and is consistent with the idea that male conversation focuses on sociability rather than intimacy. Roshan understands that participation involves "talking about yourself," but he is not clear about what form that self-disclosure is supposed to take or its limits (cf. Barnlund 1989 for a discussion of cross-cultural differences in self-disclosure in sociable interaction).

Another aspect of competence reflected in this data set is mastery of subactivities within the larger speech activity. In this case we see that the ability to shift into "jocularity," in the form of collaborative joking activity, is important. Roshan has learned how to respond to teasing (as a kind of subactivity within the larger activity of "shooting the shit"): Steve reported that in the past Roshan would have responded to Steve's ritual insult teasing in utterance 24—"Well, I'll tell you one thing; we're not gonna double date"—either with laughter or with a retort like "Fuck you, Steve," whereas by the time of the taping Roshan has learned to produce a comeback in the form of "All right, Steve, you just broke my heart and I was planning for that, you know" (in utterance 27)—playing along with the mock insult by responding with a mock hurt response. He has learned how to use the ritual insult joking as a way of displaying the strength of their friendship (cf. Davies 1984; Boxer and Cortes-Conde 1997; Davies, in press).

A third aspect of competence is what the participants refer to as the "tone" of the interaction. This tone seems to be related to Hymes' notion of "key" (1974, 57–58), although not as clearly as the issues of "seriousness" and "jocularity." In the playback interview, Steve said he had set the tone in the first, "wrong" interaction intending for it to be a "downer" and that Roshan had picked up on that tone in the "better" version. Based on these two examples and other observations, what is represented here seems to be a prototypical student stance: of world-weariness and being overburdened by school, but with a plucky attitude expressed—so that it doesn't present the speaker as needy. This stance is conventionalized in the ritual greeting and response: "What's up/"—"Not a whole helluva lot /Not much" ("'Wrong' Version," 1–2; "'Better' Version," 1–2). There is a kind of commiseration through matching stories, as well as some problem-solving (in this case in relation to the French teacher), but advice is not directly solicited. The stance seems to involve caring about academic responsibilities, while trying to "get by." Enthusiasm seems to be disallowed, which is one reason Roshan's hyperbole seems discordant. The American student's contributions are sardonic: the indirect "she gets a little moody sometimes" in utterances 34 and 36 and the subtle "Are you wearing Nikes?" in utterance 60.

A final aspect of competence, which I discuss in more detail below, involves two dimensions that the participants identified. The first has to do with "ease of interaction." Roshan is aware that he still sounds "forced"; he is aiming at a quality of ease within his participation in the speech activity such that he is literally "up to speed" in his appropriate contributions. The second has to do with a particular "tension of consciousness." A phenomenological dimension of the activity emerges in the pragmatic coaching concerning "shortening up of attention span," with the idea of hitting a "groove."

The dimensions of the discourse identified here seem to move beyond both shared background knowledge and shared orientation within a particular context. They appear to be part of a shared cognitive dimension in the form of a collaboratively constructed intersubjectivity.

The Unexpected Cognitive Focus

The cognitive focus that emerged in the coaching is conceptualized partly as "shortening up his attention span." This discourse perspective on attention differs from mainstream treatments of attention in the research on language learning.

Cognitive theories that are concerned with automaticity (the idea that as fluency develops and language use becomes automatic, the conscious effort required diminishes and more cognitive energy is freed up to pay attention to other aspects of language) make the distinction between "declarative knowledge" and "procedural knowledge": knowledge *that* versus knowledge *how*. Steve and Roshan have conceptualized the idea of "short attention span"—a form of declarative knowledge about the speech activity—but the translation of that concept into procedural knowledge is very challenging and apparently requires explicit coaching.

Discourse Perspective on Attention

A discourse perspective on attention would take as foundational Chafe's (1994) work on consciousness and the flow of language, as the out-of-awareness connection between thought and speech. It also would draw on work in the ethnography of speaking, using culturally defined units of speech events and activities as the starting point (Hymes 1972). In this case, we have a named activity; the culture or subculture has chosen to lexicalize it. Hymes' notion of "key" also is important here. In terms of "manner" or "spirit" (Hymes 1972, 57) this notion seems relevant to the analysis because this speech activity is characterized as nonserious and perfunctory (in that topics are touched on lightly and switched rapidly). Yet already we have two "keys"—and if we consider "tone," another dimension is introduced: the "downer" tone as identified by Steve.

If we turn to Goffman's (1981) idea of "footing," we have a way of trying to mark boundaries of the speech activity within the stream of interaction—the strips that occur when speakers are "shooting the shit." Such boundary-making could include a quality of attention as part of the "footing," for which we need to return to the earlier work of Schütz (1967) for the phenomenological dimension (defined as an analysis or description of how an activity is experienced by those engaging in it). Schutz's notion of consciousness includes shifting "the accent of reality" as it moves among "finite provinces of meaning," each of which has its own cognitive style.

The speech activity under investigation here clearly seems to have a particular cognitive style, partly conceptualized by the practitioners in relation to length of "attention span" and the notion of a "groove." It also has the distinctive quality, however, of being a form of joint action. "Groove" is a term from jazz, representing the idea that the participants move into a space in which they are improvising smoothly and effectively together. Such an idea relates to the notion of a specific tension of consciousness and a prevalent form of spontaneity.

Conclusion

A Male Friendship

Some mastery of this form of casual conversation may be very important for learners in establishing social networks that allow friendships to develop. Steve and Roshan note several important dimensions of the social context of the university that facilitated the initiation of their friendship. The first is that Roshan had a chance to observe Steve (both in class and at the student center) and form the impression that he might be receptive to interactions. The second point they noted is that when the first awkward conversation occurred at the student union, Steve didn't chase Roshan away because he knew that he'd see him the next day in French class. Finally, both agreed that the French conversation class provided a common interest and excuse to get together (to practice French). If Roshan had had to rely on his interactional competence alone, the friendship might never have developed.

Roshan and Steve both commented in the playback session and in the ethnographic interviews on what their friendship means. Steve said that he considers Roshan "one of my very best friends" who had helped him to "cross over" to the understanding that skin color is not important. Addressing Roshan, he said, "I'm not afraid anymore. I was still afraid before I met you." He specifically mentioned the importance of knowing that he could count on Roshan. For Roshan, the friendship with Steve helps him to understand American culture. Roshan seems to be a natural ethnographer, and this tendency is served by a member of the culture who can answer his questions. The friends also report that their now-solid friendship involves less "shooting the shit" but that Roshan still uses it quite a bit in dealing with other American men day to day.

Social Interactional Perspective

A social interactional perspective as a framework allows us to integrate current relevant perspectives on second-language development. The first perspective is the apparent dichotomy between instructed learning (in a classroom context) and naturalistic learning (outside the classroom). In Roshan's case, we have learning initiated and sustained by the motivation and agency of the learner. Schmidt's work on his own language learning in Brazil (Schmidt and Frota 1986) and on Wes's development (Schmidt 1983) notes various aspects of the learning but does not provide data of the sort reported here in relation to discourse. A language socialization perspective (Schieffelin and Ochs 1986) encourages us to follow up on such learners and find out what they are actually doing.

A second current perspective on language learning has to do with the importance of identity (Norton-Pierce 1995; MacKay and Wong 1996). Roshan wanted to learn about American culture, and he consciously looked for cues of receptivity as he attempted to make American friends. He also was nonjudgmental and willing to take risks. Rather than retreating into a defensive posture that he already "knew" English, he was willing to accommodate by developing this particular sociolinguistic skill without feeling threatened in his own sociocultural identity. It is noteworthy that in this prototypical data set Roshan presents himself in a role that is not authentic (for example, representing himself as not caring about his grades) but that he is willing to adopt as part of the performance of the speech activity (Schilling-Estes 1998). He also has consciously modified his accent and his stress patterns, purely for utilitarian reasons; he said that he was tired of having to repeat everything several times to local Americans. Steve, for his part, had already been opened up to a broader sense of his own identity and perspective on the world; he knew what it was like to experience prejudice in the United States on the basis of his Alabama accent, and he had had cross-cultural experience in France. This study has provided an example of spontaneous development of cross-cultural awareness of discourse conventions and their link to sociocultural identity. If the students had not had the opportunity to go beyond initial unsuccessful conversations, they might have rigidified their stereotypes of each other as too superficial and too intense, respectively.

Finally, Vygotskyan sociocultural theory (Lantolf 2000) fits comfortably into the idea of socialization. In the case of this data set, we have a natural situation of novice and expert, with the expert providing feedback as well as interactional scaffolding. A social interactional perspective allows us to integrate work in all of these areas with the notion of interactional competence. Boxer and Cohen (2004) point out the essential compatibility of the theoretical models of language identity, language socialization, and sociocultural theory.

Implications for Language Teaching

Turning now to implications for language teaching, we have seen that the development of a friendship, with accompanying openness and trust, allowed for conditions in which a form of pragmatic coaching could take place, offering feedback on the development of interactional competence. Teaching methodologies that attempt to create these conditions can be found in Bardovi-Harlig et al. (1991); Bardovi-Harlig (1996); Davies, Tyler, and Koran (1989); Davies and Tyler (1994); Gumperz and Roberts (1980); and Tyler (1994). The broadest implication for language teaching is to incorporate an ethnographic perspective on the uses of language, with presentation and analysis of examples of important speech activities so that students will begin to be aware, at least, of these dimensions of culture. The goal of such methodology would be to encourage and equip learners to try to form friendships and networks of various sorts with native speakers in ways that further the process of language socialization.

REFERENCES

Bardovi-Harlig, Kathleen. 1996. Pragmatics and language teaching: Bringing pragmatics and pedagogy together. *Pragmatics and Language Learning* 7:21–39.

Bardovi-Harlig, Kathleen, Beverly Hartford, Rebecca Mahan Taylor, M. J. Morgan, and Dudley W. Reynolds. 1991. Developing pragmatic awareness: closing the conversation. *ELT Journal* 45:4–15.

Barnlund, Dean C. 1989. *Communicative styles of Japanese and Americans: Images and realities*. Belmont, Calif.: Wadsworth.

Boxer, Diana, and Andrew Cohen, eds. 2004. *Studying speaking to inform second language learning*. Clevedon, United Kingdom: Multilingual Matters.

Boxer, Diana, and Florencia Cortes-Condé. 1997. From bonding to biting: Conversational joking and identity display. *Journal of Pragmatics* 27:275–94.

Canale, Michael, and Merrill Swain. 1980. Theoretical bases of communicative approaches to second language teaching and testing. *Applied Linguistics* 1, no. 1:1–47.

Celce-Murcia, Marianne. 1995. The elaboration of sociolinguistic competence: Implications for teacher education. In *Linguistics and the education of second language teachers: Ethnolinguistic, psycholinguistic, and sociolinguistic aspects,* Georgetown University Round Table on Languages and Linguistics, ed. James Alatis, Carolyn Straehle, Brent Gallenberger, and Maggie Ronkin, 699–710. Washington, D.C.: Georgetown University Press.

Chafe, Wallace. 1994. *Discourse, consciousness, and time: The flow and displacement of conscious experience in speaking and writing*. Chicago: University of Chicago Press.

Coates, Jennifer. 2003. *Men talk: Stories in the making of masculinities*. Oxford: Blackwell.

Davies, Catherine Evans. 1984. Joint joking: Improvisational humorous episodes in conversation. In *Proceedings of the Tenth Annual Meeting of the Berkeley Linguistics Society*, ed. Claudia Brugman and Monica Macaulay, 360–71. Berkeley: University of California Press.

———. 2004. Developing awareness of cross-cultural pragmatics: The case of American/German sociable interaction. *Multilingua: Journal of Cross-Cultural and Interlanguage Communication* 23, no. 3:207–23.

———. In press. Gendered sense of humor as expressed through aesthetic typifications. *Journal of Pragmatics.*

Davies, Catherine Evans, and Andrea Tyler. 1994. Demystifying cross-cultural (mis)communication: Improving performance through balanced feedback in a situated context. In *Discourse and performance of international teaching assistants*, ed. Carolyn G. Madden and Cynthia L. Myers, 201–20. Alexandria, Va.: TESOL.

Davies, Catherine Evans, Andrea Tyler, and John J. Koran. 1989. Face-to-face with English speakers: An advanced training class for international teaching assistants. *English for Specific Purposes* 8:139–53.

Goffman, Erving. 1981. *Forms of talk.* Philadelphia: University of Pennsylvania Press.

Gumperz, John J. and Celia Roberts. 1980. *Developing awareness skills for inter-ethnic communication.* Occasional paper no. 12. Singapore: SEAMEO Regional Language Centre.

Hall, Joan Kelly. 1995. "Aw, man, where you goin'?": Classroom interaction and the development of L2 interactional competence. *Issues in Applied Linguistics* 6, no. 2:37–62.

Hymes, Dell. 1972. On communicative competence. In *Sociolinguistics: Selected readings,* ed. J. B. Pride and Janet Holmes, 269–93. Baltimore: Penguin.

———. 1974. *Foundations in sociolinguistics: An ethnographic approach.* Philadelphia: University of Pennsylvania Press.

Johnson, Marysia, and Andrea Tyler. 1998. Re-examining natural context: How much does the LPI look like a conversation? In *Language proficiency interviews: A discourse approach*, ed. Richard Young and Agnes He, 23–53. Amsterdam: Benjamins.

Kramsch, Claire J. 1986. From language proficiency to interactional competence. *Modern Language Journal* 70, no. 4:366–72.

Lantolf, James P., ed. 2000. *Sociocultural theory and second language learning.* New York: Oxford University Press.

MacKay, Sandra, and Sau-Ling Cynthia Wong. 1996. Multiple discourses, multiple identities: Investment and agency in second language learning among Chinese adolescent immigrant students. *Harvard Educational Review* 66, no. 3:577–608.

Norton-Pierce, Bonnie. 1995. Social identity, investment, and language learning. *TESOL Quarterly* 29, no. 1:9–31.

Philipsen, Gerry. 1975. Speaking "like a man" in Teamsterville: Culture patterns of role enactment in an urban neighborhood. *Quarterly Journal of Speech* 61:13–22.

Schieffelin, Bambi, and Elinor Ochs. 1986. Language socialization. *Annual Review of Anthropology* 15:163–91.

Schilling-Estes, Natalie. 1998. Investigating "self-conscious" speech: The performance register in Ocracoke English. *Language in Society* 27:53–83.

Schmidt, Richard. 1983. Interaction, acculturation, and the acquisition of communicative competence: A case study of an adult. In *Sociolinguistics and language acquisition,* ed. Eliot Judd and Nessa Wolfson, 137–74. Rowley, Mass.: Newbury House.

Schmidt, Richard, and Sylvia Frota. 1986. Developing basic conversational ability in a second language: A case-study of an adult learner of Portuguese. In *Talking to learn: Conversation in second language acquisition*, ed. Richard Day, 237–326. Rowley, Mass.: Newbury House.

Schütz, Alfred. 1967. *Collected papers I: The problem of social reality.* The Hague: Martinus Nijhoff.

Tannen, Deborah. 1996. *Gender and discourse.* Oxford: Oxford University Press.

Tyler, Andrea. 1994. Effective role-play situations and focused feedback: A case for pragmatic analysis in the classroom. In *Discourse and performance of international teaching assistants*, ed. Carolyn G. Madden and Cynthia L. Myers, 116–33. Alexandria, Va.: TESOL.

7

Applied Cognitive Linguistics and Newer Trends in Foreign Language Teaching Methodology

SUSANNE NIEMEIER
University of Koblenz-Landau, Germany

Overview

Research on foreign language teaching methodology is still a relatively recent topic, although we may trace it back to the 1940s. During its brief history, it has been influenced by various linguistic theories and later on by applied linguistics. We have seen, for example, the impact of behaviorism, structural approaches, generative grammar, speech act theory, and others; these models have left their traces in textbooks and teaching materials, to a greater or lesser extent.

My contribution first briefly summarizes the recent history of the relation between linguistics/applied linguistics and foreign language teaching methodology and then mainly focuses on the cognitive linguistic (CL) perspective on language, as well as on the connections between the CL approach and its recently posited application as manifested in applied cognitive linguistics (ACL). I especially highlight the latter's potential for foreign language teaching to German learners of English. I assume that, from an ACL perspective, the rigid distinction between grammar and lexis is no longer tenable because the underlying structuring principles within both areas are comparable. I therefore comment on the inadequacy of assuming such a distinction. To show what a more holistic view of the grammar-lexis continuum would look like, I give examples from various areas of English as a foreign language (EFL) teaching, ranging from the traditional concept of lexicology to the traditional concept of grammar. Finally, I discuss the compatibility of an ACL approach with current trends within foreign language teaching methodology.

Status of Syntax and Lexis within Foreign Language Teaching Methodology

If we regard older, as well as more recent, trends in foreign language teaching methodology and their relation to linguistics/applied linguistics, all of these approaches seem to have one thing in common, notwithstanding the varying perspectives they take. They all share the traditional view of language as consisting of distinct components—namely, syntax and lexis.

To start with an example from the more distant past, teaching methods based on behaviorism regarded language learning as "habit formation"; language itself was regarded as a collection of speech patterns and structures—that is, there was a strong focus on grammar, whereas the communicative function of language was largely neglected. This view found its way into the foreign language classroom in the form of the audio-lingual method with its famous pattern drills, which often consisted of memorized grammatical templates into which lexical items were substituted (Richards and Rodgers 1986). When Chomsky in the late 1950s claimed the existence of a "language acquisition device" (LAD) (Chomsky 1957), behaviorism in language teaching lost its footing. Instead, theories concentrating on transformation drills—in which the surface structure of sentences was to be changed while the deep structure (and hence the meaning) stayed intact—became the mainstay of grammar teaching. As was the case for behaviorism, in the transformational approach language was not regarded or taught in relation to its communicative or social function. Moreover, as with the audio-lingual approach, these transformational exercises assumed a strict division between syntax and the lexicon. In contrast to current views, the focus was not on producing the language but on talking *about* the language. Even Chomsky doubted the relevance of his theories for foreign language teaching (cf. Howatt 1984). With Hymes's (1971) critique, which introduced the notion of communicative competence, a pure transformational approach came to be regarded as a limited endeavor. Yet even Hymes tacitly accepted "grammatical competence" as a separate component.

Drawing on Hymes's insights, Canale and Swain (1980) developed their applied linguistic model of communicative language teaching with its focus on "communicative competence," which included pragmatic knowledge and aimed at enabling learners to apply the rule-based language system in different communication situations. Again, however, we still find the traditional separation between syntax and lexis.

Even more recently, Long et al. (e.g., Long and Larsen-Freeman 1991), who followed the interactionist approach (which evolved into focus-on-form), never challenged the linguistic theory that formed the basis of language learning/teaching; the only aspect they challenged was the route through which language learning took place.

Another example of the nonholistic view of language is the functional-notional approach. To a certain extent Austin's (1962) and Searle's (1969) speech act theory was the linguistic basis for this approach, so foreign language teaching turned against the structure-dependent view of language and toward its meaning potential—but still never questioned the separate roles of syntax and lexis.

Although communicative language teaching probably is still the most widespread view on foreign language teaching, we are witnessing a movement back from a concentration on solely communicative competence toward a renewed interest in including a focus on more formal aspects of language, which is especially highlighted in the focus-on-form approach, aiming at reintegrating grammar into the foreign language classroom by combining formal instruction and communicative language use (Doughty and Williams 1998; Long 1991). Researchers see "the need for direct instruction and corrective feedback" (Pica 2000, 11). Another recent development is discourse-based approaches to grammar instruction, which focus on authentic language uses and structures and their meanings in discourse and text and are an application of corpus-based research (McCarthy 1991; McCarthy and Carter 1994), so that learners may be confronted with "real" language and not with specially constructed texts.

In this section I have highlighted only some aspects of the much more complex theory development in second-language acquisition (SLA) research. Wherever we look, however, we notice that the rigid separation of grammar and lexis was never challenged until the CL/ACL paradigm developed. Even if we consider current EFL textbooks in Germany and presumably elsewhere, we see that they maintain this distinction.

In the following section, I first point out key tenets of CL that are particularly useful to language teaching and then discuss these key issues within ACL.

Key Tenets of Cognitive Linguistics

CL arose in the late 1970s/early 1980s, partly out of dissatisfaction with the generative paradigm. CL regards language not as an autonomous module in our minds but as closely interacting with other mental faculties such as vision, sensorimotor skills, memory, and others. Furthermore, CL represents language as inseparably intertwined with culture. Some of its major research topics/directions are categorization, prototypicality, iconicity, and metaphorization, which I discuss in more detail in the succeeding sections. These topics also are of immediate interest to ACL and its budding research on foreign language teaching methodology.

What is unique to the CL approach is that these strategies of language usage apply not only to lexis but also to grammar. They are understood as belonging to the general mental organization principles, which apply not to language alone but also to other areas of cognition.

In recent years researchers have attempted to apply insights from CL to language learning and teaching, thereby creating the area of ACL. ACL-focused publications are still scarce, but a widespread interest is present and growing (see, for example, Achard and Niemeier 2004; Pütz, Niemeier, and Dirven 2001a, 2001b).

Applied Cognitive Linguistics

Although ACL is still in its development, researchers are getting more and more interested, especially in analyzing problems occurring in foreign language teaching and in looking for solutions within the CL paradigm. Like CL, ACL takes a holistic perspective, regarding language as part of and interacting with other mental capacities as well as with everyday knowledge. Within the history of SLA theory, ACL represents a revolutionary view on language because for the first time it questions Chomsky's LAD as the explanation for linguistic universals, on which most postbehaviorist language teaching methods seem to rely. Although ACL acknowledges certain language universals resulting from general human cognitive processes, it also emphasizes nonuniversal aspects because it regards language as inseparably intertwined with the surrounding culture.

As such, the foremost concern within ACL is the use of the language. As a usage-based model, ACL looks at language as it is actually used (e.g., it relies on corpus analyses)—which stands in contrast to the more prescriptive linguistic perspective of the generative generation. This perspective, however, does not exclude interest in the explanations of the linguistic phenomena themselves. Such explanations frequently rely on the general organizing principles mentioned above, which also entail relating language to its cultural background(s).

ACL's main aim is to make learners aware of the motivation behind linguistic phenomena and to help them understand how language works because it regards understanding as a precondition for learning. This understanding seems to be possible via the inherent explanatory power of seeing language on the whole as governed by the aforementioned structuring principles, such as categorization, prototypicality, iconicity, and metaphorization. These strategies are to be found on any level of the language. For CL (and thus for ACL as well), grammar and lexis are not regarded as separated from each other but as two poles of a continuum, underlying the same structuring elements. I provide an example for this claim in the following text (see also Niemeier 2001; Niemeier, in press; Rudzka-Ostyn 2003).

Examples of ACL Approach in the EFL Classroom

As an illustration of how an ACL approach in an EFL classroom could work, consider one area that is traditionally called "lexical" and one area that is traditionally called "grammatical." As an example from lexis I have chosen metaphors, and as an example from grammar I focus on prepositions. As I hope will become apparent, however, these two areas are closely interrelated—an aspect that no traditional approach ever points out.

Dealing with Metaphor in the EFL Classroom

It probably is not necessary to present metaphor theory within CL as such at this point. Suffice it to say that one of the earliest and until today most widely received developments within CL is Lakoff's and his colleagues' research on conceptual metaphors, starting with "Metaphors We Live By" (Lakoff and Johnson 1980). Whereas metaphor previously had been regarded mainly as a creative stylistic device, Lakoff et al. argue that relegating metaphor to stylistics misses the undeniable fact that everyday language is filled with conventional metaphors. Often we are not even aware that we are using these metaphors because they are so much a part of our language that we do not pay any special attention to them; yet there is indeed a structuring behind the widespread usage of everyday metaphors. Lakoff coined the term "conceptual metaphor" to highlight the fact that within our conceptual systems we have a metaphorical structure that allows us to conceptualize one domain in terms of another. The general pattern is to use our understanding of the physical, spatial, or social—that is, "objective"—domain to understand or conceptualize the internal, "subjective" domain.

A frequently quoted example of a conceptual metaphor is "time is money." The mapping from "time" to "money" is not conscious but a cognitive predisposition within our culture. The concept "time is money" comes to the fore in many linguistic instantiations, such as *I spent an hour with my grandmother yesterday*; *this flat tire cost me an hour*; *I lost a lot of time in the traffic jam;* and many others; there are an unlimited number of such expression. The mental structuring behind all of these expressions, however, is the "time is money" concept. We talk about time in money terms because time is an abstract concept that is difficult to express directly; therefore we turn toward a more concrete physical, spatial, or social domain such as valued physical objects—in this case money—and map it onto time. Talking about and conceptualizing *time* in terms of *money* (or a valuable physical object) highlights certain properties of *time:* that the human life span is limited, that the amount of work humans can accomplish during a particular span of time is limited, and so forth.

The meaning transfer does not happen in a conscious way; it is part of our linguistic and cultural socialization. In a culture in which people are not paid by the hour, month, or year, this exact mapping presumably would not come into existence. In this respect, however, there is no large cultural difference between Anglo-American cultures and the German culture, so we find this conceptual metaphor in German as well, although the linguistic instantiations are not completely identical. Thus, we do not "spend" time in German, but as in English we can "Zeit investieren" (*invest time*), "Zeit gewinnen" (*gain time*), "Zeit verlieren" (*lose time*), "Zeit sparen" (*save time*), "Zeit verschwenden" (*waste time*), and "ein bißchen Geduld kann sich auch auszahlen" (*a little patience pays off*).

A key notion in Lakoff's approach to metaphor is that the mappings from source to target domains are partial. Thus, when we use concepts from one domain to understand another domain, this mapping process highlights certain properties of the target domain while obscuring other properties.

In the foreign language classroom metaphors generally have appeared—until today—only in literary analysis. The everyday or conceptual metaphors in which CL is mainly interested are hardly addressed at all. Working with conceptual metaphors in the foreign language classroom may help achieve two different goals: raising learners' awareness for intercultural differences as well as structuring principles in language and thought.

Metaphors always involve cultural knowledge because they develop within a culture and often are handed down from generation to generation. Therefore, one reason to focus on metaphors in the foreign language classroom is that they can raise learners' intercultural awareness and may be used for a contrastive approach. We can see this benefit, for example, when learners actively work with metaphors in comparing conceptual metaphors, as well as their linguistic instantiations, in English and German texts of any kind and their own choice—because metaphors are everywhere. Metaphors also may be connected to the analysis of literature or used as a conscious strategy in creative writing. Working with metaphors also entails an affective element; such an approach may raise the learners' motivation because uncovering manipulation is fun and may induce learners to look more closely at language and decipher "hidden meanings." Furthermore, working with metaphors heightens learners' potential for monitoring their own output in the foreign language in a more meaningful way. The main point is that working with metaphors is a way to understand how language works, how it changes, and how meanings are created and extended. Thus, learners may develop a new perspective on language in general.

An example for different metaphorizations in the two languages in question—German and English—are color metaphors (see also Niemeier 1998). In English we find expressions such as "to feel blue," "blue movie," or "red tape," the understanding of which entirely relies on cultural background information. The meanings are metonymically related to melancholy, the fact that laws against showing such movies used to be printed on blue paper, and the fact that legal proceedings were tied together with a reddish ribbon, respectively. If we don't know about the metonymic relationships (which usually is the case), however, we interpret the meanings as metaphors, see also Niemeier 2000. We do not find any of these expressions in German; thus, learners need to know about the background culture to be able to decipher the meanings in question. For example, if a German states that he "ist blau" (literally: *feels blue*), he is actually saying that he is drunk—an interpretation that, again, relies on cultural background knowledge. Knowledge about these culture-bound metaphors and metonymies can enable listeners to avoid misunderstandings.

Furthermore, from a more functional point of view, we can state that metaphors often are used for manipulative purposes, such as in advertising or political propaganda. If news coverage of a war or political unrest metaphorically frames one party as "the bad guys" and the other as "the good guys"—and does so by exploiting common conceptual metaphors—we normally are not even aware of this kind of manipulation, so the possibility that we will see the events in any other light is limited. To take an example from advertising in Germany: A recent IKEA ad for home office furniture says "Kommen Sie doch auf einen <u>Karrieresprung</u> vorbei," by which we understand something like "do visit us for a career jump." This slogan is a play on a popular German saying inviting people for a short visit: "Kommen Sie doch auf <u>einen Sprung</u> vorbei" (literally: *Do drop in for a jump = for a short while*). We realize that common conceptual metaphors are involved here: A jump is an upward movement, so the orientational metaphor *good is up* is involved, and because a jump generally also is a forward movement, *life is a journey* is at work as well.

This advertisement is manipulative insofar as it suggests that the future home office furniture owner's career will be pushed ahead (*good is up*)—an interpretation for which there is absolutely no objective reason. Thus, by mentioning the upward movement, the ad implicitly states that buying the furniture is a positive asset that may pay off. Had the ad simply presented the information as "here is our new selection of home office furniture," this notion would not have developed. What is more, the *life is a journey* metaphor—suggesting that we move in life on a certain path—is activated by the use of the verb "vorbeikommen" (*drop in*), which in English does not mention the path of the movement as it does in German but focuses on the manner of movement. This metaphor goes hand-in-hand with the orientational metaphor *good is up* because advancing in one's job is equally conceptualized as a forward movement.

The manipulative potential of metaphors, then, is one of the reasons learners should at least be made aware of the notion of a conceptual metaphor, so that they have a chance to see as well as to react to it and realize what a powerful and flexible tool language really is. This statement, of course, is true not only for a foreign language/culture but also for the native language/culture. Once learners realize how a foreign language works and how things are conceptualized in a foreign culture, they may see their native language and culture in a different light because they realize that there are different words and ways to talk about and deal with certain topics. Thus, via the alienating effect of realizing how the foreign language/culture works, one may also arrive at a more realistic view of one's own language/culture.

Dealing with Prepositions in the EFL Classroom

If learners have already been made aware of conceptual metaphors, as a next step one might deal with metaphorization in the more abstract realm of prepositions. Prepositions, along with the tense and aspect system, are one of the most difficult areas for German learners of English, who often perceive them as being randomly distributed over the language. They cannot rely on their German mother tongue because similar prepositions often work differently in the two languages. For example, compare "at university" to "in/an der Uni." If we can represent the meanings and uses of prepositions as being systematic and motivated, this insight may help learners in their acquisition. The ACL account offers some hope in this area.

CL/ACL posit that our basic bodily experiences are spatial, as we come into life and move in space. The basic prepositions represent spatial relationships. I focus on *at, on* and *in;* although I cannot offer a full-fledged account of all the meanings here, I sketch the meaning differences on three levels: the basic meanings and the metaphorized meanings of these prepositions on two levels—temporal and abstract. This is exactly what is different in the ACL approach as compared to more traditional approaches: Prepositions are not all discussed at the same level; there is a distinction between the so-called basic (i.e., spatial) uses of the prepositions and the metaphorized uses of the prepositions. The temporal and abstract uses of the prepositions rely on the basic, spatial meanings, and the mappings keep these meanings partially intact. Thus, if one knows the basic meaning, one can easily deduce the metaphorized meanings.

I illustrate that with the three prepositions in question, starting with the basic spatial meanings. *At* is zero-dimensional; it is seen as a precise point in space (examples: *at the station, at school, at home*). *On* is one- or two-dimensional, depending on whether it is seen as a line or as a surface, because two objects are in contact or at least in very close vicinity to each other (examples: *[the picture] on the wall, [the book] on the table, [the town] on the border*). *In* is three-dimensional because one object encloses another (examples: *[the wine] in the bottle, [the spider] in the shower, [the burglar] in the flat*).

Of course these usages are not the only uses of these prepositions; all of them also can be used temporally—that is, metaphorically. The conceptual metaphor behind the temporal usages is *time is space*. Examples for the temporal *at* are *at midnight, at dinner time, at 7 P.M.* Temporal *at* is regarded as a precise point on the timeline; the preciseness and zero-dimensionality have been mapped from the spatial usage onto the temporal usage and thus have been kept intact. Examples for the temporal *on* are *on a Sunday, on my birthday, on Christmas Eve*—the day in English is regarded as the prototypical time unit expressing a stretch of time because our routine activities in life are mainly organized around days. The temporal *on* preserves the meaning of coverage (covering a stretch of time) that it already has in its basic, spatial sense. Finally, examples for the temporal *in* are *in a minute, in 1920, in the evening*. Thus, all time units shorter and longer than a day use *in*. The temporal *in* preserves the notion of enclosure that is present in the spatial *in*, where a time span is conceptualized as a container that encloses certain events—we perceive boundaries (unlike with *on*). This conception, of course, is possible only with durations in the past or the future because the present is regarded as a precise point on the time line and therefore is referred to by the temporal *at (at present)*.

What is especially important in this view of prepositions is that the spatial and temporal uses are closely connected in meaning and that they share the abstracted meaning features of *point/target, coverage/contact,* and *containment/enclosure*. Thus, the meaning aspect is highlighted, and if learners internalize the abstract meanings, they need not learn all prepositional uses by heart.

These abstracted meanings also stay intact when we consider the second kind of metaphorization that we find with prepositions, which is somewhat more complex: the abstract use of prepositions. The reason for this second metaphorization is that we do not have too many strategies for all we want to express, so we extend the basic notions that are already present in the language. "Abstract" metaphors refer to notions such as circumstance, cause, reason, purpose, subject matter, or area. Fewer characteristics of the spatial prepositions are taken over in these mappings, however, than in the mappings from spatial prepositions onto temporal prepositions; nevertheless, there *are* common denominators.

The use of abstract prepositions depends to a large extent on the accompanying verb or adjective. Examples for the abstract *at* are *At Peter's flattering remark, Helen blushed. We laughed at this story* (short bout of laughter, in contrast to "laugh about"). The abstract *at* still refers to a specific event that tends to be very short, comparable to a point in space or a point in time. Another usage of the abstract *at* is to refer to a target that is conceived of as a point (pointing to something), as in *He is good at math*. Examples for the abstract *on* include *participants should pay on arrival, a talk on birth control,* and *you are always on my mind*. The abstract *on* retains the notion of close contact or even covering a metaphorical surface; that is, payment is supposed to happen immediately after participants arrive, and the talk covers the area of birth control—thus, the notion of *coverage* or *close contact* is kept intact. In the third example, I think about the person a great deal and thus experience the situation as the person basically covering all my thoughts. Examples for the abstract *in* are *we were stuck in the traffic jam, I am interested in horses, I am in love*. The abstract *in* retains the meaning of *enclosure*: The persons in question are kept more or less in their present situation—they are enclosed by the traffic jam, they delve deeply into a topic and their interest keeps them inside this topic as if it encloses them, or they feel dominated by certain circumstances to which they surrender completely and can't easily or don't even want to get out of.

Thus, in the basic sense as well as in the metaphorical senses of the three prepositions, we have the same meaning schemata at work: *point/target* for *at*, *coverage/contact* for *on,* and *containment/enclosure* for *in*.

The question remains: How can we use such knowledge with learners? How can we help them take advantage of the systematicity found in prepositions? If we manage to convey the basic notions motivating the prepositions (i.e., point/target, coverage/contact, containment/enclosure), which are relatively easy to understand, we can make learners see the meaning aspect of prepositions as well as a connection between their different uses. This procedure helps learners understand the spatial concepts behind the basic prepositions and also their relation to the metaphorizations. They can accomplish this learning by visualizing the meaning schemata on all three meaning levels—for example, a learner can visualize an arrow for *at* (pointing, for example, at a town, at a specific time on a watch, or at a certain subject in the school report for "good at math"). For *on,* the learner might visualize the contact between a book and a table (for "book on the table") or between the day and the events on that day; the learner might visualize a problem that is weighing "heavily on my mind" by putting the problem directly above and in close contact to a person's head. Finally, a learner could visualize the different uses for *in* by referring to the liquid contained by a bottle or a watch on which the area "in the morning" is circled as contained within the rest of the day, or by drawing people caught in a snowstorm as being completely surrounded by it. All of these uses are prototypical, but they help make the concepts clear. More marginal examples can follow subsequently.

This approach may be a valid way of building up learners' knowledge about prepositions and/or restructuring their knowledge and helping them see the motivation behind the various usages. We also could teach meaning connections by showing the network of preposition meaning in a visual way, as noted above—especially for learners who have problems with more abstract explanations. Learners could then work on example sentences, taken from actual usage, and explain the reasons for the writer's/speaker's choice of preposition. In this way, they will be encouraged to pay more attention to the meaning aspect of grammar and will see that grammar is as important as lexis, for example, and that a structuring principle such as metaphorization can be found in similar ways on both ends of the lexis-grammar continuum.

ACL and Newer Trends in Foreign Language Teaching Methodology

ACL seems to tie in well with current approaches in foreign language teaching methodology ("current" from a German perspective, at least). In this section I touch briefly on some of these approaches and show their connection to a possible ACL approach.

First, I focus on what is called "holistic learning," following Bach and Timm (1996), Timm (1995), or Weskamp (2001). This approach maintains that—in contrast to traditional, mainly cognitively oriented methods—the whole person should be taken into account, with all senses involved and both hemispheres active. This model is highly compatible with an ACL approach because it takes a holistic perspective of language and regards general cognitive and perceptual processes as integrally entwined, and it does not sharply delineate language from culture or grammar from lexis, for instance. Both approaches highlight humans' everyday knowledge and regard language as an integral part of culture.

Second, I highlight the role of affect in language learning. Krashen (1981) mentions the importance of the so-called affective filter for learning. The claim—which is generally accepted—is that learners are more motivated when learning is fun and when they feel at ease. In my experience, language learners tend to be more engaged and less anxious when language learning is connected to stories, games, creativity, and authentic language usage than when it is merely concerned with grammar drills and word lists, where learners may have trouble seeing the sense of what they are supposed to learn. This observation connects affective goals with ACL because learners are asked to be creative and to seek the motivation for peculiarities in the foreign language on all levels—and thus to look for "sense" and meaning of grammar. As Langacker (2000, 9) notes, "It is not the linguistic system per se that constructs and understands novel expressions, but rather the language user, who marshals for this purpose the full panoply of available resources." Thus, the language learner himself or herself is in the center of interest and—in an ideal case at least—should learn to consider the foreign language as a flexible instrument that can fulfill exactly the communicative needs they may have at a given moment.

Third, a recent keyword in teaching methodology is the autonomous learner—that is, a learner who feels responsible for his or her learning and progress (see, for example, Little 1999). To become autonomous or at least near-autonomous, learners (at least advanced learners) should be provided with the skills to cope with language on their own, for which they need insights into the systematicity of language. Armed with these insights, learners can become more independent from teacher input and enabled to make linguistic discoveries on their own and come up with hypotheses concerning linguistic phenomena. Thus, they may work on different conceptual metaphors in English and compare them in a contrastive way with German metaphorical instantiations. In this way, they also become more sensitized to their own language output: They gain insight into patterns in the target language as well as their own language, which they can exploit as a guide to advance their understanding of the target language. ACL offers the tools for such an autonomous handling of the foreign language and language in general.

We also may want to consider the notion of action-oriented or process-oriented learning (in German, *Handlungsorientierung;* cf. Bach and Timm 1996). In this approach, language is regarded as an instrument for linguistic action or activity, and learners are to be exposed to language not in an abstract, rule-governed way; they are expected to use it, according to communicative strategies and always oriented toward a result. This notion goes hand-in-hand with ACL ideas, even if those ideas come from a different perspective—namely, that learners should handle the foreign language as a flexible tool that enables them to express their own viewpoint and fulfill their own communicative needs. In an ideal case, learners should use the foreign language autonomously and authentically. This approach presupposes that in the English classroom tasks should be as authentic and efficient as possible; ACL ideas—for example, analysis of conceptual metaphors to find "hidden meanings" in texts such as political propaganda of all kinds or advertising—seem to be very useful for this purpose. Furthermore, such experiences are relevant beyond school.

The close connection between language and culture that is the basis of the ACL approach brings us to the next point: intercultural learning, understanding of "the other" (see, for example, Kramsch 1993). The goal of intercultural learning or intercultural competence to date has been pursued mainly through texts and sometimes audio and video materials that generally are limited to transmitting facts and figures and visual/auditory impressions of the other culture. Within an ACL approach, however, intercultural awareness raising and intercultural learning also can be part of language analysis, grammar work, and vocabulary work. Learners realize that the concepts in their mother tongue are not identical to those of the target language; they discover the situatedness of language usage and may at the same time acquire schematic social knowledge about the target culture because the choice of a particular linguistic element or phenomenon is always a reflection of its social usage and thus a symptom of its cultural contextualization.

Finally, we should consider the relationship between the relatively new focus-on-form approach and ACL. Although focus-on-form still distinguishes rigidly between grammar and lexis, at least it focuses on the formal aspects of language. Hence, this approach seems to be highly compatible with the ACL approach, in which the main concern is with the "use of the language" but also with explanations of linguistic phenomena themselves. ACL's main aim is to make learners aware of the motivation behind linguistic phenomena and to help them understand how the language works.

Final Remark

In sum, I offer a short overview of the key points of ACL insofar as they are applicable to foreign language teaching and learning. ACL can be considered a holistic approach, in which language is directly interacting with other mental capacities and all linguistic elements are understood as motivated. The approach is user- and usage-centered, and the notion of culture is omnipresent; language and culture are regarded as inseparably intertwined. Probably the most important point—and the one that differentiates ACL from other approaches—is that grammar and lexis are not regarded as separated but as governed by the same organizing and structuring principles, which helps learners understand and produce the language once they have understood these principles and strategies.

Thus, ACL may be considered an effective and motivating approach, using our mental networks to their fullest potential (see Lamb 1999, 2000, showing how connections are established in our brains). A major shortcoming, however, is that there are hardly any teachers who have been trained in ACL—at least not in Germany, though the situation probably is not much different elsewhere. This training remains a task for the immediate future.

REFERENCES

Achard, Michel, and Susanne Niemeier, eds. 2004. *Cognitive linguistics, second language acquisition and foreign language teaching.* Berlin: Mouton de Gruyter.

Austin, John L. 1962. *How to do things with words.* London: Oxford University Press.

Bach, Gerhard, and Johannes-Peter Timm, eds. 1996. *Englischunterricht*, 2d ed. Tübingen: Francke.

Canale, Michael, and Merrill Swain. 1980. Theoretical bases of communicative approaches to second language teaching and testing. *Applied Linguistics* 1, no. 1:1–47.

Chomsky, Noam. 1957. *Syntactic structures*. The Hague: Mouton.

Doughty, Catherine, and Jessica Williams, eds. 1998. *Focus on form in classroom second language acquisition*. Cambridge: Cambridge University Press.

Howatt, Anthony P. R. 1984. *A history of English language teaching*. Oxford: Oxford University Press.

Hymes, Dell. 1971. *On communicative competence*. Philadelphia: University of Pennsylvania Press.

Kramsch, Claire. 1993. *Context and culture in language teaching*. Oxford: Oxford University Press.

Krashen, Stephen. 1981. *Second language acquisition and second language learning*. Oxford: Pergamon.

Lakoff, George, and Mark Johnson. 1980. *Metaphors we live by*. Chicago: University of Chicago Press.

Lamb, Sydney M. 1999. *Pathways of the brain: The neurocognitive basis of language*. Amsterdam: John Benjamins.

———. 2000. Neuro-cognitive structures in the interplay of language and thought. In *Explorations in linguistic relativity*, ed. Martin Pütz, and Marjolijn Verspoor, 173–96. Amsterdam: John Benjamins.

Langacker, Ronald W. 2000. *Grammar and conceptualization*. Berlin: Mouton de Gruyter.

Little, David. 1999. Developing learner autonomy in the foreign language classroom: A social-interactive view of learning and three fundamental pedagogical principles. *Revista Canaria de Estudios Ingleses* 38:77–88.

Long, Michael H. 1991. Focus on form: A design feature in language teaching methodology. In *Foreign language research in cross-cultural perspective*, ed. Kes de Bot, Ralph Ginsberg, and Claire Kramsch, 39–52. Amsterdam: John Benjamins.

Long, Michael H., and Diane Larsen-Freeman. 1991. *An introduction to second language acquisition research*. New York: Longman.

McCarthy, Michael. 1991. *Discourse analysis for language teachers*. Cambridge: Cambridge University Press.

McCarthy, Michael, and Ronald Carter. 1994. *Language as discourse: Perspectives for language teaching*. Harlow, United Kingdom: Longman.

Niemeier, Susanne. 1998. Colourless green ideas metonymize furiously. In *Kognitive lexikologie und syntax*, ed. Friedrich Ungerer, 119–46. Rostock, Germany: University of Rostock Press.

. 2000. Straight from the heart. Metonymic and metaphorical explorations. In *Metaphor and metonymy at the crossroads: A cognitive perspective*, ed. Antonio Barcelona, 195–211. Berlin: Mouton de Gruyter.

———. 2001. Zur Beziehung zwischen Lexik und Grammatik. In *Mehrsprachiges Europa*, ed. Dagmar Abendroth-Timmer and Gerhard Bach, 305–26. Tübingen, Germany: Narr.

———. In press. Boundedness/Unboundedness—Blick durchs Schlüsselloch. Angewandte Kognitive Linguistik für den Englischunterricht. *Zeitschrift für Angewandte Linguistik.*

Pica, Teresa. 2000. Tradition and transition in English language teaching methodology. *System* 28:1–18.

Pütz, Martin, Susanne Niemeier, and René Dirven, eds. 2001a. *Applied cognitive linguistics I: Theory and language acquisition*. Berlin: Mouton de Gruyter.

———. 2001b. *Applied cognitive linguistics II: Language pedagogy*. Berlin: Mouton de Gruyter.

Richards, Jack C., and Theodore S. Rodgers. 1986. *Approaches and methods in language teaching*. Cambridge: Cambridge University Press.

Rudzka-Ostyn, Brygida. 2003. *Word power: Phrasal verbs and compounds. A cognitive approach*. Berlin: Mouton de Gruyter.

Searle, John. 1969. *Speech acts: An essay in the philosophy of language*. New York: New York University Press.

Timm, Johannes-Peter, ed. 1995. *Ganzheitlicher fremdsprachenunterricht*. Weinheim, Germany: Deutscher Studien Verlag.

Weskamp, Ralf. 2001. *Fachdidaktik: Grundlagen and konzepte. Anglistik—Amerikanistik*. Berlin: Cornelsen.

8

Language Play and Language Learning: Creating Zones of Proximal Development in a Third-Grade Multilingual Classroom

ANA CHRISTINA DaSILVA IDDINGS AND STEVEN G. McCAFFERTY
Vanderbilt University and University of Nevada at Las Vegas

MANY STUDIES ATTEST to the importance of language play in first-language development; few investigations, however, have explored the relationship between language play and second-language (L2) learning, particularly with respect to children. In the study described in this chapter we investigated how language play created zones of proximal development (ZPD) for L2 learning in circumstances in which a Brazilian student with no language background in either English or Spanish entered a third-grade class in which all of the other students spoke Spanish as their first language. We were interested in gaining insights into the role of language play in developing metalinguistic awareness/knowledge and in affording meaning making through the creation of semiotic systems. In analyzing the data we followed the premises of activity theory and microgenesis, in addition to Newman and Holzman's (1993) perspective of Vygotsky's construct of the ZPD, which emphasizes transformational and revolutionary aspects of learning.

Language Play and Language Learning

Language play principally consists of purposely modifying either language form—through the use of mimicking, rhyme, rhythm, alliteration, puns, songs, grammatical parallelism, and so forth—or semantics, through the use of mockery, repetition, parody, fictional words, and substitutions, for example (Cazden 1974; Davidson 1974; Ely and McCabe 1994; Esposito 1980; Kuczaj 1983; Yue-Hashimoto 1980). Besides just having fun, engagement in these activities serves important functions in child development; like other forms of play, language play enables children to experiment with processes and features beyond their current level of development—which, of course, can lead to learning.

Although the relationship between language play and L2 learning has remained largely unexplored, some of the literature (Belz 2002; Lantolf 2000, 1997) emphasizes the intramental role of language play for experimentation and rehearsal. In the case of L2 learners, Lantolf (1997) argues that language play appears frequently in the L2 and, moreover, often is connected with making comparisons to other languages. Furthermore, he claims that language play is instrumental in advancing the development of learners' linguistic systems in that it includes prediction, validation, restructuring, and consolidation of newly developed understandings of the L2, thereby increasing levels of metalinguistic awareness and leading to language learning.

In addition, Belz (2002) found that language play in an emerging L2 can bring forth a sense of multicompetence. That is, through the creation and use of hybrid forms of language, learners in Belz's study came to better understand their first language as well as the L2, leading to a feeling of being part of a larger multilinguistic community, which in some cases enhanced their sense of identity.

Semiosis and Second-Language Learning

Semiotics is defined as the science of signs and signifiers (e.g., Barthes 1977; Hodges and Kress 1989; Peirce 1958; Saussure 1974). Of particular relevance to the current study is use of native, foreign, and target languages as constitutive elements of a new, hybrid system of signs, which are created by combining and recombining existing signs to express new meaning (Anzaldua 1989; Kramsch 2000; Lantolf 1993). This process, according to Kramsch (2000, 139), is not "an innocent re-labeling of the familiar furniture of the universe. It reconfigures one's whole classification system." That is, learning another language is the process of creating, conveying, and exchanging signs; it is not primarily the acquisition of grammatical elements as much of the L2 acquisition literature characterizes it.

In relation to this transformation of signs, it is important to note that although in the early stages of his thinking Vygotsky focused on the idealization of sign-mediated self regulation, by the end of his life he had become centrally concerned with meaning making and its relationship to consciousness, hypothesizing consciousness as a system of psychological processes with semantic structure (Luria 1928). Moreover, Vygotsky theorized that linguistic signs, as elements of speech (including inner speech), are correlatives of consciousness as its basic unit but not correlatives of thought and that meaning is the path from thought to words (Prawat 1999).

According to Vygotsky (1997), the structure of thought flows through phases or stages. In the early stages, thought originates as *sense* or direct embodied impressions of what things are or might be, assuming an imagistic form; in later stages, systems of signs or codes (e.g., language) take the key role. Within this process, meaning making is conceptualized as neither equal to speech (mostly process) nor equal to thought (content) but as both and in equal measure, which, combined, "mediate between holistic, imaginal thinking and the instantiation of that thinking in a verbal format" (Prawat 1999, 269). Furthermore, Prawat (1999) argues that overall this process is highly akin to Charles S. Peirce's notion of *abduction:* both hinge on imaginative, creative thinking (Houser, Kloesel, and the Peirce Edition Project 1998).[1]

The Zone of Proximal Development

Vygotsky (1978, 102) highlights play as a formative activity in relation to the ZPD. He argues that when children pretend—for example, dressing up like adults and imitating adult discourse—they are creating ZPDs because in such circumstances a child "always behaves beyond his average age, above his daily behavior." Moreover, the view of the ZPD we take in our study derives from Newman and Holtzman (1993), who espoused that much of Vygotsky's theorizing has been stripped of its original Marxist contexts and, in particular, that the ZPD has been interpreted from an instrumentalist perspective—that is, as a "tool *for* result" as opposed to the more revolutionary (Marxist) view of "tool *and* result," in which case the tool changes the users and the users change the tool as well. In other words, through interaction with people and cultural artifacts, the entire experience of learning/teaching can transform for all participants. This perspective also defines the ZPD as activity, disavowing the container metaphor, which depicts the ZPD spatially—what is or is not "in the zone."

Elaborating on this theoretical explication, Kinginger (2002, 241) notes that the revolutionary perspective of the ZPD embraces a "progressive" view of education, focusing on both process and product at once as opposed to the conservative interpretation, which favors the "transmission and reproduction of educational practices." Moreover, the revolutionary view of the ZPD stems from the dialogical approach to learning, which assumes that participants share meaning making in constructing their social, psychological, and physical world (McCafferty 2002). Reproduction, on the other hand, is essentially restricted to passing on of knowledge that students "bank" for later use (Freire 1970).

Moreover, if the ZPD were construed as simply transmission, that construal would necessarily entail an equally reduced sense of Vygotsky's (1978, 57) genetic law of development (that psychological development occurs first on the social or interpersonal plane and then on the intrapsychological plane). Of course, development is not simply the reproduction of information and behaviors: Individuals interact with their own knowledge on the basis of experience in multiple contexts; development also includes how they feel, their values, and so forth, as part of the process of *internalization*. To assume otherwise suggests a lock-step notion of development, which Vygotsky clearly rejected.

Another important aspect of learning to consider in relation to the ZPD concerns the role of imitation. In the field of L2 learning imitation has been connected with audiolingualism—that is, repetition of decontextualized language forms as associated with frequency of practice, leading to learning. For Vygotsky, however, imitation is aimed at the gathering of *sense*—that is, coming to understand aspects of future roles and activity. Importantly in relation to the ZPD, Vygotsky (1978, 88) argues that "a person can imitate only that which is within her developmental level." Furthermore, imitation and the ZPD are connected with internalization. The transformation from the social to the psychological plane takes place as revolutionary activity (above), and imitation creates just such potential.

A final consideration of the ZPD concerns the development of metalinguistic knowledge/awareness. Swain (1995) suggests that *output* (production) promotes *noticing* (conscious attention to linguistic form), which in turn promotes language learning. Therefore, when L2 learners are dialogically engaged in language play, they are increasing the possibility of acquisition according to this perspective. Swain and Lapkin (1998) further argue that although jointly reflecting on their own use of the

L2 (meta-talk) while involved in communicative tasks, learners develop awareness of the L2. This and subsequent work by Swain and her colleagues concerning dialogic learning explicitly invokes elements of the Vygotskian theoretical framework, including the ZPD (see Kinginger 2002).

Activity Theory and Microgenesis

Current research is aligned with the paradigm of Vygotskian approaches to L2 research and, more specifically, with activity theory and microgenetic analysis.[2] Although activity theory is relatively new to Western researchers (e.g., Cole 1999; Engstrom 1987, 1993, 1999; Kostogritz 2000; Kozulin 1998; Lantolf and Pavlenko 2001), it has a long tradition in the former Soviet Union (e.g., Alexie N. Leont'ev and Peter I. Zinchenko), with philosophical roots in the works of Karl Marx.

Incommensurable with traditional theories of knowledge construction that retain dualist distinctions between mind and world, activity theory set out to resolve Cartesian splits in psychology by focusing on the dialectical interrelationships between thought and the material world, mind and body, individual and society. In this respect, activity theory tries to demonstrate (through theory and practice) the inextricable relationship between mind and activity as well as the inseparability of mind/activity from the historical, cultural, and social contexts in which it is embedded (Leont'ev 2002).

To understand mediated human, social, and mental activity, Vygotsky (1978) proposed *genetic analysis* (*genetic* meaning having to do with genesis). Vygotsky (1986) points to the analysis of linguistic signs, or word, as the minimal unit in which the form, function, and genesis of consciousness could be investigated. Wertsch (1985), adding to Vygotsky's framework, proposes the observation of action that occurs on both interpersonal and intrapersonal planes (tool-mediated action) as a proper unit of analysis. Vygotsky believed, however, that an understanding of mediated forms of human behavior could not be achieved through exclusive reliance on descriptive research. For the theorist, mere descriptions of actions would yield interpretations analogous to scientific analysis. This point is important because Vygotsky's goal was to understand rather than to predict "what was uniquely human in human activity" (Vygotsky 1978).

Therefore, Vygotsky advocated a research methodology that transcended models borrowed from the positivist paradigm. From his point of view, the focus on genetic analysis was a means to understand mental processes through disclosure of their emergence and subsequent growth. That is, by observing precisely how participants integrate a system of signs and symbols into a task, the researcher can gain access to the psychological functions of human beings (Wertsch 1991). Within this framework communication plays an important role, not only as the medium of interaction but as an analogue for analysis of episodes in which communication is engaged in—for example, through gesture, facial expressions, and so forth.

The elements that compose activity are not regarded as static or as existing in isolation from each other; they are dynamically and continuously in interaction with each other. Furthermore, within activity there are contradictions or tensions among the elements. These tensions have been characterized by Engestrom (1987) and Bateson (1972) as double-bind situations (for example, as in this study, when a common language is not present among people who need to speak to each other) that prompt participants to "innovate, create, change or invent new instruments for their resolution through experimentation, borrowing or conquering already existing artifacts for new uses"(Engestrom 1987, 165, quoted in Leander 2003, 5). Our study regards identifying double binds, creating hybrid functional systems, and ultimately transforming activity as key aspects of language play and creating ZPDs.

In drawing together the foregoing discussion before turning to our study, we emphasize that language play in dialogical contexts is richly imaginative and can take many different forms. At the same time, however, it involves making meaning (including gathering sense) through novel or comic use of aspects of the linguistic system or, in the case of semiosis, by combining signs to create a hybrid system to constitute meaning. These processes produce fertile grounds for learning-leading development (the co-construction of ZPDs) with regard to language as linguistic and semiotic systems, enhancing metalinguistic knowledge—through both understanding and production—and, in turn, facilitating language learning.

The Study

Participants and Setting

Our study investigated a third-grade class, located in an urban district of the southwestern United States, that consisted of seventeen students from Spanish-speaking backgrounds (fourteen Mexicans, two Cubans, and one Guatemalan). Early in the semester Ana, a student from Brazil, entered the class. Ana's language background was varied. Although Ana spoke only Portuguese, both her grandparents were Italians and spoke Italian to her at home, as did her mother—who also spoke Portuguese to her. At school Ana's teacher spoke only English; her classmates spoke both English and Spanish to her, although initially she had no proficiency in either language.

Data Collection

Data collection for this study was part of a larger effort lasting five months, and for most of that time one of the researchers visited the classroom four times a week. During the latter part of the study, observations continued with a little less frequency (two to three times per week). Video- and audiotapes as well as anecdotal records of students' interactions were collected throughout the data collection period. These forms of data collection allowed for close examination of complex relationships between students, activity, and context (activity theory), both moment-to-moment and over time (microgenesis).

The process for data analysis was continuous and ongoing throughout all the phases of data collection as well as after completion of the fieldwork. Although we collected more than thirty hours of videotape recordings, for the sake of conciseness we examined only the events that were most pertinent to the research interests of the present study.

Findings and Discussion

Episode 1 In contextualizing this episode, it is important to mention that Ana had relied exclusively on her native Portuguese to speak with the other children when she first entered the class and that this pattern had sparked a sense of linguistic curiosity among the Spanish speakers. One of the results of this heightened awareness was an increased sensitivity among students in the class to linguistic differences in the varieties of Spanish found in the class.

A few days before episode 1 was recorded the teacher had asked the researcher, a Brazilian, to teach a song in Portuguese, hoping that it would make Ana "feel more at home." Unbeknown to the researcher at the time, the Spanish-speaking students had discovered a few days earlier that there were differences in the pronunciation of the word *gato* among them, and the word had become the subject of an inside joke. Therefore, when the researcher chose a song about a cat (*um gato*) the Spanish speakers heard yet another version of that word because the Portuguese intonation differs from that in Spanish.

The episode was recorded a few days after the singing lesson. During the intervening days (as well as at the time of the recording), the Spanish-speaking students had tried to prod Ana into speaking Portuguese, which she largely resisted, fearing that she would be made fun of—as had happened to other students.

(1) Rafael (trying to initiate a conversation with Ana): Como se dice *gato* en Portuguese? [How do you say *cat* in Portuguese?]
(2) Ana (shrugging): . . . [no answer]
(3) Andrea (attempting to maintain communication): *Gato*, Ana, como se dice? [*Cat*, Ana, how do you say it?]
(4) Rafael (continuing to attempt to get a response): Yo lo digo asi, *gato*, pero Alexandro lo dice asi, *gaaaato*. [I say it like that, *cat*, but Alexandro says it like this, *caaaat* (exaggeratedly)]
(5) Alexandro (overhearing Rafael): Teacher, Rafael is making fun of my accent again!

This interaction illustrates ongoing attention to differences in language form on the part of some of the Spanish-speaking students, although not because they were especially interested in developing their knowledge of Portuguese or varieties of Spanish per se. They were engaging in language play—more particularly, mockery. Rafael, a Cuban, focused on phonological differences by comparing Alexandro's pronunciation (Mexican) to his own in attempting to get the reluctant Ana to divulge her version of the word.

Although not the genetic root of this particular focus of metalinguistic development, the episode nonetheless demonstrates a continuance of that spark. Moreover, Rafael's comparison of the two Spanish pronunciations (line 4) is meta-talk that draws explicit attention to differences in the use of this linguistic feature. Therefore, we believe that the language play in episode 1 could have created ZPDs related to language learning and the conceptualization of language and perhaps how the participating students viewed themselves in relation to linguistic multicompetence as well. We also caution, however, that even though such learning opportunities might have been afforded, they were not necessarily realized or realized in the same way for all participants: How the students felt about being Spanish speakers in their American school and how they perceived having an "accent," for example, could have affected them quite differently.

Episode 2 This episode took place during a small-group activity in which the students, in pairs, were to read nonfiction books and then discuss what they had read. Ana and Ricardo had paired up to "read" a book on spiders that mainly consisted of large photographs and minimally descriptive text (mostly labeling). Neither knew how to read in English, and neither knew much of the other's language. They relied on narrative schema, however, to create oral text to accompany each picture, mixing Portuguese and Spanish:

(1) Ana (looking at a photograph of a tarantula): Mira, es uma . . . [Look, it's a . . .]
(improvising a term for *tarantula*): Es uma branca de neve. [It's a Snow White]

(2) Ricardo (laughing and agreeing): Si, es una blanca . . . branca de nieve y ella esta comiendo. [Yes, it's a Snow White and she is eating]

(3) Ana (turning the page and looking at another photograph of a tarantula): Y ahora a branca de neve esta dormindo, [And now Snow White is sleeping]

Ana did not know the word *tarantula* in any language. The playful term that she chose in Portuguese, *Branca de Neve,* was easily identifiable in Spanish (*Blanca de Nieve*) as "Snow White," and of course Ricardo knew that this term was not the proper name of the spider. Furthermore, we assume that Ana was referring to Snow White the Disney character, although we can't be sure because the spider the children were looking at in the book had white markings on it resembling snowflakes, which might have triggered Ana's imaginative choice. In any case, the children joined together in using the term to create meaning and to establish intersubjectivity. The use of *Snow White* also provided a discursive vehicle to play with, as evidenced by the students' continuation of the narrative as if the spider were both eating and sleeping, although there were no such representations in the book. This use of language play is comparable to other forms of play in which children, through imaginal processes, represent one thing for another—for example, when children pretend a broomstick is a horse, which they can ride.

An important means of creating ZPDs arose from the participants speaking both Spanish and Portuguese. Ana's first two words (turn 1) were Spanish (*mira* and *es*). She also started the next sentence of the same turn in Spanish (*es*) but then switched to Portuguese for the phrase "it's a Snow White." Ricardo's response (turn 2) started a repetition of Ana's term for the spider but in Spanish (*si, es una Blanca*); then he switched to Portuguese (*Branca de Nieve*). This switching indicates that he understood the meaning of the term while sustaining the code switching initiated by Ana. As such, he joined Ana in creating a hybrid code by not only interconnecting two different languages but also labeling the spider as something other than what it is. In her final turn (3), Ana's initial utterance was in Spanish (*y ahora*), after which she switched to Portuguese (*Branca de Neve esta dormindo*).

In addition, even when Ana was speaking her native Portuguese she tried to imitate Spanish intonation patterns. This strategy is in an interesting accommodation that allowed Ana to "sound Spanish," which she evidently felt was useful in interacting with the Spanish speakers and, we presume, helped her gain access to the Spanish speakers and perhaps led to increases in Spanish proficiency as well.

By appropriating each other's lexicon, by understanding one thing in terms of another, and, in Ana's case, by applying Spanish intonation to Portuguese, the children not only transformed linguistic conventions in the process of communicating; they also relied on their metalinguistic awareness/knowledge to do so. Unlike the previous episode, however, in which explicit attention was brought to bear on pronunciation through meta-talk, in this episode there was no separation of process and product. Instead, meta-awareness/knowledge developed through the act of communicating itself.

Language use in this episode also is both "tool *and* result," to use Newman and Holtzman's (1993) phrase. The children were both using and inventing sign at the same time. Moreover, this episode entailed Ricardo and Ana's imitating one another: both using Spanish and Portuguese to communicate and Ana imitating Spanish intonation when she was speaking Portuguese. If indeed Vygotsky was "moving toward a view that equates consciousness with awareness of meaning" (Prawat 1999, 268), it would appear that the two children in this episode were highly engaged at a meta-level of linguistic awareness and, as such, creating ZPDs for understanding the larger scope of sign-symbol relationships: semiotics. Moreover, we would suggest that overall the act of communicating in this episode is highly imaginal and creative, indeed, the very grounds for transformation and the ZPD.

Finally, a further affordance of the interaction in this episode concerns the development of linguistic multicompetence. Kramsch (2000) found that people who learn another language also begin to realize the relativistic nature of linguistic systems, and Belz (2002: 19) emphasizes the notion that "those who know two languages might think differently than those who know one" and that linguistic multicompetency may bring with it a changing sense of identity—i.e., belonging to a larger multilinguistic community. In this episode the children clearly demonstrated a willingness to enter into each other's linguistic worlds as well as to create one of their own making.

Conclusion

When the students in the class faced the double-bind situation of not being able to speak much of each other's language but wanting to communicate, they experienced the freedom to experiment with signs and to create a hybrid functional system for making meaning. These circumstances triggered a level of metalinguistic awareness/knowledge that was hitherto unobserved among the students. In particular, in episode 1 the students continued to concentrate on differences in Spanish pronunciation based on variety. Moreover, in episode 2 there was a collaborative effort to make meaning by combining two linguistic systems (Spanish and Portuguese), in addition to labeling one thing in terms of another. This episode demonstrates high levels of linguistic sophistication in transforming sign for communication and play; moreover, it seems reasonable to suppose that although the learners were third graders, they gained important insights into the workings of language and semiotics. Overall, episode 2 attests to the students' resourcefulness as learners and the power of dialogic interaction to make meaning in unpredictable ways.

Although we focused on the co-creation of ZPDs, we also emphasize that this process is expected to lead to internalization, and both of the episodes in the data demonstrate affordances for increased awareness of language at the meta-level. Furthermore, over the course of data collection Ana became increasingly aware that she could use the Spanish she had learned to help her understand English. For example, if she needed to know the meaning of an English word, she would first ask one of her peers what it meant in Spanish.

Although we believe that the language play episodes we captured in this study led to increased metalinguistic awareness, facilitating L2 learning, we do not advocate that teachers attempt to instigate language play in their classrooms. Instead, we point out that children largely recognize their own need to communicate and make sense of their world and, as such, spontaneously transform themselves and their activity as part of the process of meeting their goals. Indeed, after the study, the classroom teacher became keenly aware that although she had not understood what the students were saying at the time of data collection, in fact they were engaged in highly productive interactions with regard to their language learning.

NOTES

1. The process of abductive reasoning leads to the creation of new ideas and concepts. Prawat (1999) provides the example of Albert Einstein's thought experiments, which led to his theory of relativity, among others.
2. *Activity* should be regarded as cultural-historical frames—for example, what is supposed to happen in classrooms under a particular system of education in combination with the particulars of what actually happens.

REFERENCES

Andalzua, Gloria. 1989. *Borderlands/La Frontera: The new mestiza.* San Francisco: Spinsters/Aunt Lute Books.

Barthes, Roland. 1977. *Image—music—text.* Trans. S. Heath. London: Fontana.

Bateson, Gregory. 1972. *Steps to an ecology of mind.* London: Granada.

Belz, Julie A. 2002. Second language play as a representation of the multicompetent self in foreign language study. *Journal of Language, Identity, and Education* 1, no. 1:13–39.

Cazden, Courtney B. 1974. Play with language and metalinguistic awareness: One dimension of language experience. *The Urban Review* 7:28–39.

Cole, Michael. 1999. Cultural psychology: Some general principles and a concrete example. In *Perspectives on activity theory,* ed. Yrjo Engstrom, Reijo Miettinen, and Raija-Leena Punamaki, 19–38. Cambridge: Cambridge University Press.

Davidson, Anni. 1974. Linguistic play and language acquisition. *Papers and Reports in Child Language Development* 8:179–87.

Ely, Robert, and Allyssa McCabe. 1994. The language play of kindergarten children. *First Language* 14:19–35.

Engestrom, Yrjo. 1987. *Learning by expanding: An activity-theoretical approach to developmental research.* Helsinki, Finland: Orienta-Konsultit.

———. 1993. Developmental studies of work as a testbench of activity theory: The case of primary care medical practice. In *Understanding practice,* ed. Seth Chaiklin and Jean Lave, 64–103. Cambridge: Cambridge University Press.

———. 1999. Activity theory and individual and social transformation. In *Perspectives on activity theory,* ed. Yrjo Engstrom, Reijo Miettinen, and Raija-Leena Punamaki, 19–38. Cambridge: Cambridge University Press.

Esposito, Anita. 1980. Children's play with language. *Child Study Journal* 10:207–17.

Freire, Paulo. 1970. *Pedagogy of the oppressed.* New York: Herder and Herder.

Hodges, Robert, and Gunther Kress. 1989. *Social semiotics.* Ithaca, N.Y.: Cornell University Press.

Houser, Nathan, Christian Kloesel, and the Peirce Edition Project, eds. 1998. *The essential Peirce.* Bloomington: Indiana University Press.

Kinginger, Celeste. 2002. Defining the zone of proximal development in U.S. foreign language education. *Applied Linguistics* 23, no. 2:240–61.

Kostogritz, Alex. 2000. Activity theory and the new literacy studies: Modeling the literacy learning activity system. Paper presented at annual meeting of Australian Association for Research in Education, Sydney, Australia, December 4.

Kozulin, Alex. 1998. *Psychological tools: A sociocultural approach to education.* Cambridge, Mass.: Harvard University Press.

Kramsch, Claire. 2000. Social discursive constructions of self in L2 learning. In *Sociocultural theory and second language learning,* ed. James P. Lantolf, 133–53. Oxford: Oxford University Press.

Kuczaj, Stan A. 1983. *Crib speech and language play.* New York: Springer-Verlag.

Lantolf, James P. 1993. Sociocultural theory and the second-language classroom: The lesson of strategic interaction. In *Strategic interaction and language acquisition: Theory, practice, and research.* Georgetown University round table on languages and linguistics 1993, ed. James E. Alatis. Washington, D.C.: Georgetown University Press.

———. 1997. Contemporary perspectives on the acquisition of Spanish. In *Production, processing, and comprehension* vol. 2, ed. William R. Glass and Ana Teresa Perez-Leroux, 3–24. Somerville, Mass.: Cascadilla Press.

———. 2000. *Sociocultural theory and second language learning.* New York: Oxford University Press.

Lantolf, James P., and Aneta Pavlenko. 2001. (S)econd (L)anguage (A)ctivity theory: Understanding second language learners as people. In *Learner contributions to language learning: New directions in research,* ed. Michael P. Breen, 141–58. Essex, England: Pearson Educational Limited.

Leander, Kevin. M. 2003. Polycontextual construction zones: Mapping the expansion of schooled space and identity. *Mind, culture, and activity* 9, no. 3:211–37.

Leont'ev, Dmitry A. 2002. Activity theory approach: Vygotsky in the present. In *Voices within Vygotsky's non-classical psychology: Past, present, future,* ed. Dorothy Robbins and Anna Stetsenko, 45–62. New York: Nova Science Publishers, Inc.

Luria, A. R. 1928. The problem of the cultural development of the child. *Journal of Genetic Psychology* 35:493–506.

McCafferty, Steven G. 2002. Gesture and creating zones of proximal development for second language learning. *Modern Language Journal* 86, no. 2:192–203.

Newman, Frederick, and Lois Holzman. 1993. *Lev Vygotsky: Revolutionary scientist.* New York: Routedge.

Peirce, Charles S. 1958. *Collected papers of Charles Sanders Peirce,* vols. 1–6, ed. Arthur W. Burks, Cambridge, Mass.: Harvard University Press.

Prawat, Richard S. 1999. Social constructivism and the process-content distinction as viewed by Vygotsky and the pragmatists. *Mind, Culture, and Activity* 6, no. 4:255–73.

Saussure, Ferdinand. 1974. *Course in general linguistics.* London: Fontana.

Swain, Merrill. 1995. Three functions of output in second language learning. In *For H. G. Widdowson: Principles and practices in the study of language: A festschrift on the occasion of his 60th birthday,* ed. Guy Cook and B. Seidlhofer, 125–44. Oxford: Oxford University Press.

Swain, Merrill, and Sharon Lapkin. 1998. Interaction and second language learning: Two adolescents working together. *Modern Language Journal* 82:320–37.

Vygotsky, Lev S. 1978. *Mind in society.* Cambridge, Mass.: Harvard University Press.

———. 1986. *Thought and language.* Cambridge, Mass.: MIT Press
———. 1997. The problem of consciousness. In *The collected works of L. S. Vygotsky, vol. 3: Problems of the theory and history of psychology*, ed. R. W. Rieber and J. Wollock, 129–38. New York: Plenum.
Wertsch, James. 1985. *Vygotsky and the social formation of mind.* Cambridge, Mass.: Harvard University Press.
———.1991. *Voices of the mind: A sociocultural approach to mediated action.* Cambridge, Mass.: Harvard University Press.
Yue-Hashimoto, A. O. 1980. Word play in language acquisition: A Mandarin case. *Journal of Chinese Linguistics* 8:181–204.

9

Cognates, Cognition, and Writing: An Investigation of the Use of Cognates by University Second-Language Learners

ROBIN CAMERON SCARCELLA AND CHERYL BOYD ZIMMERMAN
University of California at Irvine and California State University, Fullerton

Background and Rationale

The role of cognates in second-language (L2) teaching has baffled researchers for many years. Many linguists have claimed that cognates are useful to L2 learners, both in comprehension and in production, arguing that cognate knowledge can be mastered easily and can be readily applied by L2 learners. For instance, some researchers have suggested that Spanish learners of English should be able to understand cognates such as *medicine* (*medicina*), *electricity* (*electricidad*), and *kilometer* (*kilómetro*) when they encounter them in speech and print. Linguists have also debated, however, the extent to which L2 learners actually are able to use and exploit their knowledge of cognates or even perceive the relationships between words in their first and second languages. (For reviews of these positions, see Whitley 2002 and Carroll 1992.)

Although there is considerable controversy regarding the usefulness of cognates to L2 learners, contemporary trends in education have resulted in an emphasis of etymology in instruction. *The California English and Language Arts Content Standards, Grades Four through Twelve* emphasize "knowledge of affixes and roots, along with their word meanings and *origins*" (California Department of Education 1997,102; emphasis added). For example, learners are asked to apply knowledge of Greek, Latin, and Anglo-Saxon roots and affixes to draw inferences concerning the meaning of subject matter terminology. One reason for the emphasis on word origins in the state of California is that more than 1.5 million children in California's public schools are learning English as a second language (ESL), and more than 80 percent of the ESL students in California speak Spanish (Rumberger 2000). Researchers believe that these learners will benefit from a study of etymology because many Spanish words have English cognates, and cognates are thought to be a host of "free words." *The California Reading/Language Arts Framework* states that "students in grades three through twelve who have strong literacy skills in their primary language can be expected to transfer many of those skills to English and progress rapidly in learning English" (California Department of Education 1999, 233).

The instructional emphasis on etymology—and, sometimes by extension, cognates—is based in large part on the implicit assumption that lexical knowledge transfers from Spanish into English. That is, educators assume that vocabulary proficiency in Spanish actually transfers to vocabulary proficiency in English. There is a tacit belief in the transferability of vocabulary knowledge across languages—in this case, Spanish and English. (For a related discussion of transfer, see, for instance, August 2004.)

Lamentably, although roots and affixes, along with their etymology, play a central role in the California Reading and Language Arts Standards, in California high school English textbooks the instruction of etymology is rarely presented with explicit linking to the implications for teaching Spanish-speaking students. Instead, it has mainly been presented as though all students were native speakers of English. Only recently, with the production of new textbooks designed for L2 learners, have such linkages been made in ESL instruction. In these new books, Spanish-English cognates are identified and taught explicitly.

Regrettably, little can be inferred about the transfer of vocabulary knowledge from Spanish to English from California assessment data. Despite the heavy emphasis on assessment in California, scores on the vocabulary sections of standardized exams do not yield useful information about students' specific vocabulary strengths and weaknesses. Although the California Test of Standards and California Achievement Test-Version 6—required of children enrolled in public schools in California—assess knowledge of roots and affixes, these tests do not yield detailed information about students' vocabulary knowledge. Standardized tests such as the ones given in California do not include a sufficient number of test items pertaining to specific aspects of the students' vocabulary knowledge to provide valid data.

Unfortunately, because of methodological difficulties involving the challenge of investigating naturally occurring language and controlling confounding variables (such as avoidance, discussed below), even researchers have had difficulties exploring lexical transfer. Consequently, research on the nature of lexical transfer has been quite limited. Much of the existing research focuses on the transfer of phonological properties of words rather than syntactic or morphological features (see Durgunoglu 1997, 1998; Durgunoglu, Snow, and Geva 2001; Durgunoglu and Öney 1999); receptive rather than productive knowledge (see Jiménez, García, and Pearson 1996; Nagy et al. 1993); concrete, high-frequency words rather than abstract, academic words (for a review, refer to Nation 2001); and management of vocabulary instruction (such as the best teaching methods and handling specific difficulties encountered by particular groups of learners) rather than on the development or use of vocabulary in an L2. (For discussion, see Laufer 1998.)

Arguments Supporting the Usefulness of Cognate Knowledge

In brief, the importance of cognates to reading ability has been well documented. Considerable research has focused on the effect of cognitive knowledge on Spanish-speaking students' reading ability in English. Several researchers have reported that Spanish-speaking children who are skilled readers in English exploit their knowledge of Spanish cognates (such as *enfermo* and *infirm)* in figuring out the meanings of unknown English words (Jiménez, García, and Pearson 1996; Nagy et al. 1993).

One reason cognate knowledge might be particularly helpful to Spanish speakers who are learning to read in English is that a large number of Spanish-English cognates occur in academic text. Lobo (1966) suggests that 3,000 English words have cognates in Spanish, and a few simple rules allow these words to be expanded into 10,000 Spanish items. Moss (1992) argues that technical text can be expected to contain at least 30 percent cognates. Moreover, Whitley (2002) suggests that not only are Spanish cognates frequent in academic English but the relationships are close. He points out that some words are almost identical in both languages (for instance, *fundamental/fundamental, vision/visión, persona/personal,* and *doctor/doctor*), and other words have only minor, predictable changes in spelling (e.g., *dialect/dialecto, pharmacy/farmacia*, and *emotion/emoción*).

Arguments Refuting the Usefulness of Cognate Knowledge

Despite research supporting the usefulness of cognate knowledge in reading comprehension, the usefulness of cognate knowledge in production is complex and not clearly established for L2 production (see Carroll 1992). Although there are many Spanish cognates in English, they differ in many ways. For instance, their apparent similarity invites the transfer of phonological features from Spanish into English, even when these features should not be transferred. Cognates also differ in terms of the contexts in which they are used. For instance, Meara (1993) suggests that the English *embargo* has a specific technical sense that *embargo* does not have in Spanish and that these cognates differ in formality. According to Whitley (2002) common, everyday Spanish words such as *aumento, socorro*, and *renunciar* do not have the formal quality suggested by the English words *augment, succor,* and *renounce.* Hence, L2 students who speak Spanish as a first language might avoid them in formal English writing. Cognates also differ in terms of their frequency of use. That is, the members of the cognate pair are not necessarily used with the same frequency in their respective languages (Santos Maldonado 1997, 85), possibly leading students to over- or under-use cognates in their L2. In addition, cognates often have multiple meanings that do not match in both English and Spanish. The word *cuestión* in Spanish, for example, is rarely used to mean *question*. Instead, the word *pregunta* is used. (*Cuestión* is reserved to indicate *a matter of + noun phrase.*) Furthermore, dialect differences in vocabulary use also can affect the cognate use. For instance, the word *provocar* means *provoke* in most Spanish-speaking countries, but it means *be appealing* in Colombia and Venezuela (Whitley 2002). A Colombian could not exploit his or her knowledge of cognates to figure out the meaning of the word *provoke* in English.

In addition to these differences in cognate meanings in Spanish and English, learners face additional linguistic obstacles in trying to understand or use cognates correctly in their L2 (Whitley 2002). For example, Whitley points out that some forms are so similar that they can be confused; students tend to overextend cognate meanings and create words that do not exist. They might say, for example, *protectic* instead of *protective* because *-ic* is a derivative suffix with which they are familiar (Nation 2001).

In this chapter, we are concerned with the possibility that adult L2 learners might lack the lexical and morphological ability to benefit from their knowledge of cognates and that their inability to use cognates effectively might undermine their writing. As a measure of cognate knowledge, we consider the use of cognates in essays. As a measure of morphological ability, we consider the use of derivational suffixes in sentences as morphological units that distinguish nouns, verbs, adjectives, and adverbs. Before turning to our study, we first define terms and discuss the literature on difficulties involved in learning academic words.

Definitions of Terms

Researchers have defined the term *cognate* in different ways. Moss (1992) uses the *Oxford Dictionary of English Etymology* to define the term: "Akin, descended from a common ancestor (from the Latin *co+gnatus*)." Whitley (2002) explains that linguists often use this narrow definition. He suggests that many linguists regard words as cognates only "if they have been inherited from the same ancestor language" (Whitley 2002, 305). Whitley goes on to argue that linguists would not find such words true cognates if their resemblance were coincidental or if one or both of the words were borrowed from a third language. Meara, Lightbown, and Halter (1994) define *cognate* more broadly, as a word with a similar form and meaning in the learner's L1 and L2. (See Carroll 1992 and Nagy et al. 1993 for similar definitions.) Following these researchers, we define *cognate* as an English word with similar form and meaning in Spanish. Like others, we ignore linguists' narrow definition of *cognate*; we note that over the past 1,000 years or so English and Spanish have traded many vocabulary items, mostly borrowed from the French, often to express technical or academic knowledge (Whitley 2002). For the sake of focus in this investigation, we exclude false cognates (such as *embarazada/embarrassed*, *rato/rat*, *lectura/lecture)* that are similar in form but have different meanings in the two languages and come from different etymological sources. Because we are interested in cognates in the L2 production of university students, we focus on the use of cognates that share morphological and semantic information with Spanish words and appear on the Academic Word List (Coxhead 2000). Throughout this chapter we refer to these words as *cognates/academic words*. Such words are characteristic of academic English.

Academic English represents the advanced forms of English needed to communicate effectively in academic settings. Without this variety of English, students are unable "to enter and complete higher education and to advance in the labor market" (Scarcella and Rumberger 2000, 1). Knowledge of academic English includes fluency in academic vocabulary.

Simply stated, the term *academic vocabulary* refers to words that are common to a wide range of academic texts and are not as common in nonacademic texts (Nation 2001). Academic words are not to be confused with technical terms used in specific disciplines (e.g., *cell, nucleus, molecule*); they are the generally useful "scientific vocabulary" (Barber 1962) or "subtechnical vocabulary" (Cowan 1974) used across all academic disciplines (e.g., *accommodate, inhibit, deviate).* Academic words also are not to be confused with basic or general service words that are very common across all genres—usually defined as the 2,000 most frequent word families as indicated in the General Service List (West 1953). For the purpose of this study, we chose words from the Academic Word List (Coxhead 2000)—a list of 570 word families identified from an academic corpus of 3.5 million words from the fields of arts, science, law, and commerce (see Nation and Waring 1997).

Difficulties in Learning Academic Words

Academic word knowledge is difficult in part because academic words occur with relatively low frequency, they often occur within contexts that are less familiar to students, and they are cognitively complex and abstract. In addition, academic vocabulary learning is challenging because of the complexities of knowing a word. To *know* a word involves considerable knowledge about its meaning(s), written form, spoken form, grammatical behavior, collocations, register, associations with other words, and frequency (Nation 1990). Word knowledge is acquired incrementally over time through multiple exposures to the word (Schmitt 2000).

What makes academic words particularly difficult for L2 learners is mastery of derivative forms. Previous studies have demonstrated the problematic nature of learning derivatives in an L2. For example, a longitudinal study designed to track the gains of L2 graduate university students over one academic year found that the learners gained an average of 330 words but knew only 15 percent of their derivatives (Schmitt and Meara 1997). One group of studies has shown that it was uncommon for learners to know the derivatives in all four word classes (Schmitt 1999), that improvement in derivational knowledge did not occur over the period of one year in a language-rich environment (Schmitt 1998), and that adjective and adverb forms were especially problematic (Schmitt 1998; Schmitt and Zimmerman 2002). Other studies have demonstrated that gaps in derivative knowledge influence the writing of L2 students. For example, for L2 students who failed a placement exam for a university writing program, more than 10.6 percent of the errors were related to derivational morphology (Bardovi-Harlig and Bofman 1989). Other studies examine similarities between English and Spanish derivations and suggest implications for L2 development and teaching (see Osburne and Mulling 2001). Whitley (2002), for example, points out that Spanish L1 students learn that there is a good chance that English words ending in *-ance*, *-ity*, *-ic(al)*, *-ist*, *-ment,* *-tion*, and *-ize* have corresponding Spanish words ending in *-ancia*, *-idad*, *-ico*, *-ista*, *-mento*, *-ción*, and *-izar*. He also argues that Spanish-speaking students need to put little effort into figuring out the meanings of English words ending in *-al*, *-ble* and *-sis* because these word endings are identical in English and Spanish.

The foregoing literature provides preliminary evidence that cognates facilitate students' recognition of word meanings in reading and descriptions of academic language use. There are gaps in the literature, however, concerning the effect of cognate knowledge on language production, including academic writing. Even less is known about the importance of cognate knowledge in the use of derivative forms of academic words and the use of these words in writing. In light of the absence of research on cognates and language production, we undertook the study described in the following sections.

The Study

On the assumption that Spanish L1 speakers potentially have access to cognates whereas Asian L1 speakers do not, we explored whether Spanish L1 speakers use more academic cognates than Asian L1 speakers in writing. We also investigated how Asian L1 and Spanish L1 speakers fared on a test of English academic word derivatives, consisting of English words with Spanish cognates. Experiment 1 examines the frequency of use of cognates/academic words in the written essays of these learners. It considers variables such as first language, length of residence in the United States, and verbal SAT score that might affect the use of cognates/academic words. Experiment 2 investigates English L2 learners' derivative knowledge of cognates/academic words, exploring the knowledge of Asian L1 and Spanish L1 students. Participants in both experiments were drawn from the same population but from different intact classes.

Whereas students who participated in the first experiment could avoid the use of cognates/academic words if they did not know them, students in the second experiment were required to use them in the correct word class. This methodology enabled us to control for avoidance. Schachter (1974), Kleinmann (1977), and others considered this problem in their investigations of L2 development. Their results indicate that students avoid using grammatical features such as relative clauses when they have not mastered these features. Building on this research, others investigated avoidance in lexical use by Hebrew and English L2 learners. For example, Blum-Kulka and Levenston (1983) found, "Learners tend to avoid words for which no precise equivalents occur in their mother tongues, especially when the semantic components of such words require them to make distinctions they are not used to making at the level of single words. An example is the verb *ibec* (to insert in a suitable place). This is replaced by *hixnis* (insert) or *sim* (put) or by paraphrase" (Blum-Kulka and Levenston 1983, 124). For a different study on lexical avoidance, see Melka (1997).

Experiment 1

In the first experiment, we explored the following research questions:

1. To what extent do university ESL students use academic words/cognates in their writing?
2. Will Spanish-speaking ESL students use more cognates/academic words than Asian language–speaking ESL students?

The participants in the first experiment were 113 university ESL students. Of these students, twenty-four were Spanish speakers and eighty-nine were Asian language speakers (forty-nine spoke Vietnamese, fifteen spoke Korean, and twenty-five spoke Chinese). All of the students had advanced proficiency in English, as determined by the University of California (UC) Writing Assessment, and were enrolled in advanced ESL writing courses. All of the Spanish speakers had been schooled in Mexico or Central America and reported that they were highly fluent in reading and writing in Spanish. Approximately half of the students were men, and half were women. Participants' scores on the verbal portion of their SATs ranged between 400 and 550 (see table 9.1). Both groups had lived in the United States about seven years. Although the Asian L1 students had slightly higher verbal SAT scores than the Spanish L1 students, differences between the two groups were not significant.

To determine ESL writing placement levels, we gave the UC Writing Assessment to the students. The assessment includes a short reading passage in which the students were asked to respond in an expository essay to an excerpted article written by Miguel Bustillo that argues that education helps individuals achieve the American dream. The essays were scored by ESL faculty graders who had been trained by the Educational Testing Service. The following example text, which comes from a student's essay, illustrates the kind of academic writing we evaluated.

> Since the time of birth, our brains are always gaining knowledge consciously or unconsciously. Until our last breath we will learn something new about ourselves, others, the world, and many things. Education has a great impact on the direction of a person's life aside from bringing good job, U.S. citizenship, the American Dream. . . . The immigrants' thirst for knowledge has overcome the obstacle. With a good knowledge of the English language, the immigrants realize that they are living a better life. Teacher, because you taught me English, I am now living a better life. Education also has the power to enrich and to open a person's mind. Knowledge has the ability to get rid of ignorance and bigotry. Education opens a person's mind to ideas and to things that he or she has never been exposed to before.

We used Cobb's (2002) Vocabprofile to scan the selected essays, decompose them into lexical frequency zones, and determine the students' ability to use academic words (see Cobb 2002; see also Cobb and Morris 2002). The Vocabprofile calculates the percentage of academic words in each student's essay, along with type-token frequency and total number of words. In native English speaker writing, generally 10 percent of the words consist of academic words and 80 percent of the words consist of high-frequency words. The remainder consists primarily of proper nouns and technical words (see table 9.2). In the L2 writer example above, the Vocabprofile revealed that the student used academic words such as *immigrants-imigrantes* and *ignorance-ignorancia*.

Table 9.1.
Background characteristics of participants in experiment 1

Background characteristics	Asian (n = 89)		Spanish (n = 25)	
	Mean	*SD*	Mean	*SD*
Length of residence (years)	7.73	2.88	7.89	4.13
Verbal SAT score	471.49	78.5	420.00	69.35

Table 9.2.
Typical native-speaker results

Words used in texts (%)	Four levels of words
70	Words on a list of 1,000 most frequently used word families
10	Words on a list of the second 1,000 most frequently used word families
10	Academic Word List words
10	Off-list words that do not appear on the above lists

Source: Cobb (2002).

Eighty-eight percent of words the student used were basic high-frequency words, and only 3 percent of the words were academic words.

The results indicate that L1 Spanish students used significantly fewer cognates/academic words than the L1 Asian language students. Whereas 5 percent of the words in the Asian L1 essays consisted of academic words/Spanish cognates, only 3 percent of the words in the Spanish L1 essays were academic words/Spanish cognates. Differences were significant ($p < .005$). Neither group used as many academic words as native speakers (10 percent), as reported in the literature (Cobb 2002).

Because the ESL students did not use many academic words, their writing did not look scholarly. In the foregoing example, the student used general words (such as *good* and *thing*) and repeated the same words many times. In addition, she made many vocabulary errors. These errors often were caused by her inaccurate use of idioms (such as *open a person's mind*). They also were caused by her failure to follow English grammatical restrictions on words. (For instance, the student used the indefinite article *a* before a noncount noun: *a good knowledge*.) Less obvious, however, is that the student's inability to use academic words such as *survive* resulted in the use of everyday, common words such as *live*. These words do not have as many related derivative forms as academic words and therefore cannot add to the text's cohesion in the same way academic words do. Had she used the academic words *minimize*, *remove*, *diminish*, *negate*, *displace*, or *terminate* instead of *get rid of*, her essay would have looked more scholarly; had she used related academic word forms (such as *minimum*, *minimal*, *minimize*, or *remove* and *removal*), the essay might have been more cohesive.

Experiment 2

In the second experiment, we examined the following research question: How do Asian L1 and Spanish L1 ESL students do on a test of academic word derivatives in English? (Recall that the test consists of Spanish-English cognates.) Motivation for this question comes from our desire to provide information concerning how well advanced ESL undergraduates at a major university know academic word derivatives. In addition, we wish to offer a starting point for further investigation of Spanish cognate knowledge and academic words in L2 production.

The participants were thirty-four university ESL students who were enrolled in two intact classes. We compared the performance of these students with the performance of thirty-four native English speakers, as reported in the literature (Schmitt and Zimmerman 2002). The thirty-four ESL students had the following characteristics: an average length of residence in the United States of 7.8 years (with a standard deviation of 3.8 years); an average verbal SAT score of 473 (with a standard deviation of 84 points); and advanced writing proficiency, as measured by the UC Writing Assessment. All students had graduated in the top 10 percent of their high school graduating classes. Of the students, four were Spanish L1 speakers and thirty were Asian L1 speakers. The reason for the small number of students in the Spanish L1 group was the availability of these students in the two participating intact classes—reflecting the fact that relatively few Spanish L1 students (first-generation Latinos) are admitted to UC campuses. The Spanish L1 students in this study reported that they had been schooled in Mexico or Central America and were proficient in reading and writing in Spanish.

We gave the students the Test of English Derivatives (Schmitt and Zimmerman 2002). The directions and an example with the academic word/cognate *stimulate/estimular* follow.

Test of Derivatives
In this section, look at each word and write the correct form in each sentence. If there is more than one possibility (e.g., more than one adjective form), you only need to write one. If there is no form, put an "X" in the blank on the left. Sometimes the form will not need changing, as it is already correct (such as STIMULATE in the example below).

Example:

stimulate

stimulation	noun	A massage is good ____.
stimulate	verb	Massages can ___ tired muscles.
stimulating	adjective	A massage has a ___ effect.
X	adverb	He massaged ___.

There were sixteen items on the test, and all words were considered Spanish/English cognates. Participants were tested together in a single class session of about fifty-five minutes. Although they were given as long as they needed to complete the Test of Derivatives, they completed the test in thirty minutes or less. All necessary instructions were included in the directions.

The Pearson correlation coefficient for SAT verbal scores and scores on the Test of Derivatives (total score) was strong, $r = .51$. The results suggest that whereas native English speakers score about the same on all word forms—achieving a score of about 90 percent (see Schmitt and Zimmerman 2002)—the ESL students find adjective and adverb forms more problematic than noun and verb forms. They scored an average of 39 percent. Although we can make no generalizations because of the small number of Spanish speakers, the Spanish speakers in this study did worse than the

Asian L1 learners on the derivative test, scoring an average of 36 percent in comparison to the Asian L1 learners' average of 43 percent.

All ESL students made interesting mistakes when they attempted to use derivational morphology. Notable mistakes are listed below (see table 9.3).

Discussion

Fluent use of L2 words requires not only that L2 words be known but also that they be retrieved rapidly from memory and used correctly. Morphologically related words share a representation in memory (Costa and Caramazza 1999; Feldman 1995; Taft 1994; Tyler and Nagy 1989). This organizational principle holds for words belonging to one language as well as different languages, so that a Spanish-English bilingual has one representation containing both the English words *govern* and *government* and the Spanish words *gobernar* and *gobierno.* (For discussion, see De Bot et al. 1995; Jiang 2000.) According to this view, learning cognates does not involve creating new entries in memory but adding new information to existing entries. In the case of academic writing in English, simply knowing the meaning of a word does not give learners with cognate knowledge much advantage over their peers without such knowledge. Writers need productive knowledge of words. Cognate knowledge informs them only of word meanings, not ways to use words in sentences, such as the grammatical means of combining words, registral variation, collocations, and so forth (Nation 2001).

Although knowledge of cognates assists L2 learners in reading, the learners in our study are not using many academic words in their writing. (Recall that the Vocabprofile text analysis showed that the ESL students in this study used an average of 4 percent academic words in their essays.) The second experiment suggests that advanced ESL students, whether they are Spanish or Asian L1, are deficient in their ability to produce derivative forms. One possible explanation for the Spanish speakers' low scores on the derivative test is that even though they may have known the Spanish-English cognates, they overlooked even obvious similarities between words

Table 9.3.
Examples of student errors on test of derivatives

Word	Noun	Verb	Adjective	Adverb
assumption			assumptious, assumptional, assumulating	assumptively
inevitable	inevitation	inevitite, inevitate, inevitabled	inevited	
precise	precisement, precisetance	precises	precisive, preciant, precised preciseling	precisety preciseling

in their L1s an L2s and may not have fully utilized the help offered by cognates. Further study is necessary to substantiate this finding.

The line between *receptive* and *productive* vocabulary knowledge is blurred, in part because of the notion of avoidance and L2 proficiency level. Melka (1997) observes that beginners tend to generalize equivalences in both reception and production but that at more advanced levels they hesitate to use cognates about which they are unsure. As one might expect, many Spanish speakers might avoid cognate use in writing because they are familiar with the difficulties associated with the use of false cognates (Lightbown and Liben 1984; Meara, Lightbown, and Halter 1994, 1997).

Knowledge of Spanish vocabulary might contribute to the use of academic words, but this contribution might not be automatic. Among the factors contributing to the effective use of cognates are students' L1 proficiency, awareness of cognates, and grammatical proficiency in English. Factors that facilitate learning of a new word include a combination of unproblematic pronunciation, derivational regularity, and morphological transparency (Laufer 1998).

The fact that the ESL students found adjective and adverb forms more problematic than noun and verb forms could indicate that for the items tested, adjective/adverb suffixes were more predictable than noun/verb suffixes. It also could be related to their frequency in academic text (Schmitt and Meara 1997; Schmitt 1998), as well as the students' lack of exposure to academic text (Nation 2001).

Future studies must address several methodological concerns. The nature of the students' proficiency in Spanish and English calls for further investigation. More specifically, students who self-reported high Spanish proficiency may not have known the Spanish cognates, which would have affected the results. The nature of the task and the experimental linguistic stimuli on the Test of Derivatives undoubtedly plays a critical role in lexical production and should be explored further. A further concern is the fact that academic words are polysemous and have various frequency rates. Future studies might control for word frequency and the number of word meanings of the cognates. Furthermore, we tested only adult university students in intact classes. We were unable to obtain large numbers of Latino students in either experiment—particularly the second one—and our findings therefore cannot be generalized.

Conclusion

In learning English words, Spanish L2 learners may have an advantage over L2 learners whose L1 is not a romance language because many English words have Spanish cognates, and Spanish L2 learners may be able to figure out the meanings of the English words on the basis of their knowledge of Spanish. We question the assumption, however, that lexical knowledge transfers effortlessly or successfully in both reading and writing. We suspect that cognate knowledge is more useful in improving L2 reading comprehension than in improving L2 writing.

We suspect that the results of our study might reflect the instruction that many students receive in their high school English courses. In these courses, linkages between the students' L1s and English are rarely made, and the use of vocabulary—including the ways words are combined with other words as well as their derivative use—has been largely overlooked. Teachers have concerned themselves largely with teaching word meanings.

This situation is unfortunate, given the heavy emphasis on writing. (California students are required to take writing exams as part of the California High School Exit Exams, as well as the California Standards Exams. Many students who go on to college also take writing exams such as the SAT I, the UC Subject A Exam, and the California State University [CSU] English Placement Test.) Overall, students in California have not fared well on writing tests. More than 50 percent of the students who attend CSU and UC campuses fail to pass these exams and require special classes before they take freshmen writing courses. This study suggests that students' use of academic words might be one obstacle to their writing success.

Highly educated UC students, who have graduated in the top 10 percent of their high school classes, are doing very poorly with regard to their use of academic words. Adult L2 learners who are poor writers of English have given evidence that they lack the ability to use Spanish/English cognates in their writing. Although cognate knowledge might facilitate comprehension, its effect on production seems to be limited. Analyses of our writing data indicates that Spanish speakers' knowledge of Spanish academic words/cognates is not a reliable predictor of their writing proficiency in English. Moreover, the data suggest that it is not enough to teach Spanish-speaking students Spanish-English cognates; we recommend that educators identify the set of academic word cognates and teach Spanish-speaking adolescents these cognates explicitly, when possible, linking the instruction of etymology to cognates and emphasizing the use of cognates in the context of academic writing.

REFERENCES

August, Diane. 2004. *Acquiring literacy in English.* Report on National Institute of Child Health and Human Development project, Transfer of reading skills in bilingual children. [Subproject 2 of "Acquiring Literacy in English: Cross-linguistic, Intralinguistic, and Developmental Factors" Research Program with Margarita Calderón, María Carlo, and Catherine Snow.] Washington, D.C.: Center for Applied Linguistics. Available at http://www.cal.org/acqlit/subproject2/ (accessed September 17, 2004).

Barber, Charles L. 1962. Some measurable characteristics of modern scientific prose. In *Contributions to English syntax and philology,* ed. Charles L. Barber, 21–43. Gothoburgensis: Studies in English. Goteborg, Sweden: Acta Universitatis.

Bardovi-Harlig, Kathleen, and Theodora Bofman. 1989. Attainment of syntactic and morphological accuracy by advanced language learners. *Studies in Second Language Acquisition* 11:17–34.

Blum-Kulka, Shoshana, and Edward Levenston. 1983. Lexical-grammatical pragmatic indicators. *Studies in Second Language Acquisition* 9:155–70.

California Department of Education. 1997. *The California English and Language Arts content standards.* Sacramento: California Department of Education. Available at http://www.cde.ca.gov/be/st/ss/engmain.asp.

———. 1999. *The California English Language Arts framework: Kindergarten through grade twelve.* Sacramento: California Department of Education. Available at http://www.cde.ca.gov/ci/rl/cf/index.asp.

Carroll, Susanne E. 1992. On cognates. *Second Language Research* 8, no. 2:93–119.

Cobb, Thomas. 2002. *Vocabprofile.* [Updated July 2002] Montreal, Canada: University of Quebec. Available at http://www.er.uqam.ca/nobel/r21270/cgi-bin/webfreqs/web_vp.cgi (accessed September 20, 2002).

Cobb, Thomas, and Lori Morris. 2002. Vocabulary profiles as a predictor of TESL student performance. Paper presented at American Association for Applied Linguistics, Salt Lake City, Utah.

Costa, Albert, and Alfonso Caramazza. 1999. Is lexical selection language specific? Further evidence from Spanish-English bilinguals. *Bilingualism: Language and Cognition* 2:231–44.

Cowan, J. Ronayne. 1974. Lexical and syntactic research for the design of EFL reading materials. *TESOL Quarterly* 8:389–400.

Coxhead, Averil. 2000. A new academic word list. *TESOL Quarterly* 34:213–38.

De Bot, Kees, Albert Cox, Annedi Schaufeli, and Bert Weltens. 1995. Lexical processing in bilinguals. *Second Language Research* 11:1–19.

Durgunoglu, Aydin Yücesan. 1997. Reading in two languages. In *Tutorials in bilingualism: Psycholinguistic perspectives*, ed. Annette M. B. de Groot and Judith F. Kroll, 255–76. Mahwah, N.J.: Lawrence Erlbaum Associates.

———. 1998. Acquiring literacy in English and Spanish in the United States. In *Literacy development in a multilingual context: Cross-cultural perspectives,* ed. Aydin Yücesan Durgunoglu and Ludo Verhoeven, 135–46. Mahwah, N.J.: Lawrence Erlbaum Associates.

Durgunoglu, Aydin Yücesan, and Banu Öney. 1999. A cross-linguistic comparison of phonological awareness and word recognition. *Reading and Writing* 11:281–99.

Durgunoglu, Aydin Yücesan, Catherine Snow, and Esther Geva. 2001. Theoretical issues in literacy development of ELL students. *International Dyslexia Association Commemorative Booklet,* 21–26. Baltimore: International Dyslexia Association.

Feldman, Laurie B., ed. 1995. *Morphological aspects of language processing.* Hillsdale, N.J.: Lawrence Erlbaum Associates.

Jiang, Nan. 2000. Lexical representation and development in a second language. *Applied Linguistics* 21:47–77.

Jiménez, Robert T., Eugene García, and David Pearson. 1996. The reading strategies of bilingual Latina/o students who are successful English readers: Opportunities and obstacles. *Reading Research Quarterly* 31:90–112.

Kleinmann, Howard. 1977. Avoidance behavior in adult second language acquisition. *Language Learning* 27:93–107.

Laufer, Batia. 1998. What's in a word that makes it hard or easy: Some intralexical factors that affect the learning of words. In *Vocabulary: Description, acquisition and pedagogy*, ed. Norbert Schmitt and Michael McCarthy, 140–55. Cambridge: Cambridge University Press.

Lightbown, Patricia M., and G. Liben. 1984. The recognition and use of cognates by L2 learners. In *Crosslinguistic perspective for second language research*, ed. Roger Anderson, 393–417. Rowley, Mass.: Newbury House.

Lobo, Felix. 1966. A 10,000 Word Spanish vocabulary expanded from 3,000 English cognates. Ph.D. diss., Georgetown University.

Meara, Paul. 1993. The bilingual lexicon and the teaching of vocabulary. In *The bilingual lexicon*, ed. Robert Schreuder and Bert Weltens, 279–97. Philadelphia: John Benjamins.

Meara, Paul, Patricia Lightbown, and Randall Halter. 1994. The effect of cognates on the applicability of yes/no vocabulary tests. *Canadian Modern Language Review* 50:296–311.

———. 1997. Classrooms as lexical environments. *Language Teaching Research* 1:28–47.

Melka, Francine. 1997. Receptive vs. productive aspects of vocabulary. In *Vocabulary: Description, acquisition and pedagogy*, ed. Norbert Schmitt and Michael McCarthy, 85–102. Cambridge: Cambridge University Press.

Moss, Gillian. 1992. Cognate recognition: Its importance in the teaching of ESP reading courses to Spanish speakers. *English for Specific Purposes* 11:141–58.

Nagy, William, Eugene García, Aydin Yücesan Durgunoglu, and Barbara J. Hancin-Bhatt. 1993. Spanish-English bilingual students' use of cognates in English reading. *Journal of Reading Behavior* 25:241–59.

Nation, Paul. 1990. *Teaching and learning vocabulary.* Rowley, Mass.: Newbury House.

———. 2001. *Learning vocabulary in another language.* Cambridge: Cambridge University Press.

Nation, Paul, and Robert Waring. 1997. Vocabulary size, text coverage and word lists. In *Vocabulary: Description, acquisition and pedagogy,* ed. Norbert Schmitt and Michael McCarthy. Cambridge: Cambridge University Press.

Osburne, Andrea G., and Sylvia S. Mulling. 2001. Use of morphological analysis by Spanish L1 ESOL learners. *IRAL* 39:153–59.

Rumberger, Russell. 2000. Educational outcomes and opportunities for English language learners. Presentation to California State Legislature, Joint Committee to Develop the Master Plan for Education, Kindergarten through University. Available as occasional paper of the Linguistic Minority Research Institute, University of California at Santa Barbara. Available at http://lmri.ucsb.edu/resdiss/2/pdf_files/091300_rumberger_masterplan3.pdf (accessed September 17, 2004).

Santos Maldonado, Carmen. 1997. Lexical processing in uneven bilinguals: An exploration of Spanish-English activation of form and meaning. *Edinburgh Working Papers in Applied Linguistics* 8:76–97.

Scarcella, Robin, and Russell Rumberger. 2000. Academic English—Key to long term success. *University of California Linguistic Minority Research Institute Newsletter* 4:1. Available at http://www.lmri.ucsb.edu/resdiss/2/newsletters.htm.

Schachter, Jacquelyn. 1974. An error in error analysis. *Language Learning* 24:205–14.

Schmitt, Norbert. 1998. Tracking the incremental acquisition of second language vocabulary: A longitudinal study. *Language Learning* 48:281–317.

———. 1999. The relationship between TOEFL vocabulary items and meaning, association, collocation, and word class knowledge. *Language Testing* 16:189–216.

———. 2000. *Vocabulary in language teaching.* Cambridge: Cambridge University Press.

Schmitt, Norbert, and Paul Meara. 1997. Researching vocabulary through a word knowledge framework: Word associations and verbal suffixes. *Studies in Second Language Acquisition* 19:17–36.

Schmitt, Norbert, and Cheryl Boyd Zimmerman. 2002. Derivative word forms: What do learners know? *TESOL Quarterly* 36:145–71.

Taft, Marcus. 1994. The morphology of the mental lexicon: Internal word structure viewed from a psycholinguistic perspective. In *Morphological structure, lexical representation and lexical access*, ed. Sandra Dominek and Marcus Taft, 271–94. East Sussex, N.J.: Lawrence Erlbaum Associates.

Tyler, Andrea, and Nagy, William. 1989. The acquisition of English derivational morphology. *Journal of Memory and Language* 28:649–67.

West, Michael. 1953. *A general service list of English words.* London: Longman, Green and Co.

Whitley, M. Stanley. 2002. *Spanish/English contrasts.* Washington, D.C.: Georgetown University Press.

Discourse Resources and Meaning Construction

10

Intonation, Mental Representation, and Mutual Knowledge

ANN WENNERSTROM
University of Washington

AN IMPORTANT PART of the research program in cognitive linguistics involves using linguistic structure as an entry point to better understand cognitive processes. In this chapter, I argue that just as certain lexicogrammatical structures have been claimed to interact with cognitive processes and constructions, certain intonation patterns also interact with cognitive processes and constructions. Therefore, in our search for a better understanding of these relationships we would be well served to include intonation analysis among our methodologies.[1]

Rather than argue for a particular cognitive model, I draw from three popular existing models (which are not necessarily incompatible): Clark's (1992) model, in which community membership is a crucial element in constructing a mental representation of discourse; Fauconnier's (1985) mental space theory, in which discourse is represented by a network of interconnected mental spaces; and Lakoff's (1987) theory of idealized cognitive models (ICMs), in which new situations are processed with respect to stored prototypes (as in Rosche 1978). I illustrate with excerpts of conversations and lectures how an intonation analysis is consistent with each of these models and, in some cases, can actually shed new light on cognitive constructions beyond what might be revealed in lexicogrammatical structure.

I consider two main intonation patterns, both from English (though other languages may have similar patterns): the high-pitched intonation of contrast (henceforth "contrast intonation") and the low pitch of accessible information (henceforth "given intonation"). Contrast intonation—often referred to as "contrastive focus" or "contrastive stress"—usually is manifested as an L+H* pitch accent (Pierrehumbert 1980) aligned with the stressed syllable of the contrasting word. This syllable is higher in pitch than would be expected within the normal declination of the intonation contour and may be louder and of longer duration. Given intonation, which also has been called "deaccentuation" (Ladd 1980; Terken and Hirschberg 1994), can be either a lack of prominence or a more deliberate lowering gesture for items that the speaker believes to be accessible to hearers in the discourse (Chafe 1994; Ladd 1980; Wennerstrom 2001).[2] Given intonation usually is associated with lower amplitude as well. I have argued elsewhere (Wennerstrom 1998, 2001) that both of these intonation patterns function as cohesive devices in discourse. A contrast, by definition, juxtaposes two ideas in an adversative or concessive relationship (Rudolph 1996)—an association that can be considered a cohesive link. Likewise, given intonation necessarily involves a cohesive relationship between the low-pitched item and some prior item or idea.

These pitch patterns frequently align with lexicogrammatical structure. Some contrasts involve lexical antonyms (e.g., *up* versus *down*; *early* versus *late*) or complementary members of lexical sets (e.g., *Monday* versus *Tuesday*). Likewise, given intonation often is associated with a word that is cohesive through the classic relationships defined for cohesion by Halliday and Hasan (1976)—direct repetition, synonymy, various proforms and substitutions, and so on. The following example illustrates lexical and intonational alignment. In this exchange, two men in their forties are reminiscing about a small-town boyhood activity of high jumping by rigging up some makeshift equipment in their yards. Starting in line 9, Brian begins a story about the plight of a left-handed jumper. The words *left* and *right*, antonyms within the superordinate set of lateral directions, are contrasted throughout lines 10–12. Contrast intonation (indicated with underlining) coincides with these words. Meanwhile, the verb *jump* in line 10, a repetition in the talk of high jumping, has given intonation (indicated with a low arrow ↳).

1. High jumping[3]

(1)	Brian:	Yeah, a galvanized pipe for a cross bar, n'. .
(2)	Steve:	Yah . . they had a lot . lot better than .
(3)		at least y'know the inner tubes n' . .
(4)		ya had y- . at least somethin' . comfortable to land on,
(5)		Mom and dad . . in the uh . . cross the other way
(6)		all they had wasss . . sawdust . . /just like we did in grade school.
(7)	Brian:	\hhhhhhhhhhhhhhhhhhh
(8)	Steve:	Landing on the sawdust wasn't much fun. . .
(9)	Brian:	Yeah. . . . part a their . high jumpin' there at Whitman, we'd ah . . Ken Magnuson . he
(10)	^	was a . . . left handed jumper, so he'd always ↳ jump on the other side of the ↳ pen
(11)	^	and we were right handed jumpers, we'd . . so . we'd fluff up all the sawdust on the . .
(12)	^	lefthand side, because that's where we'd always land n'. .
(13)		he didn't have any sawdust over on his side.

Perhaps more interesting than intonational and lexicogrammatical alignment, however, are cases in which these patterns occur in the absence of clear lexicogrammatical cues. As examples throughout the remainder of this chapter show, contrast can be based not on existing lexical oppositions but on ad hoc categories set up for the purpose of the discourse at hand. (In fact, Deppermann 2004 has claimed that such nonlexical contrasts constitute the majority of cases.) Such contrasts always involve a third, superordinate category—also ad hoc—that subsumes both elements of the contrast, creating a framework within which the contrast is made. Furthermore, only one member of a contrast need appear in the text; both the contrasting element and the superordinate category may be inferred. Likewise, items with given intonation may never have been mentioned before, so that their antecedent must also be inferred. In short, these given and contrast intonation patterns are a good starting point for a discussion of cognitive processes because they involve inference and the construction and juxtaposition of categories.

To illuminate such cases, I turn to the cognitive linguistics literature, beginning with Clark's (1992) notions of mutual knowledge and community membership. In discourse, Clark says, the choice of linguistic structure is based on participants' judgments about their mutual knowledge. Assessments of mutual knowledge, in turn, depend on three elements: what is mutually perceivable in the immediate physical environment; what has been mentioned in prior discourse; and what is understood by virtue of community membership. In the third case, the idea is that knowledge is stored in memory encyclopedically (by topics and events, organized into frames, schemas, and scenarios), and it is cross-referenced with an index of "who knows what" for both individuals and communities. Thus, in communication, participants make judgments about their common community membership, from which they assess what kinds of knowledge and assumptions—generic and specific—might be familiar to hearers. This assessment affects linguistic choices: how much detail needs to be specified, whether one can use definite reference, and so on. As succeeding examples show, the way intonation patterns are used reflects speaker judgments about what is mutually known and thus what assumptions are being made about community membership among the participants.

The role of intonation in these assessments can be illustrated with two examples. The first (transcript 2) involves a group of friends—white, American graduate students in their early thirties—who are discussing one member's (Travis's) experience living in Nepal. Regarding the cliché that Western tourists always get sick in Nepal, Travis explains that Nepali natives also get serious diseases, which they *just live with* (line 8). He uses contrasting pitch in two utterances of the word *live,* although there is no inherent lexical counterpart in the contrast (as in *live* versus *die*, for example). As figure 10.1 shows,[4] the first utterance of *live* has the more exaggerated pitch, though the second *live* is also high relative to surrounding words. The opposite element is not mentioned in the text but must be inferred.

2. Living with *giardia*

(1) Sadie: You'd think they'd / get resistant to it eventually though.
(2) Mindy: \You mean lotta kids die?
(3) Travis: I don't think it's I mean it's not pos /sible to be resis /tant t:::o (.5)
(4) Mindy: \mmm \mmm
(5) Travis: I mean I think=
(6) Mindy: =t' that kind of thing=
(7) Travis: =yeah. I mean even- (.4)
(8) ^ they just live with giardia and they live with amoebas you know.

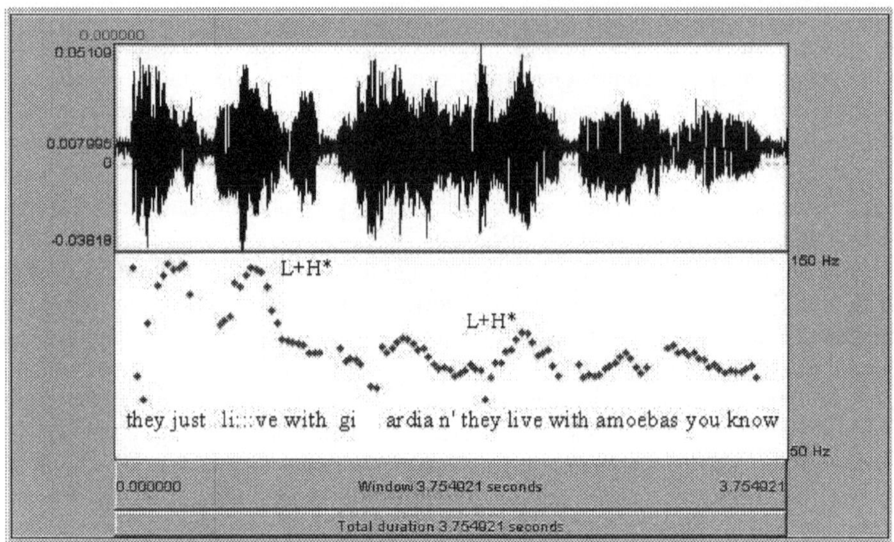

Figure 10.1. An ad hoc contrast on *live* without lexical antecedant

In Clark's (1992) model, this ad hoc contrast might be interpreted with reference to the communities involved: Travis has lived in Nepal but Sadie and Mindy have not. Travis can judge the community of Sadie and Mindy as having a scenario of Western medicine and health norms in which one would try to fight and cure most diseases rather than living with them. A superordinate category—lifestyle choices surrounding diseases—also can be inferred. The speaker can be economical and not spell out these details in the text. It is noteworthy that this contrast interpretation is triggered more by intonation than by lexicogrammatical structure. If we changed the intonation of *giardia* and *amoebas*, for example, to extended plateaus or "listing contours"—*they just live with gia::::rdia:: ; they live with amoe:::::::ba:::s*—line 8 could be interpreted not as a contrast but as a list of diseases and a comment on how difficult the lives of Nepalis are.

This analysis is consistent with Deppermann's (2004) observation that in conversation, many contrasts have moral implications: They clarify and exemplify dispreferred social behaviors—or, in his words, they "warrant a deviation category." In example 2, the speaker implies that members of this (less-traveled) Western community might think it strange to *live* with diseases because curing them should be the norm. From such implied contrasts, then, we can learn what speakers are taking for granted about community membership and what sort of mutual knowledge and values they assume.

Example 3 illustrates given intonation associated with an item that has no direct antecedent in the text. The excerpt is from a lecture on correlation in which a genetics study of ducks is described. In the description of the study, the lecturer uses the word *parents* four times between lines 3 and 6 with given intonation and no antecedent (line 3 is illustrated in figure 10.2). In Clark's (1992) terms, the speaker thus reveals assumptions about the community membership of the audience: "Typical" American undergraduates belong to a generally educated academic community, which she presumes to be familiar with a basic genetics schema. Given these judgments, she can treat the word *parents* intonationally as given, although it is neither an exact repetition nor a synonym of a prior item.

3. Ducks and their parents

(1) . . . and the question that was being addressed by this particular study, (.5)
(2) was whether (.6) crossbreeds, (.4)
(3) ∧ so (.2) ducks that had (.4) a- one mallard →parent and one pintail →parent, (.5)
(4) if you look at them, (1.4) and (.1)
(5) ∧ you notice that a particular duck looks more like the pintail →parent than it does like (.2)
(6) ∧ th- the mallard →parent (.5) is it also true that its behavioral charact- behavioral
(7) characteristics (.3) will be more like the pintail.

In sum, followers of Clark's (1992) model can apply intonation analysis to learn what speakers are taking for granted about the mutual knowledge and values of the communities to which the participants belong. This analysis could be especially important in studies of discourse in which speech communities meet; for example, in the case of marginalized groups in the school system, such an analysis might provide information that would be helpful in the design of instructional materials.

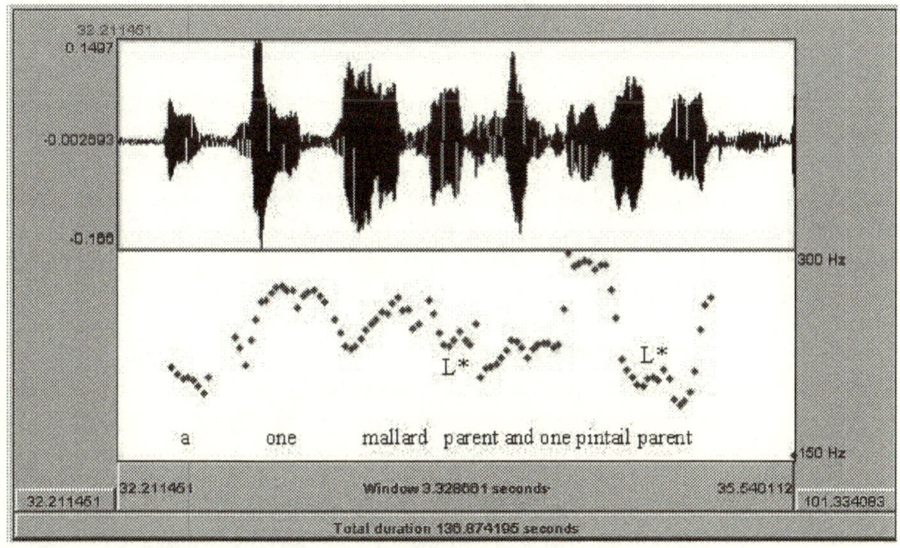

Figure 10.2. *Parents* has given intonation but no antecedent

Next I turn to a second set of claims about conceptual structure: Fauconnier's (1985) mental space theory. In essence, his idea is that mental representation in discourse involves the participants' setting up of one or more temporary mental spaces that contain referents, events, and their properties and relations. Mental spaces can be underspecified by linguistic structure because we fill in the gaps with background knowledge. The elements of one mental space are connected to the elements of other mental spaces via several relations, such as identity of reference, time, space, and metaphorical extension.

Part of this research program involves identifying linguistic structures called "space builders" that trigger—or, in Fauconnier's words, "give instructions for" (1985, 20)—the establishment of mental spaces, the elements in them, and the connections among them. Space builders may be grammatical: For example, Sweetser (1996) investigated how conditionals trigger mental spaces for hypothetical worlds. They may be lexical: Michaelis (1996) looked at the adverbial *still* as a trigger for a present-time mental space linked to an earlier-time mental space when the action of the verb also was in force.

Turning to intonation, I submit that contrast and given intonation also are linguistic structures that trigger certain mental space configurations in the minds of participants in discourse, just as lexicogrammatical structures have been claimed to do. Contrast intonation is a mental space builder that triggers the construction of a new mental space for the contrasting element. Further, it triggers a "generic space" (Fauconnier and Turner 2002) in which the superordinate category that encompasses both of the contrasting members also is constructed. Given intonation "points to" an element that is already available in the mental space network. This analysis is reminiscent of Fauconnier's (1985) discussion of definite and indefinite articles, in which the definite article also is said to "point to" an element already in a mental space whereas the indefinite article triggers the addition of a new element.

The next set of examples illustrates these relations as we return to the two men reminiscing about high jumping (reprinted from 1 as 4). Steve makes an ad hoc contrast between *inner tubes* (line 3) and *sawdust* (line 6)—hardly lexical antonyms. The superordinate framework for the contrast also is an ad hoc category: "surfaces to land on in backyard high jumping"—mentioned in line 4 as *somethin' comfortable to land on*. This contrast is paired with a second one between two locations: Brian's yard, which had the inner tubes, and "mom and dad's" place (line 5), where there was only sawdust to land on.

4. High jumping

(1) Brian: Yeah, a galvanized pipe for a cross bar, n'. .
(2) Steve: Yah . . they had a lot . lot better than .
(3) ∧ at least y'know the inner tubes n' . .
(4) ya had y- . at least somethin' . comfortable to land on,
(5) Mom and dad . . in the uh . . cross the other way
(6) ∧ all they had wasss . . sawdust . . /just like we did in grade school.
(7) Brian: \hhhhhhhhhhhhhhhhhh

(8) Steve: Landing on the <u>saw</u>dust wasn't much fun. .

(9) Brian: Yeah. . . . part a their . high jumpin' there at Whitman, we'd ah . Ken Magnuson . he

(10) ∧ was a . . . <u>left</u> handed jumper, so <u>he'd</u> always →jump on the <u>other</u> side of the →pen

(11) and we were <u>right</u> handed jumpers, we'd . . so . we'd fluff up all the sawdust on the . .

(12) <u>left</u>hand side, because that's where <u>we'd</u> always land n'. .

(13) he didn't have any sawdust over on <u>his</u> side.

Drawing on Fauconnier's (1985) model, I suggest that as soon as we hear the contrast intonation on *inner tubes* in line 3, we are triggered to construct a new mental space for the expected contrast. The result, sketched in figure 10.3, consists of three mental spaces: an input space with high jumping onto inner tubes in Brian's yard; a second contrast space with empty slots for the anticipated landing surface and place; and a third, generic space created to encompass the superordinate categories. Other elements in the input space (such as the activity itself, the boys, and so forth) also appear in the contrast space and the generic space because it is anticipated that they will be common to all. The potential nature of these links is indicated with dotted lines. As the discourse continues, these lines can be solidified, the contrast slots can be filled in appropriately, and other adjustments can be made in the network if necessary.

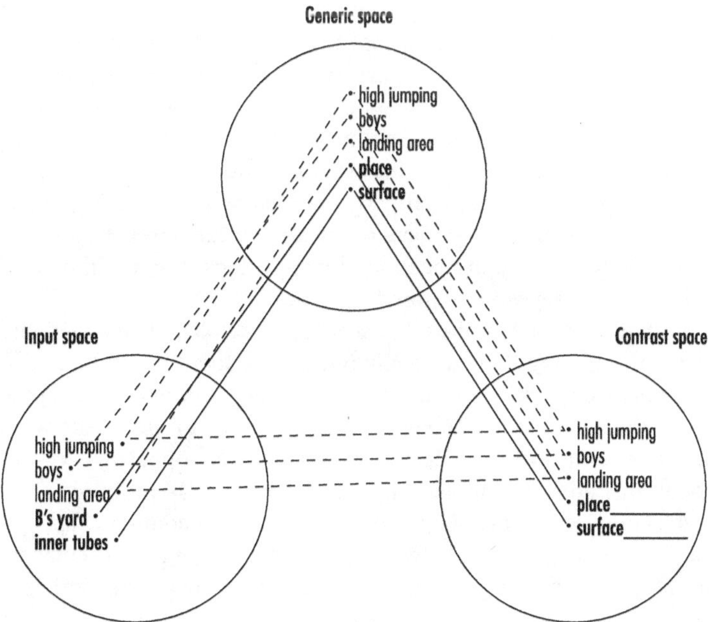

Figure 10.3. Mental space network triggered by contrast intonation

We can notice that the word *pen* in line 10, though not mentioned previously, is treated intonationally as given. This intonation can be said to "point to" an element already in place in the mental space network. In high jumping, a pen is the area that encloses the landing surface (inner tubes or sawdust). Rather than creating a new mental space or adding a brand new element to an existing space, the speaker's intonation "points to" what should already be present. Although I would not have chosen the word *pen*, I can easily elaborate my own existing mental space for this discourse by adjusting the label from "landing area" to "pen" throughout the mental space network.

I turn last to Lakoff's (1987) idealized cognitive models (ICMs) and his discussion of categories and prototypes. According to Lakoff, as we go through life we develop conceptual categories to understand and store our experiences in the world. Categories are organized radially around central prototypes, which are further organized into more complex structures called ICMs. As Lakoff (1987, 45) puts it, ICMs are "theories of some subject matter." Cultures and individuals make decisions about what categories in the realm of experience need to be distinctive and what constitutes a prototypical case for each category. In any new situation we can compare the present circumstances to our ICMs and thus engage in cognitive processes such as recognition, reasoning, inferencing, making judgments, and so on.

One of Lakoff's methodologies is to identify linguistic structures from languages of the world—for example, classifier words in Dyirbal and Japanese—to demonstrate how human classification systems are organized. As with the other models, we see a methodology in which linguistic form acts as an entry point to conceptual structure.

Once again, I argue that the intonation patterns I am discussing are another kind of linguistic structure that gives us a tool to understand categorization and ICMs. Contrast by definition involves a category-based organization scheme in which two elements are juxtaposed within a third superordinate category. Ad hoc categories are especially interesting in this regard. As Barsalou (1983) discovered through a series of experiments in which subjects performed word association and listing tasks, even ad hoc contrasts showed prototype effects. In other words, the subjects consistently judged certain items as better members of the ad hoc categories than others. Therefore intonation, which highlights category juxtapositions, can reveal more about categories and their prototypes in the mind of a speaker.

Example 5 illustrates a contrast between a prototype and an actual situation, as Steve of the high-jumping dialogue again reminisces about his childhood. This time he relates an episode in which his older brother duped him into mowing the lawn by pretending it was fun, to avoid doing the chore himself. In line 4, the word *handlebars* has contrast intonation but does not have a lexical opposite. Within Lakoff's (1987) model, this ad hoc contrast might be interpreted as follows: If we posit an ICM in which equipment typically is proportioned so that adult-sized people can use it effectively, there is a contrast between this prototype and our mental representation of the little boy mowing the lawn and having to reach upward to grasp the handlebars.

5. Reaching the handle bars

(1) Steve: n' then finally. after he'd mow a couple a times n . .
(2) he sai- y'know d'you wanna do this? he said- it's really a lot of fun . .
(3) hhh ((barely audible laugh)) I don wan- h
(4) ∧ yea::h y'know I could hardly reach the top of the handlebars but . . .
(5) ((breath in)) I start m- mowin' 'n . . next thing you know .
(6) Don wasn't around any more h h huh .
(7) he was in the house ?and he was h h tahuh . .
(8) an' . from that point on, I basically became the lawn mower . .
(9) person for our . for our yard.

The final example, transcript 6, involves given intonation with no antecedent for the low-pitched item. Steve and Brian, who in previous text have said that they enjoy skiing, are talking about some friends who went on a ski vacation in midweek, taking time off from work. In line 3 Steve says, sarcastically: *must be nice!* Brian then comments in line 4 that their ski trip *ticked Brandon off* (Brandon being another friend). The crucial word is *off,* with given intonation: Normally, the verbal compound *ticked óff* would have stress on the particle, but in this context Brian treats it intonationally as given. Again, proponents of Lakoff's model might interpret this intonational choice with reference to an ICM of "normal work-a-day life" in which one doesn't just breeze off to the slopes in midweek. In that context, Steve's sarcasm and the fact that Brandon was *ticked off* is given. One obviously could be envious of people who behaved contrary to the prototypical, socially sanctioned work ethic.

6. Ticked off

(1) Brian: They went up . last Tuesday, Jeff and Shell took the day off n' .
(2) went snow ski hhh ing h=
(3) Steve: =((sarcastic)) must be nice=
(4) Brian: ∧ =huh yeah . ticked Brandon →off cause he didn't getta go.
(5) Steve: /hhhhh
(6) Brian: \hhhhh

To conclude, I have explored three cognitive models in which past investigations have shown how lexicogrammatical structure of discourse interacts with conceptual structure. I have proposed that in such research, an additional type of linguistic structure—namely, intonation—can fruitfully be included as part of the methodology. The facts are particularly striking with ad hoc contrasts and inferred cohesive relationships, where the lexicogrammatical structure alone may not reveal the full story. The pitch patterns of contrast and given intonation can be used as an entry point for understanding the relationships between language and the mind.

Acknowledgments

Transcripts used with kind permission from "Dialects of the Pacific Northwest," an ongoing project at the University of Washington Phonetics Laboratory by Alicia Beckford Wassink and Richard Wright.

NOTES

1. Chafe (1994, 1998) has long made a similar argument using different types of evidence.
2. I believe (Wennerstrom 2001) that deaccent overlaps in some cases with Pierrehumbert's (1980) L* pitch accent, whose discourse meaning is described in Pierrehumbert and Hirschberg (1990) as salient but mutually believed.
3. Data for examples 1, 4, 5, and 6 are from "Dialects of the Pacific Northwest."
4. The top half of the graph indicates the amplitude (roughly the volume); the bottom half shows the pitch. Figures 10.1 and 10.2 were made with Praat software.

Transcription Conventions

. . .	unmeasured pause
(.3)	measured pause
a::::	extended syllable
/text	overlapping speech
\text	
=	latch (no pause between speakers)
,	continuing intonation boundary
.	final intonation boundary
-	cutoff intonation
<u>contrast</u>	contrast intonation
↳	given intonation
hhh	laughter syllables
((text))	metacomment

REFERENCES

Barsalou, Lawrence W. 1983. Ad hoc categories. *Memory and Cognition* 11:211–27.

Chafe, Wallace L. 1994. *Discourse, consciousness, and time: The flow and displacement of conscious experience in speaking and writing.* Chicago: University of Chicago Press.

———. 1998. Language and the flow of thought. In *The new psychology of language: Cognitive and functional approaches to language structure,* ed. Michael Tomasello, 93–111. Mahwah, N.J.: Lawrence Erlbaum Associates.

Clark, Herbert H. 1992. *Arenas of language use.* Chicago: University of Chicago Press.

Deppermann, Arnulf. 2004. Lexical contrasts and conversational contrasting. In *Syntax and lexis in conversation,* ed. Auli Hakulainen and Margret Selting. Amsterdam: John Benjamins.

Fauconnier, Gilles. 1985. *Mental spaces: Aspects of meaning construction in natural language.* Cambridge, Mass.: MIT Press.

Fauconnier, Gilles, and Mark Turner. 2002. *The way we think: Conceptual blending and the mind's hidden capacities.* New York: Basic Books.

Halliday, Michael A. K., and Ruqaiya Hasan. 1976. *Cohesion in English.* London: Longman.

Ladd, D. Robert. 1980. *The structure of intonational meaning.* Bloomington: Indiana University Press.

Lakoff, George. 1987. *Women, fire, and dangerous things: What categories reveal about the mind.* Chicago: University of Chicago Press.

Michaelis, Laura A. 1996. Cross-world continuity and the polysemy of the adverbial *still.* In *Spaces, worlds, and grammar,* ed. Gilles Fauconnier and Eve Sweetser, 179–226. Chicago: University of Chicago Press.

Pierrehumbert, Janet. 1980. *The phonology and phonetics of English intonation.* Ph.D. diss., Massachusetts Institute of Technology.

Pierrehumbert, Janet, and Julia Hirschberg. 1990. The meaning of intonational contours in discourse. In *Intentions in Communication,* ed. Philip R. Cohen, Jerry Morgan, and Martha E. Pollack, 271–311. Cambridge, Mass.: MIT Press.

Rosche, Eleanor. 1978. Principles of categorization. In *Cognition and categorization,* ed. Eleanor Rosche and B. B. Lloyd, 27–48. Hilldale, N.J.: Lawrence Erlbaum.

Rudolph, Elisabeth. 1996. *Contrast: Adversative and concessive relations and their expressions in English, German, Spanish, Portuguese on sentences and text level.* Berlin: Walter de Gruyter.

Sweetser, Eve. 1996. Mental spaces and the grammar of conditional constructions. In *Spaces, worlds, and grammar,* ed. Gilles Fauconnier and Eve Sweetser, 318–33. Chicago: University of Chicago Press.

Terken, Jacques, and Julia Hirschberg. 1994. Deaccentuation of words representing "given" information: Effects of persistence of grammatical function and surface position. *Language and Speech* 37, no. 2:125–45.

Wennerstrom, Ann. 2001. *The music of everyday speech: Prosody and discourse analysis.* New York: Oxford University Press.

———. 1998 Intonation and second language acquisition: A study of Chinese speakers. *Studies in Second Language Acquisition* 20, no. 1:1–25.

11

Linguistic Variation in the Lexical Episodes of University Classroom Talk

ENIKO CSOMAY
San Diego State University

Background

The linguistic characteristics of texts have been researched from two major perspectives over the past three decades: one describing the internal discourse organization of texts and the other focusing on the typical linguistic characteristics of texts and text types. Studies of the first type usually have been qualitative, providing detailed analyses of the discourse patterns in individual texts (e.g., Fox 1987; Mann, Matthieson, and Thompson 1992). In contrast, studies of the second type provide quantitative results, using lexical and grammatical features for their analyses while generally ignoring higher-level discourse structures (e.g., Biber 1988, 1995; Reppen, Fitzmaurice, and Biber 2002).

The linguistic studies analyzing university classroom discourse reflect these two major research traditions. On one hand, researchers investigate the discourse patterns of academic lectures by focusing on lexical patterns and their relationship either to coherence (Tyler 1995) or to the micro and macro structures of class sessions (DeCarrico and Nattinger 1988). Other studies concentrate on the subunits in lectures and identify the linguistic markers of topic shifts (e.g., Hansen 1994) or relate the subunits to various communicative purposes (Young 1994) in the classroom. Although these studies are invaluable in our understanding of the discourse patterns in lectures, most of the analyses are carried out on a few selected texts; hence, the findings are not generalizable.

On the other hand, most recent studies have provided us with comprehensive linguistic characterizations of university classroom discourse, relying on quantitative analysis of a wide range of co-occurring linguistic features. Using Biber's (1988) dimensions of textual variation across registers, Csomay (2000) concludes that university classrooms exhibit linguistic features of both academic prose and face-to-face conversation. In describing the dimensions of textual variation within the academic context, Biber (2003) compares the linguistic characteristics of classrooms to language used in other academic registers (e.g., textbooks). Finally, Csomay (2002a) investigates linguistic variation across class sessions and describes variation in language use related to the level of instruction and the degree of interactivity (i.e., monologic versus interactive classes). Although these studies are able to draw generalizations concerning patterns of linguistic variation across texts, they fail to show variation within texts.

My goal in this chapter is to provide a linguistic characterization of lexically coherent discourse units found in university classroom texts, using quantitative measures for the analysis. The discourse units characterized this way correspond to varying communicative purposes and provide the foundation to further describe text-internal linguistic variation.

More specifically, I first apply Youmans's (1991) Vocabulary Management Profile (VMP) to trace the overall lexical patterns in discourse. On the basis of this lexical profile and a quantitative segmentation technique developed for the study, I identify two major discourse units: lexical episodes and transitional units. Corresponding to lexical episodes is the introduction of new lexis in a stretch of discourse; primary reliance on repeated vocabulary marks transitional talk between the lexical episodes. Second, I classify lexical episodes into types on the basis of their shared linguistic characteristics, using Biber's (2003) dimensions of academic discourse. Finally, I associate these lexical episode types (involved narrative, procedural, content-oriented) with varying communicative purposes and present them in a partial taxonomy.

Analytical Procedures

I took three major analytical steps to achieve the main goals of the study: segment class sessions into discourse units; identify multidimensional characteristics of lexical episodes; and identify lexical episode types on the basis of their multidimensional characteristics of academic discourse.

Segment Class Sessions into Discourse Units—The VMP

The VMP tracks the introduction of newly occurring vocabulary into the discourse. To identify newly occurring vocabulary items, the text is processed via a "sliding window" of 100 words, and new vocabulary items are counted in that window at each word. That is, at the start the window is positioned at the beginning of the text and contains words 1–100. Then the window "slides" one position and contains words 2–101. The window continues to slide one position at a time, allowing analysis of overlapping 100-word chunks of the target text, until the end of the text is reached.

The VMP keeps track of every word introduced in the text prior to the point of analysis, while keeping track of the "new" words entering the window. A word counts as new if it had not occurred in the text before. Thus, a word could occur only once in the window but *not* be counted as new because it had been used earlier in the text. The value of the VMP can change plus or minus 1 every time the window slides one position. Because we use a 100-word window for the analysis, the VMP has a potential range of 0–100. That is, at each position of the window there can be anywhere from 0 to 100 new words occurring in that 100-word chunk of text. In practice, however, the VMP ranges from 5 to 40.

Using the method described above, we gain a VMP value for each word sliding through the window. If we plot the VMP values for each word, we obtain the visual representation of the dynamic change in alternating repeated and newly occurring vocabulary items in a discourse. Figure 11.1 shows the VMP for a 1,500-word

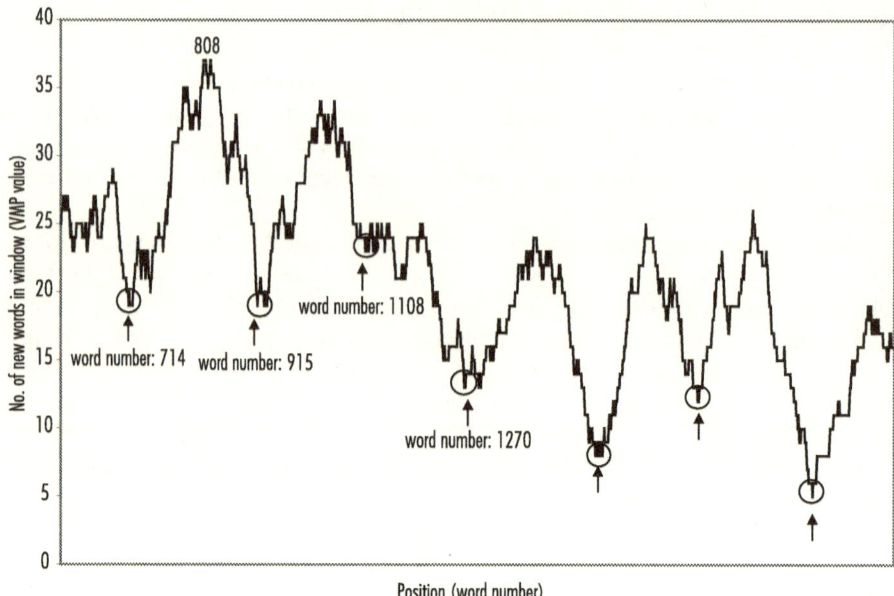

Figure 11.1. VMP patterns for a 1,500-word text segment in university classroom discourse

segment from a university classroom text (from word position 500 to word position 2,000), where each data point represents the number of new lexical items in the 100-word window at that point in the text.

Showing the patterns of "old" and "new" vocabulary in the discourse this way, we can identify the vocabulary patterns in a text. A steady introduction of new vocabulary items is associated with the beginning of a lexical episode (e.g., 714–808 in figure 11.1). A steady decline in the VMP (as in positions 1,108–1,270 in figure 11.1) represents recycling of old vocabulary and is interpreted as the coda of a lexical episode. The former is called a "lexical episode"; the latter is called a "transitional unit." Extract 1 illustrates the onset of a lexical episode (positions 714–808 in figure 11.1); the new words entering the discourse are capitalized.

Extract 1: Philosophy

Teacher: . . . What do they say that is relevant to the question of how we (714) ought to behave? We can look for the ANSWERS to THOSE questions, we will be TRYING to DEVELOP an EXISTENTIALIST ethic. It's PRETTY CLEAR that Sartre . . . and I'll be TALKING PRIMARILY about Sartre, REJECTS most of the STANDARD FORMS of ethics that you encounter in the HISTORY of WESTERN PHILOSOPHY. Not all of these ethical THEORIES FOCUS on RULES and PRINCIPLES, but most of them do. Most ethical theories TRY to ASCERTAIN the FUNDAMENTAL principles of MORALITY. JOHN STEWART LILL in the NINETEENTH CENTURY DID EXACTLY that, he said what is the (808) most basic and fundamental principle of right and wrong.

After these textual measures were developed, a two-step computational tool was developed to automatically recognize lexical episodes on the basis of the numeric VMP values computed in the previous step. In this study, lexical episodes are identified through three points: the peak and the two surrounding valley points in the VMP value. First the important VMP peaks were identified. "Important" peaks represent a high point in the VMP following a sustained increase from the preceding valley—at least a ten-point difference in the VMP between a peak and a valley point (i.e., ten new words used in the overall discourse).

Second, the boundaries surrounding the important peaks were identified through the sliding slope measures of a best-fitting regression line. The slope of the regression line could be closest to 0.0 only at the deepest valley points on the two sides of the peaks (for a more detailed description, see Csomay 2002b).

The final step in preparing for the linguistic analysis was to build a corpus of lexical episodes. The classroom texts were taken from the Test of English as a Foreign Language (TOEFL) 2000 Spoken and Written Academic Language (T2K-SWAL) Corpus. This corpus (about 2.7 million words) was designed to represent the language used in the different registers associated with the academic setting in universities of the United States (Biber et al. 2002). Using this corpus and applying the methodology described above, a total of 2,200 lexical episodes were extracted from 176 (about 1.2 million words) university classroom teaching texts.

Identify Multi-Dimensional Characteristics of Episodes

The second step in the analytical procedures was to document the linguistic characteristics of lexical episodes. The multidimensional analysis developed by Biber (1988) shows parameters of linguistic characteristics that work together. In his latest study, Biber (2003) counted more than ninety linguistic features (cf. Biber et al. 1999) to identify four underlying dimensions characteristic to academic discourse: oral versus literate discourse, procedural versus content-focused discourse, narrative versus nonnarrative orientation, and academic stance. The linguistic features identified on these four dimensions (table 11.1) were used to characterize lexical episodes in this study.

Identify Lexical Episode Types on the Basis of Their Linguistic Characteristics

Lexical episode types are identified on the basis of their linguistic characteristics on the four dimensions. To identify groupings of episode types, statistical measures—cluster analytical methods—are used. In applying cluster analysis, the ultimate goal was to find linguistic similarities in lexical episodes rather than to focus on the linguistic differences they may exhibit. That is, through statistical methods, lexical episodes with similar linguistic characteristics group together into a cluster reflecting shared communicative purposes. At the same time, the different clusters interpreted as lexical episode types distinctly "differ from one another in that they have different linguistic characterizations and correspondingly different functional emphases" (Biber 1995, 321).

Table 11.1.
Selected linguistic features on the four dimensions of academic language

Dimensions	Negative features	Positive features
1	Literate discourse	Oral discourse
	Prepositions	THAT omission
	Attributive adjectives	Demonstrative pronoun
	Passives	Present tense
	Nouns (group, human, mental)	Adverbials (time, place, hedges)
	Causative verbs	1st, 2nd, 3rd person pronoun
		Discourse particles
2	Content-focused discourse	Procedural discourse
	Content words in one-text-only	2nd person pronoun
	Size attrib. adj.	Modals (predictive and necessity)
	Past tense	Nouns (group, moderately common)
	Moderately common adverbs	Verbs (moderately common, activity, causative)
	Occurrence verbs	TO-clause controlled by Desire verbs
	BY passives	
3	Non-narrative orientation	Narrative orientation
	Noun (technical concrete, concrete, quantity)	Past tense
		3rd person pronoun
		Nouns (human, mental)
		Verbs (mental, common, communication)
		THAT omission
4	Wh- Questions	Academic stance
	WH- questions	Adverbials (factual)
	Stranded prepositions	THAT clause with Noun
		Adverb (likelihood, attitudinal)

Source: Biber (2003).

Findings

Based on the four dimensions of academic discourse (see foregoing discussion), three clusters were identified. The three clusters were interpreted as three lexical episode types, which were then examined for their communicative purposes.

Lexical Episode Types

Three major lexical episode types were identified: involved narrative, procedural, and content-oriented. Figure 11.2 summarizes the characteristics of each episode type with respect to the mean dimension scores on three of the four dimensions of academic language.

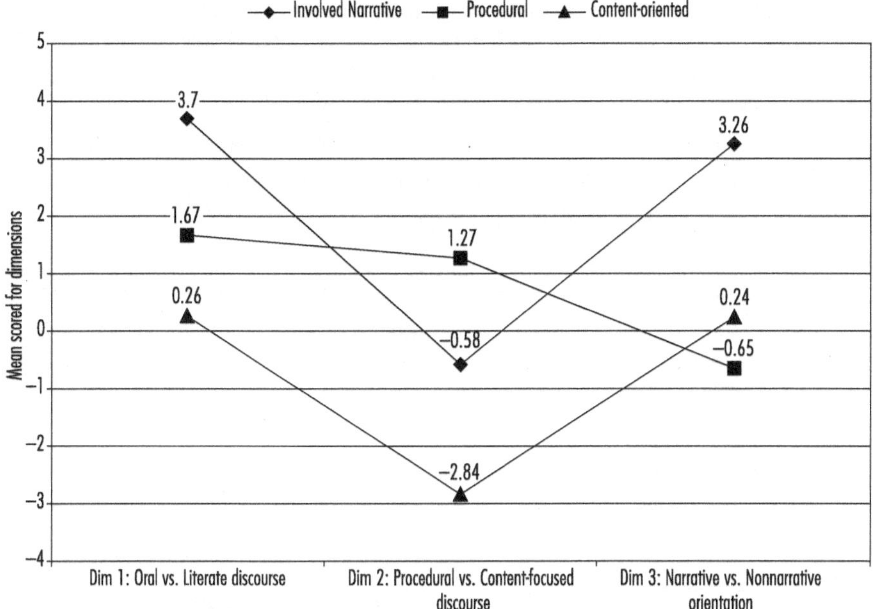

Figure 11.2. Three lexical episode types on three dimensions of academic language

As figure 11.2 shows, involved narrative episode types show the highest positive scores on two dimensions: oral discourse and narrative orientation. Procedural episodes show the highest scores on procedural discourse, and content-oriented episodes exhibit linguistic features associated with literate and content-focused discourse.

Involved Narrative Lexical Episodes The first lexical episode type, involved narrative, is distinguished by the high frequency counts of linguistic features on two dimensions: the positive side of dimension 1 and dimension 3. Positive dimension 1 features include, for example, first-, second-, and third-person pronouns, contractions, non–past tense, demonstrative pronouns, and so on—reflecting an involved, interactive style and showing personal stance. Positive dimension 3 features include past tense, animate and cognitive nouns (e.g., knowledge, fact, understanding), mental verbs (e.g., know, think, believe) (see Biber et al. 1999), and verbs commonly used in the T2KSWAL corpus as a whole (e.g., be, think, go). Extract 2 shows part of a text segment exhibiting these features.

Extract 2: Humanities

Teacher: yeah. so, I I I would agree that that B. doesn't have a terribly effective presentation style.

Student: especially when he's sick

Teacher: no presence

Student: no, he does not.

Student: well and it was interesting to me that this sort of big deal public lecture thing seemed to me to be the least well thought out and sort of coherent, I mean the, the forty five minute, or ya know forty minute whatever he did in here was absolutely stunning. ya know, ya know and I

Teacher: I have marvelously organized notes based on what he was saying

Student: yeah, and I felt like he, um had thought about what he was gonna say

Student: but don't you think this is his round,

Student: could be, could be

Student: the classroom is his world. I mean standing up in front in the pioneer room

Student: yeah, that's true, after meeting him it is less it it it did seem less of his, uh domain.

Student: yeah

Student: because he is a very good speaker just sitting with him at lunch and asking him questions and

Student: right

Student: ya, know

Student: plus he's sick to death of medicine, I mean he's not interested in talking about medicine.

Student: every form of writing, every [unclear statement]

Student: well I have [unclear statement] being in the mood for medicine. I mean he said this was eighteen months ago

Student: every time he talked about it, he made that [unclear]

Student: he said that it might as well been a lifetime ago, he said, he said, I'm more interested in talking about where I am now and these researches that I'm doing. I mean he's been away from medicine for quite awhile and now he went back . . .

The foregoing extract shows a lexical episode in which the grammatical features on the positive side of dimension 3 and positive dimension 1 are present.

With regard to the functional interpretation of this lexical episode type, involved narrative episodes were associated with situations in which information related to personal experiences was shared or concepts were explained and interpreted through relating text or visual input to personal experiences, feelings, and beliefs. Alternatively, this lexical episode type occurred in phases in which the teacher elaborated on or summarized known information.

Procedural Lexical Episodes The next episode type, procedural episodes, exhibited linguistic features on the positive side of dimension 2—for example, predictive modals (e.g., will), desire verbs with *to* clauses (e.g., want), second person pronouns (you, your), or nouns occurring moderately frequently in the entire corpus (e.g., chapter, exam, week, note, word, fact). These features are displayed in a high number in extract 3. Linguistic features on the negative side of dimension 3, such as (technical) concrete nouns (e.g., book, case, formula, exam) or quantity nouns (e.g., week, today) also appear frequently in this segment.

Extract 3: Engineering

Teacher: the medium high is is is about (eight at eighteen) hundred and then the other is twenty four hundred ok that. We'll try it again if you still have problems talk to me after class anybody else have comments or questions? Ok . . . um . . . a couple of things just remind you in *case* you are not . . . in *case* you haven't just kept a quick eye on the *syllabus* that we have the exam scheduled a *week* from *today* . . . *uh exam* one covers through the first two *chapters* so I wanted to bring that to your attention um just in your preparation between now and then uh if you look at the problems or going through your *book* or whatever um the *exam* will be closed *book* but you can bring in a *sheet* of *notes* in other words you can make a legal cheat *sheet*. . . uh and you and the thought process there is I don't want you to spend all *exam* time thumbing through your *book* looking for a formula to match up or an example problem to match up but I don't also don't want you to spend your time memorizing the *formula* and worrying whether you properly memorized a *formula* when in fact all I want you [unclear words] be able to use it so.. in your *notes* . . .</EXT>

Extract 3 shows a lexical episode in which the grammatical features on the positive side of dimension 2 and negative dimension 3 are exhibited.

Procedural episodes reflect instructional and/or communicative purposes such as sharing information related to either the classroom context (e.g., how to go about the midterm test) or professional experiences (e.g., what kinds of activities students will be engaged in once they leave the program), presenting the methods of a classroom project, or explaining concepts step by step while relating visual input to prior knowledge (e.g., interpreting a graph).

Content-Oriented Lexical Episodes The third lexical episode type, content-oriented episodes, relied on linguistic features such as prepositional phrases, relative clause constructions (reflecting elaboration), past tense, or content words that occurred in one class session only. Extract 4 is an example of a content-oriented episode.

Extract 4: Humanities

Student: . . . By eighteen twenty, Americans had **moved** INTO another century, not only IN time but IN thought. IN the way they perceive themselves IN the world. They had **experienced** the social and cultural transformation as great as any IN American history. The transformation MARKED **BY** the search FOR an American identity and **BY** the climax and fall of the enlightenment IN America. The American Revolution **seems to** present Americans WITH an opportunity to realize an ideal world. To put the enlightenment INTO practice, to create the **kind** OF ordered society and illustrious CULTURE

> THAT man since the Greeks have **yearned** FOR. WITH the revolution and the IDEAS IN enlightenment that accompany to contain WITHIN themselves the SOURCES OF their own disillusionment and destruction. BY eighteen twenty the enlightenment OF America **was** over. The ideals OF the revolution **changed** and **perverted**, yet the transformation **was** so complicated, so **undeliberate**, so [unclear], so much a **medley**, OF responses [unclear] events that Americans scarcely **knew** how they **got** FROM one point TO the other. They **began** the revolution BY then IN a world they **felt** very much a part OF. They **ended** by perceiving their destiny IN America itself, BY becoming a peculiar and unprecedented **kind** OF republic. It was so - it was an **unattended** revolution FOR the character they **saw** revealed IN Andrew Jackson and the hundreds OF Kentucky romantic, undisciplined, and untutored heroes OF the battle OF New Orleans **was** scarcely the character they **saw** IN seventeen seventy six. The [unclear] nationalism [unclear] AT the end OF the war OF eighteen twelve. It **represented** both a repudiation OF the classic ideals OF the REVOLUTION and an attempt to come to terms WITH largely unanticipated society that **emerged** FROM the revolution. A new CULTURE that had been **created** both because and IN spite of the REVOLUTION. WITH the peace OF Ghent and the end OF the Napoleonic WARS the new American republic seemed at last secure and ready to comprehend itself.

The relatively few linguistic features from positive dimension 1 are shown through the relatively few cases of underlined words (non–past tense; first-, second-, third-person pronouns; etc.). The linguistic features from negative dimension 2 in this segment are in ***bold italics*** (past tense, *by* passives, content words occurring in one text only, etc.). In addition, some features (e.g., prepositions, relative clauses, and some nouns) on the negative pole of dimension 1 are highlighted by capital letters.

This episode type was associated with purposes that reflected a strong informational focus. They occurred when a monologue-like teaching style was adopted or texts were read out loud (as in extract 4). Content-oriented episodes also reflected situations in which the explanation of a particular concept was supported by visual aids (e.g., through writing on the board).

Partial Taxonomy of Lexical Episode Types and Their Communicative Purposes

As the foregoing examples show, lexical episode types sharing similar linguistic characteristics have similar communicative purposes. The communicative tasks identified in the lexical episodes as found in university classroom discourse are shown in table 11.2.

The communicative purposes listed in this partial taxonomy all relate to information. This finding may not be surprising. The present research set out to analyze units in university classroom discourse that were marked for vocabulary items newly entering the discourse and were interpreted to largely correspond to new topics and new information occurring in the stretch of discourse. In most cases, each lexical

Table 11.2.
Partial taxonomy of communicative tasks as found in lexical episodes of university classroom talk

Communicative Purpose	Episode Type		
1. Share information on			
a. classroom procedures	P		IN
b. personal experiences			IN
c. professional experiences	P		
d. study skills	P		
2. Transmit information through			
a. lecturing		C	
b. reading a text aloud		C	
3. Interpret/explain information through relating			
a. text or visual input to			
• prior knowledge	P		
• personal experiences, feelings, beliefs			IN
• new information in the class session		C	
b. conceptual information to			
• visual illustration in context (e.g., board in the classroom, diagram in the book)		C	
4. Summarize/elaborate on information expected as known			IN
5. Report on project(s) by			
a. student	P		
b. teacher			IN
6. Demonstrate how something works (e.g., a computer program)	P		

Note: IN = involved narrative; C = content-oriented; P = procedural.

episode has a clear topical focus and a single communicative purpose. Although each episode is lexically coherent, there is variation in the way information is conveyed in these episodes.

Based on the partial taxonomy presented here, we can see what kinds of communicative tasks the different lexical episode types are most likely to exhibit. For example, there is a clear distinction between content-oriented episodes (information transmitted via lecturing or via reading a text out aloud) and procedural or involved narrative episodes (information shared through personal anecdotes or through talking about professional experiences). A most interesting point about the variation in the way information is conveyed comes out when information is related to textual or visual input (point 3 in table 11.2). Although content-oriented lexical episodes use visuals (either textual or figurative) to support new information (e.g., writing on the board), both procedural and involved narrative episodes use visuals (textual as well as figurative) as primary sources for presenting new information, based on which prior knowledge or personal aspects of the theme are connected. This distinction suggests a fundamentally different approach to conveying information in the classroom.

Summary and Future Directions

The primary goal of the present study was to provide a linguistic characterization of lexically coherent discourse units found in university classroom texts, using quantitative measures for the analysis. Based on the linguistic patterns in the discourse units, three major lexical episode types were identified (involved narrative, procedural, and content-oriented), each exhibiting varying communicative purposes in the thread of discourse.

In its approach, the present study complements earlier studies in three areas: linguistic analyses of discourse patterns in university classroom talk; corpus-based analyses of discourse units and textual variation; and identification of discourse units in texts. First, the research described here contributes to the analysis of classroom discourse patterns in which discourse units are identified and assessed through vocabulary novelty that participants experience in the discourse event of a class session. This approach offers a new perspective to analyzing classroom discourse patterns not only in the university setting; it also could be extended to other instructional settings (e.g., English as a Second Language/English as a Foreign Language classrooms).

Second, the lexically coherent discourse units were analyzed by using corpus-based analytical techniques, providing a comprehensive linguistic analysis of those units. By segmenting discourse using reliable measures and by developing a taxonomy of lexical episode types on the basis of their lexicogrammatical characteristics, we can establish the foundations for describing patterns of text-internal variation.

Third, empirical methods were developed to identify discourse units in (classroom) discourse, providing replicable findings of the present research. Although the discourse units have been predefined on the basis of their perceived communicative and instructional purposes in earlier classroom-based studies, the present research recognized those purposes after the units had been identified and characterized on the basis of reliable measures.

Although the study provides new perspectives for analyzing classroom discourse and points to future directions in this area, it also has limitations. First, the methodology could be improved for a more precise identification of topical units in discourse. Although the VMP tracks the introduction of new vocabulary items into a discourse, which often marks new topics in the unfolding discourse, vocabulary novelty is identified relative to the discourse stretch occurring prior to the point of analysis. Hence, this methodology fails to identify a lexical segment as "important"—that is, denoting a new topic—if recycled vocabulary is used, leaving out the possibility of new topics worded with recycled vocabulary in the same stretch of discourse. This pattern may be an important characteristic of classroom discourse, however, because class participants may approach different topics while verbalizing those topics with words they already have used once during that session. Applying a modified version of Hearst's (1997) TextTiling, an alternative methodology to identify topical units with greater precision is suggested by Biber et al. (2004). Second, more discourse units could be analyzed. In this analysis, only lexical episodes were included in the linguistic analysis. The discourse units that use recycled vocabulary and serve as links between lexical episodes were called "transitional units." These units were not included in the present linguistic analysis; they are equally important, however, in overall discourse patterns. Compared to lexical episodes, they may be very similar or, indeed, very different in their linguistic characteristics and their communicative functions.

Finally, another limitation is related to psycholinguistic and pedagogical issues. This research is unable to show the cognitive difficulty students may encounter while they are exposed to or involved in any of the lexical episode types (although the study did not set out to investigate this area). Moreover, because of the lack of data measuring student performance, no conclusions can be drawn about whether classes exhibiting episodic patterns of particular lexical episode types are instructionally more effective than classes exhibiting another pattern. However, the three lexical episode types displayed differences in the way new information was linked to the actual textual input or to the visuals in class. This finding provides complementary linguistic evidence on classroom literacy events (Poole 2003), and from a teacher educational perspective it is a particularly important area of research. The results could provide teachers with evidence of how language is used in the different communicative tasks performed in the classroom.

In conclusion, descriptive studies of this kind are useful and could complement other classroom-based research because they offer replicable findings, rely on data collected from naturalistic settings, and provide data for the linguistic characterizations of what actually happens in a large number of classrooms.

REFERENCES

Biber, Douglas. 1988. *Variation across speech and writing.* Cambridge: Cambridge University Press.

———. 1995. *Dimensions of register variation: A cross-linguistic perspective.* Cambridge: Cambridge University Press.

———. 2003. Variation among university spoken and written registers: A new multi-dimensional analysis. In *Corpus analysis: Language structure and language use*, ed. C. Meyer and P. Leistyna, 47–70. Amsterdam: Rodopi.

Biber, Douglas, Stig Johansson, Geoffrey Leech, Susan Conrad, and Edward Finegan. 1999. *Longman grammar of spoken and written English.* London: Longman.

Biber, Douglas, Susan Conrad, Randi Reppen, Patricia Byrd, and Marie Helt. 2002. Speaking and writing in the university: A multidimensional comparison. *TESOL Quarterly* 36:9–48.

Biber, Douglas, Eniko Csomay, James K. Jones, and Casey Keck. 2004. Vocabulary-based discourse patterns in university registers. In *Corpora and discourse,* ed. Allen Partington, John Morley, and L. Haarman. Bern: Peter Lang.

Csomay, Eniko. 2000. Academic lectures: An interface of an oral/literate continuum. *NovELTy,* 7, no. 3:30–48.

———. 2002a. Variation in academic lectures: interactivity and level of instruction. In *Using corpora to explore linguistic variation*, ed. Randi Reppen, Susan Fitzmaurice and Douglas Biber, 203–24. Philadelphia: John Benjamins.

———. 2002b. Episodes in university classrooms: A corpus-linguistic investigation. Ph.D. diss., Northern Arizona University.

DeCarrico, Jeanette, and James R. Nattinger. 1988. Lexical phrases for the comprehension of academic lectures. *English for Specific Purposes* 7:91–102.

Fox, Barbara A. 1987. *Discourse structure and anaphora. Written and conversational English.* Cambridge: Cambridge University Press.

Hansen, Christa. 1994. Topic identification in lecture discourse. In *Academic listening: research perspectives,* ed. John Flowerdew. New York: Cambridge University Press.

Hearst, Marti A. 1997. TextTiling: Segmenting text into multi-paragraph subtopic passages. *Computational Linguistics* 23, no. 1:33–64.

Mann, William C., Christian M. Matthiessen, and Sandra A. Thompson. 1992. Rhetorical structure theory and text analysis. In *Discourse description: Diverse linguistic analyses of a fund-raising text,* ed. William C. Mann and Sandra A. Thompson. Amsterdam: John Benjamins.

Poole, Deborah. 2003. Linguistic connections between co-occurring speech and writing in a classroom literacy event. *Discourse Processes* 35, no. 2: 103–4.

Reppen, Randi, Susan Fitzmaurice, and Douglas Biber, eds. 2002. *Using corpora to explore linguistic variation.* Philadelphia: John Benjamins.

Tyler, Andrea. 1995. Patterns of lexis: How much can repetition tell us about discourse coherence? In *Linguistics and the education of language teachers: Ethnolinguistic, psycholinguistic, and sociolinguistic aspects,* ed. J. E. Alatis, C. A. Straehle, B. Gallenberger, and M. Ronkin. Georgetown University Round Table on Languages and Linguistics. Washington, D.C.: Georgetown University Press.

Youmans, Gilbert. 1991. A new tool for discourse analysis: The Vocabulary Management Profile. *Language* 67:763–89.

Young, Lynne. 1994. University lectures—macro-structure and micro-features. In *Academic listening: Research perspectives*, ed. John Flowerdew, 159–76. New York: Cambridge University Press.

12

The Unofficial Businesses of Repair Initiation: Vehicles for Affiliation and Disaffiliation

HANSUN ZHANG WARING
Teachers College, Columbia University

IN CONVERSATION ANALYSIS (CA), repair refers to practices for addressing problems in speaking, hearing, and understanding (Schegloff, Jefferson, and Sacks 1977). The main CA interest in repair has been in its structural properties. For example, repair is composed of trouble source (TS), repair initiation (RI), and repair completion. In the following segment from Schegloff, Jefferson, and Sacks (1977, 364), "Yeah" is the trouble source, "He is?" is the repair initiation, and "Well he was" is the repair completion.

Ken: Is Al here today?
Dan: Yeah.
(2.0)
Roger: → He is? hh eh heh
Dan: Well he was.

Repair can be initiated by "self"—the trouble source turn speaker—or "other"—someone other than the trouble source speaker—and completed by "self" or "other." In the foregoing case, the repair is other-initiated and self-completed. Self-initiation of repair can occur in several positions. Other-initiation of repair, however, overwhelmingly occurs in one position: the next turn following the trouble source turn, as shown in the example above. The notion of next turn repair initiation (NTRI) is reconsidered in Schegloff (2000) and Wong (2000). Both Schegloff and Wong describe cases in which other initiations of repair are delayed either within or beyond the next turn. Although the study of repair tends to focus on its structural properties, Schegloff (1997) points out that other-initiated repairs can be used to accomplish other actions. In fact, he considers it a "worthy and important topic" to explore the role of other-initiated repair "as a vehicle or instrument for doing displays of doubt, nonalignment, disagreement, challenge, rejection, etc." (Schegloff 1997, 505).

This essay focuses specifically on some cases of other initiations of repair found in graduate seminar discussions. These other initiations of repair are structurally interesting: They either resemble a third- or fourth-position repair (Schegloff 1992) or appear in a somewhat "delayed" position. More important, however, they are employed to do something other than addressing problems in speaking, hearing, or understanding. They serve as vehicles for conveying affiliation and disaffiliation.

The data corpus on which this study is based was collected over the course of a semester in a major graduate school of education on the east coast of the United States. It consists of five 90-minute taped sessions of a graduate seminar with a mixture of native and nonnative English-speaking participants. The first three sessions, from which the first two segments discussed in this chapter are drawn, also had been videotaped. The data were transcribed in detail using the system developed by Gail Jefferson (see transcription conventions).

Repair Initiations as a Vehicle for Affiliation

For the purposes of this chapter, "affiliation" refers to the seeking of reconciliation. For example, when a third person strives to create some sort of alignment between two other parties, he or she is doing affiliative talk. Although this definition of affiliation is somewhat at odds with the idea of agreement or like-mindedness often associated with affiliation in the CA literature (e.g., Egbert 1997), it is in broad consonance with Heritage's (1984, 268) notion of affiliation as being "supportive of social solidarity."

The cases that contain the affiliative sort of repair initiation manifest a common sequential trajectory, as follows:

1. Trouble source turn
2. Interactional deadlock
3. Repair initiation

Note that the interactional deadlock could entail repeated indications of questions being unsatisfactorily answered, the mere absence of uptake, or the presence of two diametrically opposed positions. In what follows, I show how this sequential trajectory is manifested in actual interaction and the sort of affiliative work that repair initiation is employed to accomplish within this trajectory.

In the following segment, the seminar participants are discussing an article that compares reading strategies used by proficient and nonproficient first-language and second-language readers. The trouble source is Tamar's description of her difficulty in understanding the advantage of using an authentic reading problem rather than a planted problem in the design of the study. The repair initiation appears after two unsuccessful attempts by Ellen and the professor, respectively, to address Tamar's difficulty.

Segment [01]

(1) TS Tamar: ((lines omitted)) Now, one thing I had trouble with she
(2) kinda mentions in passing. She says that most research
(3) used planted reading problems, whereas she's using an
(4) authentic problem, and she says there was an advantage to
(5) it, but I couldn't figure out wh:y. She says something

(6)		about the unitary ah ahm problem but I- I- I don't really see
(7)		why and she doesn't really (.) if somebody understands
(8)		what she means, uh I have [proble:m
(9)	Ellen:	[W- I- I just- I mean that (.) it makes (.)
(10)		sense to me that if you create a problem? ( ) students?
(11)		then you don't really (.) then you're testing a fake
(12)		problem? I mean I can
(13)		[see how that] would be a [flaw.]
(14)	Tamar:	[y↑Y::::eah.] [but] how would that uh not (.)
(15)		but you'll still be able to see the metacognitive
(16)		[process in trying to=
(17)	Ellen:	[((slowly opens mouth and slightly tilts head to the left))
(18)	Tamar:	= [↑so:lve it.=
(19)	Ellen:	[((closes mouth))
(20)	Tamar:	=[No?=
(21)	Prof:	[.hhh
(22)	Ellen:	=((scrunches face))
(23)	Prof:	The ↑other one has to [do with (.)=
(24)	Ellen:	[((looks to professor and then looks
(25)		down))
(26)	Prof:	=((lines omitted)) Probably as she was doing research for
(27)		this other study, she found, ↑oh, ↑look at this, here's a
(28)		place where person after person after person after person
(29)		run into this problem. So then she looked at that problem in
(30)		more depth and that became the study.=
(31)	Tamar:	=[>↑Yeah! ↑right!<=
(32)		((looks away from the professor and down))
(33)	Libby:	[((raises head from normal position))
(34)	Tamar:	=[but why is that better than
(35) RI	Libby:→	[(If)((leans forward))YOUR QUESTION IS(.)IS
(36)		[NA:TURAL DATA BETTER THAN]ELICITED?
(37)	Prof:	[I- ↑it's a genuine problem.]
(38)	Tamar:	°>Okay<°. Huh? ((looks toward Libby))
(39) RI	Libby:→	Is your question why is natural data in a situation like this
(40)		better than what it would be like [eli:cited?]
(41)	Tamar:	[a planted problem] yeah.=

(42) Libby: =°yeah.°=

(43) Prof: =but a planted problem might not ever occur in exactly that

(44) form in real lan- in real [reading.]

(45) Tamar: [°Yeah.°]=

(46) Ellen: =or some of your subjects may not- I mean it might be a

(47) planted problem and they will just skip it.

(48) Tamar: °Yeah.°

(49) Prof: I mean (.) like here too,

(50) [some'v them [just skip it.=

(51) Tamar: [Well [We:ll

(52) =yeah maybe ((continues to end of turn))

The first attempt to address Tamar's question is made by Ellen as she self-selects in line 9 and claims that she could see why testing a "fake" problem is flawed. For Ellen, perhaps, the derogative connotation implicated in the word "fake" speaks for itself. Yet for Tamar, Ellen fails to target the core of the question. Not surprisingly, Tamar hastens to point out (lines 14–18) that one would still be able to see the metacognitive process in trying to solve the fake problem. In other words, using a fake problem would not necessarily compromise the goal of the study. In line 23 the professor attempts an alternative answer to Tamar's initial question. The professor does so by offering a history of the study—namely, the authentic problems arose from the author's previous project and became part of the natural extensions of her research. Again, however, this information does not seem directly relevant to the issue of why an authentic problem is superior to a planted one.

This perceived "failure" to address Tamar's original question can be observed from several perspectives. First, the emphatic tokens ">↑Yeah! ↑right!<" in line 31 indicate that Tamar is registering upgraded agreement, not receipt of new information. Hence, through this particular turn design, Tamar is treating the professor's prior explanation as non-news and thus inconsequential to her concern. Heritage and Raymond (2002) point out that upgraded agreement can indicate that a "fight" to claim access to knowledge is going on. If that were the case here, we would conclude with the same analysis: Tamar is asserting that she already knew what the professor just said, thereby indirectly suggesting that the professor's explanation has failed to address her question. Second, the raised pitch and quick pace of ">↑Yeah! ↑right!<" add a somewhat dismissive tone of "Sure, of course, we know that" to the agreement tokens. Third, by looking away Tamar indicates her disengagement and, perhaps, disaffiliation from what the professor just said. Finally, Tamar goes on to reissue her original question, thereby rendering the professor's response as inadequate. An interactional deadlock is in place.

In line 35 Libby initiates repair on Tamar's original question. The official business of this repair initiation, of course, is to display the speaker's difficulty in understanding the trouble source, thereby seeking clarification of the trouble source.

The unofficial business of this repair initiation, I argue, is to seek some sort of way "out" of the interactional deadlock. If Libby indeed had trouble understanding Tamar's original question, she had ample opportunities to seek clarification much earlier. Moreover, Libby's turn design also suggests her orientation toward breaking the interactional deadlock. For example, the phrase "in a situation like this" (line 39) underscores the notion that the issue is not whether "authentic" is better than "planted" but why the distinction matters in this particular situation—a point that both Ellen and the professor appear to have overlooked. In addition, by using research lingo such as "natural data versus elicited" in place of "authentic versus fake problem," Libby may be entertaining the prospect that the supposedly more standardized "common language" might facilitate the understandings among Tamar, Ellen, and the professor. In other words, Libby's repair initiation displays her understanding that Tamar's question has not been answered satisfactorily and contributes a possible solution to the problem. It constitutes a ratified but unaddressed participant's (Goffman 1981) resource in resolving an unfolding opposition (cf. Waring 2002a) and perhaps rebuilding social solidarity. This particular use of repair initiation might echo Jacobs' (2002, 1410–14) finding on a mediator's employment of questioning as a means to keep the focus of discussion on track and maintain neutrality. Below is a schematic representation of the sequential organization of segment [01]:

Turn 1 *TS*	Tamar (A):	raises problem of understanding
Turn 2	Ellen (B):	addresses problem of understanding
Turn 3	Tamar (A):	rejects B's account
Turn 4	Prof (C):	addresses problem of understanding
Turn 5	Tamar (A):	rejects C's account
Turn 6 *RI*	Libby (D):	rephrases A's problem in Turn 1, based on prior 4 turns

Constituting the interactional deadlock also can be the absence of uptake. At the beginning of the next segment, Tamar questions whether English as a second language (ESL) students in a specific discipline should be given reading materials within the discipline as they are learning to read in English. This question turns out to be a trouble source for a repair initiation later on.

Segment [02]

(1) TS Tamar: [wh- what should ESL- what materials should ESL
(2) students be readin- suppose ESL students in engineering,
(3) should they be given articles in engineering on the
(4) assumption that it would be easier for them because we
(5) know already [° ( ) °]
(6) Kelly: [or they have an interest in it.]=
(7) Tamar: =Yes. interest motivation and more um background
(8) knowledge, o:r should they be given (.) general type of (.)

(9) a:h (.) articles? (.)I guess where the kno:wledge (.) doesn't
(10) come into play [a lot?
(11) Kelly: [They're more readable?
(12) (0.2)
(13) Tamar: Would be maybe more readable. yeah.=
(14) Prof: =I- It also points out (.)ling- w-
(15) [((turning to Libby))when we talk-
(16) Libby: [actually I could comment on that
(17) Prof: [>I was going to< sa:y huhhuhhuhhuh
(18) Libby: [huh huh huh huh huhhuhhuhheh
(19) Tamar: °Okay?°
(20) Libby: I- I uh: (.) one of the articles that I read, was making the
(21) case that in fact. ((52 lines omitted where Libby goes to
(22) great extent illustrating with two cases the subsequent
(23) point)).hhh so (.) in fact for a very specialized audience,
(24) they do better within their↑ge:nre.
(25) (0.5)((no nonverbal response from the group))
(26) than when stuff is (.)rewritten fo:r them.
(27) (0.9)((only slight nodding from Prof))
(28) RI → but- but was your question also (.) whether (.) we need to
(29) give (.) ESL students in English for Specific purposes a
(30) general language background as opposed to a specific
(31) language background?=
(32) Tamar: =Yeah. no should we desi:gn them as specific uh uh
(33) program at all, or should everybody ( )just be taking um
(34) gen-general u:h English.
(35) (0.1)
(36) Libby: °Okay.°

In line 16, in responding to Tamar's question, Libby launches an elaborate account of how a specialized audience would find an original text easier than a simplified version. Libby's central claim concerns the readability of an original text versus a simplified version for a specialized audience, whereas Tamar questions the applicability of specialized versus general materials to ESL students within a specific discipline. The two issues are merely tangentially related. As Libby finishes her "comment" in line 24, there is a 0.5-second silence during which no sign of any nonverbal response from the group can be observed. Libby then produces an increment in line 26, which incurs another 0.9-second silence. Again, very few nonverbal responses can be observed except for the professor's slight nodding. Hence, the situation constitutes an interactional deadlock.

In line 28 Libby initiates repair on Tamar's original question. Again, the official business is to display trouble understanding the original question. The unofficial business, however, is to seek a way out of the deadlock. Presumably, the lack of uptake makes Libby think that she might have misinterpreted Tamar's question, and she then proceeds to offer a reanalysis in the repair initiation. When Tamar does proffer the repair by restating her question, however, Libby responds only with a softly uttered "°Okay°." She does not go on to argue that what she said before addressed the question in some way, nor does she try to answer the newly clarified question with a fresh start—perhaps a further indication that Tamar's question served more as a springboard for Libby's comment than a problem to be solved. Meanwhile, the simple "°Okay°" constitutes a sequentially adequate response to Tamar's clarification. Libby is under no further obligation to speak. The floor is open once again. Thus, what Libby *is* able to accomplish by initiating the repair is to relinquish a turn that has become difficult to pass on (cf. Egbert 1997 on repair initiation used to exit one conversation while entering another). Schematically, segment [02] proceeds as follows:

Turn 1 *TS*	A (Tamar):	raises question regarding implication of research
Turn 2	B (Libby):	comments extensively
Turn 3	A+others:	silence
Turn 4 *RI*	B (Libby):	initiates repair on/proffers candidate understanding of A's question in Turn 1

One might notice that the sequential structures of the two foregoing segments resemble those of a third-position repair (the first segment below) in Schegloff (1992, 1303) or fourth-position repair (the second segment below) in Schegloff (1992, 1321):

TS	Annie:	Which one::s are closed, an' which ones are open.
	Zebrach:	Most of 'em. this, this, [this this ((pointing))
→	Annie:	[I 'on't mean on the shelters. I mean on the roads.
TS	Marty:	Loes, do you have a calendar,
	Loes:	Yeah ((reaches for her desk calendar))
	Marty:	Do you have one that hangs on the wall?
→	Loes:	Oh, you <u>want</u> one.
	Marty:	Yeah

In the seminar data, however, the one who initiates the repair is not necessarily the one who produced or acknowledged the trouble source turn earlier. This may be accounted for by appeal to the nature of multiparty interaction, in which for each trouble source there are multiple recipients. Furthermore, the sequences that come between the trouble source and the repair initiator are much more extensive in the seminar data. This "lengthiness" may be a function of seminar discussion, in which ideas and positions are constantly being deliberated until they are fully substantiated and solidly grasped. Finally and most centrally, an alternative agenda other than a genuine problem of understanding motivates the repair initiation in the seminar discussion.

Repair Initiation as a Vehicle for Disaffiliation

In the foregoing cases, repair is initiated to reconcile some interactional rift. Repair also can be initiated to accomplish disaffiliative actions. The idea that repair initiation can act as a harbinger of disagreement is not new. I offer a more specific account of how repair initiation works as a vehicle for disaffiliation—not necessarily disagreement—in multiparty interaction. Such disaffiliation can consist in launching an implicit/incipient disagreement or a refusal to back down from an earlier assertion. The sequential trajectory of disaffiliative repair initiation is characterized by a delay and looks as follows:

1. Trouble source turn
2. Delay
3. Repair initiation

Segment [03] contains an example of repair initiation used to convey implicit disagreement. Jack points out that although he was able to become a fluent reader in his native language, English, simply through extensive reading, the same process did not seem to apply in his learning to read in Chinese. When Libby attributes his difficulty to age, Jack initiates repair on this attribution:

Segment [03]

(1)	Tamar:	W- you don't have much [input from Chinese as=
(2)	Libby:	[input.
(3)		=you would have from English.=
(4)	Jack:	=B-there're a lot of materials [I mean-
(5) TS	Libby:	[different age too.
(6)		right? Jack?
(7)	Jack:	Mm
(8)		(0.9)
(9) RI	→	How do you mean [different age.
(10)	Prof:	[You're older now.=
(11)	Jack:	=olde-
(12)	Prof:	heh heh [heh heh heh
(13)	Tamar:	[heh heh heh
(14)	Jack:	It should be easier. I'm [brighter].

In lines 5–6, Libby suggests that Jack's failure to achieve proficiency through extensive reading in a second language can be attributed to the fact that he was at a different age than when he was learning to read in his first language. What Libby says here turns out to be the trouble source of Jack's repair initiation in line 9: "How do you mean different age." I argue that this "repair initiation" is doing something other than initiating repair—it is conveying implicit disagreement. Jack's disagreeing orientation is visible in a series of sequential positions: the lack of immediate uptake after Libby's "different age too," the ambiguous minimal response "Mm" after Libby's consecutive attempts at solicitation ("right? Jack?"), and the 0.9-second gap that ensues. All signs converge to indicate that a dispreferred response is under way (Pomerantz 1984). Within this sequential environment, it is difficult to interpret Jack's "How do you mean different age?" as a genuine initiation of repair.

These sequential details are not the only resources that one can invoke, however, to understand the interactional business accomplished in Jack's repair initiation. Some contextual background might also help. This discourse takes place in an advanced reading seminar in applied linguistics. The class members have already taken base courses such as second language acquisition (SLA), in which age is treated as an important factor that affects the learning of languages. Upon hearing Libby's mention of "age" in explaining his learning process, it should not be difficult for Jack, as someone who shares an SLA background with Libby, to figure out the underlying argument of Libby's assertion: Younger is better. Thus, whatever is done in "How do you mean different age?" it is not a display of Jack's trouble of understanding. The strongest piece of evidence for this interpretation is Jack's subsequent overt counterargument that "older" means "brighter" (line 14). Jack's repair initiation can simply be his way of ensuring that Libby's assertion, with which he is about to disagree explicitly, is indeed the one he thinks it is.

Unlike the previous segment, in which disaffiliation lies in the display of implicit disagreement, disaffiliation also can appear in a speaker's refusal to back down from an original claim. The following extract begins with Kelly's expression of frustration with the particular format of an article, in which references to authors and dates are not listed inside parentheses in the text. When someone points out that this "frustrating" format is in fact the established format of the *Modern Language Journal* ("MLJ"), Kelly initiates repair on this newly acquired information.

Segment [04]

(1) Kelly: ((lines omitted)) the set up the setup of the article just
(2) wasn't any of the academic things we just read because he
(3) hasn't- he took his own approach to writing it, but I don't
(4) know if it's just I've seen it different, it's still a very viable-
(5) I mean it's the approach that okay.=It's okay to write like
(6) this but (.) to me, it made it so difficult to get through it
(7) because I was really frustrated (.) without evidence and
(8) without you know parenthesis that says the person and
(9) when they did the research an- (0.4)
(10) Prof: That's- that's- that's the style of the uh
(11) [Modern Language Journal.

(12) Tamar: [The MLJ format.
(13) TS Prof: The MLJ Format.=
(14) Tamar: =It's horrible I think.
(15) RI Kelly: → This one is [MLJ format?=
(16) Prof: [Yes.
(17) Tamar: =Yeah.
(18) Prof: This this one is this [this yeah
(19) Ellen: [( )
(20) Kelly: Right. right. well I mean it's so funny because there's not
(21) even enough- really enough number- or I guess there is but
(22) (.) before I even started the article I took a look at the
(23) bibliography and I said NO::: this person really knows (
(24))((laugh))looking forward to like reading all the names
(25) and everything ((laugh)) yeah I mean I figured that was what
(26) the numbers were. I did go look at it at some point but-
(27) Prof: Yeah I mean that that part is required by the journal.
(28) Kelly: yYYeah.=

I argue that Kelly's repair initiation "This one is MLJ format?" in line 15 is doing something other than dealing with problems in understanding. It is produced to convey disaffiliation—her refusal to back down from an earlier assertion. First, it occurs not in the next turn but the turn after the next, following Tamar's latching comment in line 14: "It's horrible I think." The delay is noticeable because both the professor's and Tamar's turns in lines 10–13 are clearly addressed to Kelly. Kelly, as the next speaker, could have either admitted to not knowing the specifics of MLJ format or indicated that she had never heard of the term MLJ. Note, however, that both options imply some sort of "fault" or inadequacy on Kelly's part. In light of what Kelly could have said, then, her reticence in line 14 works to withhold some sort of "giving in." Second, by emphasizing "This" in saying "This one is MLJ format?" Kelly emphasizes her disbelief—thereby veiled criticism—that a writing style such as this could be what people refer to as the MLJ format, while perhaps concealing that she does not know MLJ. Third, in lines 16–18, both the professor and Tamar, treating "This one is MLJ format?" as requesting confirmation, confirm that what Kelly refers to as the author's own approach is indeed the MLJ format. To forestall further confirmation, Kelly says in line 20, "Right. right," disallowing the professor's proceeding on the analysis of Kelly's repair initiation as "requesting confirmation." Finally, the status of this repair initiation as veiled critique is made more evident in Kelly's subsequent talk, where she gives a further account of what she considers to be the format's confusing numbering system (lines 20–26).

This segment represents another case in which repair initiation acts as a disguise under which something else—a veiled critique, coupled with a refusal to back down in the service of saving one's intellectual "face" (Tracy 1997)—is accomplished.

"This one is MLJ format?" looks like an other-initiated repair. It is treated as an other-initiated repair. Yet it accomplishes much more interactionally. In sum, Kelly's critique-implicative repair initiation signals a refusal to unquestionably accept a correction and back down from an earlier claim. This stance is consistent with a student's identity claim of intellectual competence and growing independence in a graduate seminar (Waring 2001, 2002b).

Conclusion

I have described some cases of repair initiations that are not only structurally interesting but, more important, function in ways other than dealing with problems in speaking, hearing, and understanding. By proposing an alternative understanding of the trouble source, the affiliative repair initiation operates to ensure that an earlier question can be properly addressed, a heated argument can be resolved, and threatened intersubjectivity can be restored. One also can use repair initiation to construct some sort of disaffiliative action, such as an implicit or incipient disagreement or a refusal to back down from an earlier position.

Both types of repair initiations appear to be cases in which Schegloff (1997, 505) might point out that their analysis as mere repair initiation would be inadequate. I take a step further and argue that it is not that something else is accomplished along with initiating repair. It is that in the disguise of repair initiator, something else is accomplished *instead of* initiating repair. That is the sense in which I understand the role of repair initiation as a "vehicle" or "instrument." In particular, the problem of understanding displayed in these data seems more claimed than real.[1] In some cases the repair initiation speaker, by virtue of her subsequent response to the repair, shows that she clearly is not experiencing any problem understanding the trouble source turn. In other cases, it seems that rather than initiating a process to deal with problems in understanding, the repair initiation marks some sort of epiphany in one's understanding and thus may be more fittingly analyzable as initiating a solution to an understanding problem. In other words, the production format of a repair initiator is used as a disguise under which an alternative agenda is carried out.

To answer the question of why these repair initiations look the way they do and do the work they do, I propose two possible interpretations. As several audience members at the 2003 Georgetown University Round Table (GURT 2003) pointed out, multiparty interaction might play an important role in determining the shape of these repair initiations. The nature of multiparty interaction may contribute, for example, to the delay of the repair initiation as well as the presence of extended sequences that come before the repair initiation. I also suggest that the type of affiliative and disaffiliative work accomplished in these repair initiations is in keeping with the nature of seminar discussion. The central task of collaborative reading analysis in seminar discussion necessarily involves disagreement, critique, and various forms of communication breakdown. The disguise of repair initiation provides members of the seminar with an interactional resource to advance their potentially disaffiliative claims (via disaffiliative RI) and to find a way out of the interactional deadlock once a stalemate is reached (via affiliative RI). It allows them to accomplish these actions subtly but effectively.

Acknowledgments

An earlier version of this essay was presented at the 2002 International Conference on Conversation Analysis (ICCA-02) in Copenhagen, Denmark. I gratefully acknowledge insightful comments made by Jean Wong, Irene Koshik, Naomi Geyer, Paula Korsko, and the GURT 2003 participants on various earlier drafts.

NOTE

1. In Schegloff, Jefferson, and Sacks's (1977) original conceptualization of repair, the issue of whether the problem in understanding is real or claimed remains unspecified—which, I think, leaves the question of what can count as repair initiation fairly open ended.

Transcription Conventions

. (period) Falling intonation

? (question mark) Rising intonation

, (comma) Continuing intonation

- (hyphen) Marks abrupt cutoff

:: (colon(s)) Prolonging of sound

never (underling) Stressed syllable or word

WORD (all caps) Loud speech

°word° (degree symbols) Quiet speech

>word< (more than and less than) Quicker speech

<word> (less than and more than) Slowed speech

hh (series of h's) Aspiration or laughter

.hh (h's preceded by dot) Inhalation

[ ] (brackets) simultaneous or overlapping speech

= (equal sign) Contiguous utterances

(2.4) (number in parentheses) Length of a silence

(.) (period in parentheses) Micropause—0.2 second or less

( ) (empty parentheses) Nontranscribable segment of talk.

((gazing toward the ceiling)) (double parentheses) Description of nonspeech activity

REFERENCES

Egbert, Maria M. 1997. Some interactional achievements of other-initiated repair in multiperson conversation. *Journal of Pragmatics* 27:611–34.

Goffman, Erving. 1981. *Forms of talk*. Philadelphia: University of Pennsylvania Press.

Heritage, John. 1984. *Garfinkel and ethnomethodology*. Oxford: Basil Blackwell.

Heritage, John, and Geoff Raymond. 2002. *The terms of agreement: Indexing epistemic authority and subordination in talk-in-interaction*. Plenary address delivered by John Heritage at International Conference on Conversation Analysis (ICCA-02), Copenhagen.

Jacobs, Scott. 2002. Maintaining neutrality in dispute mediation: Managing disagreement while managing not to disagree. *Journal of Pragmatics* 34:1403–26.

Pomerantz, Anita. 1984. Agreeing and disagreeing with assessments: some features of preferred/dispreferred turn shapes. In *Structures of social action: Studies in conversation analysis*, ed. Maxwell Atkinson and John Heritage, 57–101.Cambridge: Cambridge University Press.

Schegloff, Emmanuel A. 1992. Repair after next turn: The last structurally provided defense of intersubjectivity in conversation. *American Journal of Sociology* 97:1295–1345.

———. 1997. Practices and actions: Boundary cases of other-initiated repair. *Discourse Processes* 23:499–545.

———. 2000. When "others" initiate repair. *Applied Linguistics* 21:205–43.

Schegloff, Emmanuel A., Gail Jefferson, and Harvey Sacks. 1977. The preference for self-correction in the organization of repair in conversation. *Language* 53:361–82.

Tracy, Karen. 1997. *Colloquium: Dilemmas of academic discourse.* Norwood, N.J.: Ablex Publishing.

Waring, Hansun Z. 2001. Balancing the competing interests in seminar discussion: Peer referencing and asserting vulnerability. *Issues in Applied Linguistics* 12:29–50.

———. 2002a. Displaying understanding through substantive recipiency. *Research on Language and Social Interaction* 35:453–79.

———. 2002b. Expressing noncomprehension in seminar discussion. *Journal of Pragmatics* 34:1711–31.

Wong, Jean. 2000. Delayed next turn repair initiation in native/non-native speaker English conversation. *Applied Linguistics* 21:244–67.

13

Pragmatic Inferencing in Grammaticalization: A Case Study of Directional Verbs in Thai

KINGKARN THEPKANJANA AND SATOSHI UEHARA
Chulalongkorn University, Thailand, and Tohoku University, Japan

DIRECTIONAL VERBS refer to verbs that denote movements described in terms of their directionality with respect to a landmark.[1] The Thai directional verbs examined in this chapter are *khɯ̂n,* "ascend"; *loŋ,* "descend"; *khâw,* "enter"; *ʔɔ̀ɔk,* "exit"; *pay,* "go"; and *maa,* "come." These six verbs can occur as single verbs in simple sentences and as initial as well as noninitial verbs in serial verb constructions. It is generally known that directional verbs across languages are likely to grammaticalize into different types of grammatical markers that indicate meanings in spatial, temporal, and attitudinal domains. In this essay we introduce another type of grammaticalized marker that has evolved from the six directional verbs. We limit the scope of our study to the directional verbs appearing in the following pattern: NP1 TV NP2 DV (NP = noun phrase, TV = transitive verb, DV = directional verb). These directional verbs indicate a change of location of an entity crucially involved in an agent's action, which entails that the agent is successful in performing the action. Therefore, we refer to the six directional verbs with this usage as "success markers." A sentence with a success marker can be considered a resultative construction that expresses a change of location rather than a change of state. Sentences (1)–(6) illustrate these directional verbs under investigation.

(1)	*khǎw*	*yók*	*klɔ̀ŋ*	*mây*	*khɯ̂n*	
	he	lift	box	not	ascend	
	"He tried to lift a box but was not successful."[2]					
(2)	*khǎw*	*kòt*	*pùm*	*mây*	*loŋ*	
	he	press	button	not	descend	
	"He tried to push the button down but was not successful."					
(3)	*khǎw*	*cɔ̀ʔ*	*kamphææŋ*	*mây*	*khâw*	
	he	pierce	wall	not	enter	
	"He tried to pierce the wall but was not successful."'					
(4)	*khǎw*	*láaŋ*	*khrâap*	*sòkkapròk*	*mây*	*ʔɔ̀ɔk*
	he	wash	stain	dirty	not	exit
	"He tried to wash the stain out but was not successful."					

(5) *khǎw* *khěn* *rót* *mây* *pay*
he push car not go
"He tried to push the car away but was not successful."

(6) *chǎn* *taam* *tamrùat* *mây* *maa* *sàk* *thii*
I call upon police not come even time
"I kept calling upon the police but they did not show up (even once)."

In this chapter we examine the degree of grammaticalization of success markers at the present stage and investigate the role of pragmatic inferencing—especially metonymic processes—that motivates the grammaticalization of Thai directional verbs into success markers. The approach we used in this study corresponds to what Traugott (1986) terms "internal semantic reconstruction," which refers to the study of synchronic senses of a lexical item to hypothesize the historical order in which those senses arose. In accounting for pragmatic inferencing in this study, we have taken the cognitive-functional approach. This approach provides descriptions and explanations of linguistic phenomena that are psychologically plausible and connects linguistics to other behavioral and cognitive sciences.

Success Markers as a Type of Grammaticalized Form of Directional Verbs

This section divides into two subsections. In the first subsection we discuss syntactic and pragmatic contexts in which success markers take place. In the second subsection we review the arguments presented in Thepkanjana and Uehara (in press)—that success markers are grammaticalized markers. Then we argue that they are located at early stages of the grammaticalization path.

Contexts in Which Success Markers Take Place

In this section, we discuss the syntactic and pragmatic contexts in which success markers take place. Both types of context are important because they constitute a factor that gives rise to the grammaticalization of directional verbs into success markers.

Syntactic Contexts of Success Markers The success markers under investigation appear after the transitive verb phrase that incorporates the notion of motion in some way. The motion may be transparent, as in *yók klɔ̀ŋ,* "lift a box," and *khěn rót,* "push a car." It may be merely implied, as in *kin ʔaahǎan,* "eat food," and *plùuk tônmáy,* "plant a tree." The verb phrases that co-occur with success markers are semantically characterized by the fact that the agents of the actions named by these verb phrases have certain goals in mind in carrying out the actions. Each verb phrase consists of two semantic components: the agent's intended and executed action and the agent's further intention that this action lead to a particular desired result. Setting in motion an entity that is crucially involved in an agent's action can either wholly or partially constitute the agent's goal. For example, the agent's goal in eating food is not only to move the food down into the body but also to satisfy a desire for food and to survive. In the case of eating, moving an entity to a new location is merely part of the agent's larger goal. In addition, there are varying degrees of intrinsicness of the agent's goal to the inherent semantics of the co-occurring verb phrase. In other words, the agent's goal may be weakly implicated or strongly implicated. The agent's goal is more likely to be attained in the latter case than in the former case. Some Thai examples that illustrate an agent's goal that is weakly implicated in the semantics of the co-occurring verb phrase appear in sentences (7)–(12). All of these examples are negative sentences, for the sake of naturalness (see next subsection).

(7) *chǎn tii khày mây khûn*
I beat egg not ascend
"I tried to beat the eggs fluffy but was not successful."

(8) *chǎn thúp tapuu mây loŋ*
I hit down nail not descend
"I tried to hit the nail down but was not successful."

(9) *chǎn hàn núa mây khâw phrɔ́? nǐaw mâak*
I cut meat not enter because tough very
"I tried to cut the meat but was not successful because it was very tough."

(10) *chǎn láaŋ khrâap sokkapròk mây ?ɔ̀ɔk*
I wash stain dirty not exit
"I tried to wash the stain out but was not successful."

(11) *khǎw khěn rót mây pay*
he push car not go
"He tried to push the car away from him but was not successful."

(12) *khǎw taam tamrùat mây maa sàk thii*
he call upon police not come even time
"He kept calling upon the police but they did not show up (even once)."

Co-occurring verb phrases with the strong implication indicate that the agent's intention in setting an entity in motion is very likely to be fulfilled. Some examples of such verb phrases are *khlûan (rót),* "move (car)"; *pìt (pràtuu);* "close (door)"; *phaŋ (kamphææŋ),* "demolish (wall)"; *chìik*, "tear"; *láaŋ,* "wash"; *tàt,* "cut off"; and *phàa,* "cut in half." These verbs are illustrated in sentences (13)–(17).

(13) *chǎn khlûan rót mây pay*
I move car not go
"I tried to move the car but was not successful."

(14) *chǎn pìt pràtuu mây loŋ*
I close door not descend
"I tried to close the door but was not successful."

(15) *chǎn hàk kìŋmáy mây ɔ̀ɔk*
I break twig not descend
"I tried to break the twig but was not successful."

(16) *chǎn*	*khôon*	*tônmáy*	*mây*	*loŋ*
I	fell	tree	not	descend

"I tried to fell the tree but was not successful."

(17) *chǎn*	*chìik*	*phâa*	*mây*	*ɔ̀ɔk*
I	tear	cloth	not	exit

"I tried to tear the cloth but was not successful."

Notice that the motions expressed in all of the foregoing examples are of the physical type. It also is possible for a motion to be in the abstract realm, as shown in examples (18)–(22).

(18) *chǎn*	*khěn*	*lûukchaay*	*mây*	*khɯ̂n*	*ciŋ ciŋ*
I	push	son	not	ascend	really

"I tried to push my son to success but was not successful."

"I tried to push up my son but was not successful." (literal translation)

(19) *chǎn*	*yú?*	*phɯ̂an*	*mây*	*khɯ̂n*
I	convince	friend	not	ascend

"I tried to convince a friend to take an action but was not successful."

(20) *chǎn*	*àan*	*laaymɯɯ*	*khɔ̌ɔŋ*	*khun*	*mây*	*ʔɔ̀ɔk*
I	read	handwriting	of	you	not	exit

"I tried to read your handwriting but was not successful."

(21) *chǎn*	*khít*	*khrooŋrɯ̂aŋ*	*mây*	*ʔɔ̀ɔk*
I	think	plot	not	exit

"I tried to think of the plot of the story but was not successful."

(22) *fàaykháan*	*khôon*	*rátthabaan*	*mây*	*loŋ*
opposition	turn upside down	government	not	descend

"The opposition tried to overthrow the government but was not successful."

There are two ways in which the verb phrases in sentences (18)–(22) can be interpreted as indicating nonphysical motions. In the first way, verb phrases are metaphorically interpreted, as in sentences (18) and (22). Although the motions in (18) and (22) are not physical, they are still semantically transparent in the meanings of the verb phrases. The motion verbs *khěn,* "push," in (18) and *khôon,* "fell," in (22) are metaphorically interpreted as to push somebody to success and to overthrow an established organization, respectively. In the former case, changing the place of a person in the physical realm is mapped to changing the status of a person in the abstract realm. In the latter case, making a tree collapse is mapped to destroying an organization. In the second metaphorical interpretation, the whole actions expressed by the verb phrases must be conceptualized metaphorically, as in sentences (19)–(21). In other words, the second interpretation involves the notion of metaphorical concept postulated by Lakoff and Johnson (1980). In their view, metaphors refer not to linguistic expressions but to a person 's conceptual system, which is metaphorical in nature. One type of metaphorical concept discussed in their work that is pertinent to the issue in question is "orientational metaphors," which deal with the concept of spatial orientation and arise from our physical and cultural experiences—for example, *happy is up; sad is down; more is up; less is down*. Orientational metaphors play an important role in human conceptualization because most of our fundamental concepts of human beings are organized in terms of one or more spatialization metaphors. In (19) the metaphorical concept at work is *taking action is up*, which is grounded in our experiential basis that taking an action is moving upward. The metaphorical concept that is operative in (20) is *understanding is out*, which is based on our experience that if we understand something we have the impression that the sense of that thing comes out and reaches us. The metaphorical concept at work in (21) is *figuring out something is out*. This metaphorical concept is based on the physical experience that when we try to come up with something or to figure out something, our thinking takes place in our head. When we are successful in figuring it out, it will come out of our head and may be known to other people. In summary, the notion of motion in examples (18)–(22) arises from metaphorical processes, albeit in different ways. In (18) and (22), the motion arises from the metaphorical use of the main verbs. In (19)–(21) the whole actions expressed by the verb phrases must be understood in a metaphorical way, which gives rise to the metaphorical concepts described above.

Notice that there must be semantic agreement between the direction of motion associated with the verb phrase and that inherent in the lexical source of a success marker. For example, in the egg-beating example in (7), because the eggs become fluffy as a result of the agent beating them, the direction of the motion of the eggs must be upward.

Pragmatic Contexts of Success Markers Verb phrases co-occurring with success markers inherently suggest that the agent's intention in carrying out an action has been fulfilled. This observation may make us wonder why we need success markers in the first place. We argue that those verb phrases normally imply that the agent's goal in performing an action is attained. If we want to emphasize fulfillment or nonfulfillment of the agent's goal, however, we can add a success marker to obtain such a pragmatic effect. The appearance of a success marker requires a marked context because those verb phrases by default imply such success on the part of the agent. Hence success markers are not found frequently in affirmative (as opposed to negative) of declarative (as opposed to interrogative) sentences. They are more prevalent in negative sentences and in interrogative sentences.

Success Markers versus Directional Verbs versus Directional Markers

In this section we review the arguments presented in Thepkanjana and Uehara (2004) that success markers are syntactically and semantically distinct from directional verbs, which are their lexical sources, and from directional markers, which are another type of grammaticalized form also developed from directional verbs. The three forms coexist synchronically.

To see whether success markers are syntactically and semantically distinct from directional verbs, one can take them out of sentences in which they appear after the verb phrases and combine them with the nouns denoting the entities that are in motion in the original sentences, yielding simple sentences as in the (b) sentences below. We have found that some of the (b) sentences are acceptable, whereas others are either questionable or unacceptable. We list only unacceptable (b) sentences[3] here because of limited space.

(23) a. *khǎw* *yók* *klɔ̀ŋ* *mây* *khɯ̂n*
he lift box not ascend
"He tried to lift a box up but was not successful."

b. * *klɔ̀ŋ* *mây* *khɯ̂n*
box not ascend

(24) a. *khǎw* *kòt* *pùm* *mây* *loŋ*
he press button not descend
"He tried to push the button down but was not successful."

b. * *pùm* *mây* *loŋ*
button not descend

(25) a. *chǎn* *hàn* *nɯ́a* *mây* *khâw* *phrɔ́ʔ* *nǐaw* *mâak*
I cut meat not enter because tough very
"I tried to cut the meat but was not successful because it was very tough."

b. * *mîit* *mây* *khâw*
knife not enter

The fact that success markers cannot readily occur as single directional verbs in simple sentences even with the nouns denoting the entities in motion in the (a) sentences proves that they are not full-fledged directional verbs. We have further shown that they are syntactically and semantically distinct from directional markers in that the former can be negated whereas the latter cannot. Examples (26)–(28) illustrate that directional markers cannot be negated.

(26) **khǎw* *sòŋ* *nǎŋsɯ̌ɯ* *mây* *pay*
he send book not go

(27) **khǎw* *wîŋ* *mây* *khâw*
he run not enter

(28) * *khǎw* *nam* *ʔaahǎan* *mây* *maa*
he bring food not come

Furthermore, directional markers can co-occur with one another in sentences, whereas success markers cannot. There must be only one success marker in a sentence. Examples (29) and (30) illustrate that there can be more than one directional marker in a sentence, whereas examples (31) and (32) show that there cannot be more than one success marker in a sentence.

(29) *khǎw dəən ɔ̀ɔk maa*
he walk exit come
"He walked out and toward the speaker."

(30) *khǎw lóm loŋ pay*
he collapse descend go
"He fell down and away from the speaker."

(31) * *khǎw yók klɔ̀ŋ mây khûn pay*
he lift box not ascend go

(32) * *khǎw cɔ̀? kamphææŋ mây khâw maa*
he pierce wall not enter come

Degree of Grammaticalization of Success Markers

We argue in this section that success markers are still considered as located at early stages of grammaticalization because of many reasons. First, some of the original meanings and the grammaticalized meanings of success markers co-exist synchronically. On this basis, intermediate stages on this grammaticalization path can be said to be "synchronic contextual variations" of directional verbs (Heine 2002, 83). According to Heine (2002, 84–86), the grammaticalization path consists of four successive stages. Because different stages tend to be reflected in the form of different contextual clusters, Heine calls some of the stages on the grammaticalization path "contexts." These four stages are (I) initial stage, (II) bridging contexts, (III) switch contexts, and (IV) conventionalization. At stage I a morpheme expresses a "normal" or source meaning and occurs in an array of contexts. At stage II there is a specific context giving rise to an inference, which can be interpreted as a new meaning. The old and new meanings are not yet incompatible, however. At stage III there is a new context that does not allow for an interpretation in terms of the source or old meaning. The source or old meaning is incompatible with the new meaning in the new context. At stage IV the new meaning becomes conventionalized and does not need to be supported by the context that gave rise to it.

Each grammaticalized marker can be synchronically located at any intermediate stage of grammaticalization. It does not have to be a "conventionalized" marker, which is located at the final stage. According to Heine's (2002) characterizations of these stages, success markers can be considered grammaticalized forms located at the second stage, which is bridging contexts. This stage starts the grammaticalization process by triggering the inferential mechanism such that there is another meaning that is a more plausible interpretation of the lexical item in question. The new meaning actually is a conversational implicature pragmatically associated with the lexical item in context and is to be conventionalized later. A lexical item at this stage may be associated with different "new" meanings as well as "old" meanings. The new meanings may be, but need not be, conventionalized or grammaticalized at later stages.

Because the "old" and "new" meanings of success markers still coexist and are not yet incompatible, success markers are regarded as forms located at the second stage of grammaticalization. Furthermore, the fact that there must be agreement between the direction inherent in the motion expressed or implied by the verb phrase and that inherent in the lexical source of each success marker suggests that the direction in each success marker has not yet been neutralized. This observation is another piece of evidence that success markers have not yet been "conventionalized" or fully grammaticalized. In the following section, we discuss how pragmatic inferences give rise to "new" meanings of success markers.

Pragmatic Inferences that Motivate the Grammaticalization of Directional Verbs into Success Markers

Grammaticalization is considered a kind of language change. According to Hopper and Traugott (1993), three motivations of language change have been widely discussed in recent literature: child language acquisition, the role of communities and different types of contact with them, and the role of speakers and hearers negotiating meaning in communicative situations. This study discusses the third motivation, which is manifested in the form of pragmatic inferences derived during the interaction between speaker and hearer. Different types of pragmatic inferencing—namely, metaphoric and metonymic inferencing—operate in grammaticalization. Metonymy is the type of pragmatic inferencing that primarily motivates the grammaticalization of directional verbs into success markers. Our argument is based on the hypothesis concerning pragmatic strengthening and subjectification in grammaticalization advanced by Traugott (1982, 1988, 1989, 1990) and Traugott and König (1991).

This section is divided into two subsections. The first subsection presents Traugott's hypothesis concerning the role of metonymy as a type of pragmatic inferencing in grammaticalization. The second subsection discusses how metonymy motivates the grammaticalization of directional verbs into success markers in Thai.

The Role of Metonymy in Grammaticalization in General

Metaphoric processes traditionally have been regarded as central to semantic change, including grammaticalization. However, many arguments have been put forward—especially by Traugott—that grammaticalization is primarily motivated by metonymic processes. Traugott's central claim is that meaning changes at early stages of grammaticalization are pragmatic and associative. Metonymic processes play a role in motivating meaning change at these early stages. From a pragmatic perspective, the fundamental process operating in an interaction between speaker and hearer is the principle of informativeness and relevance, which can be essentially stated, "Be as informative as possible, given the needs of the situation" (Atlas and Levinson 1981). According to this principle, the speaker seeks the highest level of expressivity when he or she communicates but simultaneously puts bounds on the communication for economy's sake, which results in the use of old forms to express new meanings. This principle drives the speaker to be increasingly specific through grammatical coding and at the same time invites the hearer to select the most informative interpretation among competing meanings expressed by an utterance.

All linguistic utterances have both semantic and pragmatic meanings. Pragmatic meanings are derived by a pragmatic mode of inference called "abduction" (Givón 1989), which involves analogical reasoning—postulating hypotheses on the basis of guesswork and intuition by taking wider contexts into consideration. Thus, abduction is pragmatic, context-dependent, and based on similarity and relevance. Givón (1989) claims that abduction is required to fully understand the meaning of an utterance the speaker makes in a certain context. Abduction is closely associated with metonymic inferencing.

Antilla (1972) suggests that there are two types of semantic transfer that result in semantic changes: metaphor and metonymy. Metaphor is semantic transfer through a similarity of sense perception, whereas metonymy is semantic transfer through contiguity. Metonymy points to or indexes covert meanings of a linguistic expression and operates across interdependent syntactic constituents. Metaphoric change involves specifying a thing, usually in an abstract domain, in terms of another in a more concrete domain, which is not present in the context. On the other hand, metonymic change involves specifying one meaning of an expression in terms of another that is present, but usually covert, in the context.

In a verbal interaction, abduction and metonymic inferencing give rise to conversational implicatures, which are pragmatically associated with an utterance and are inferred in context. These pragmatic meanings are "contiguous" to the conventional meanings of an utterance. What happens at early stages of grammaticalization of a lexical word is that the conversational implicatures associated with an utterance containing that word become conventionalized by frequent use. Traugott refers to this conventionalization as "pragmatic strengthening." Traugott (1989, 1990) also suggests that the direction of change at early stages of grammaticalization is the shift from meanings grounded in objectively identifiable extralinguistic situations to meanings grounded in text-making to meanings grounded in the speaker's attitude toward or belief about what is said. Thus, grammaticalization results in a semantic shift from more to less objectified meanings or, in other words, from less subjectified to more subjectified meanings. According to Traugott, the process of subjectification plays a dominant role in grammaticalization.

Traugott and König (1991) argue that the development of grammaticalized connectives such as *while, since,* and *rather than* results from metonymic processes. In the following section, we discuss how metonymic processes play a role in the grammaticalization of directional verbs into success markers in Thai.

The Role of Metonymy in the Development of Success Markers in Thai

As we mentioned in section 1 of this chapter, the construction in which success markers take place can be regarded as a type of resultative construction. This construction indicates that the agent volitionally performs an action that affects an entity and results in a change of location of the entity. The change of location of the affected entity entails that the agent is successful in performing the action. In discussing semantic types of resultative predicates in Thai, Thepkanjana and Uehara (2004) point out that there are two types of object-oriented resultative predicates—namely, the type that indicates a change of state and the type that indicates a change of location of an affected entity. The latter type is what we are dealing with in this study. The changed location can be physical, abstract, or figurative. The former type indicates a change of state of an affected entity after undergoing an action performed by an agent. The latter type is linguistically realized as one of the six directional verbs—*khûn,* "ascend"; *loŋ,* "descend"; *khâw,* "enter"; *ʔɔ̀ɔk,* "exit"; *pay,* "go"; and *maa,* "come"—as noted above, whereas the former type is linguistically realized as a stative verb, such as *taay,* "be dead"; *saʔàat,* "be clean"; *khàat,* "be torn"; and *hàk,* "be broken." The latter type is unique in that it incorporates many semantic properties at the same time: a direction of motion of an affected entity, the resulting event of the agent's performance of an action, and the completion and success of the agent's action. As we argue above, the six directional verbs that function as the resultative predicate are a type of grammaticalized form of directional verb. In this section, we argue that the semantic elements mentioned above are present in the six grammaticalized markers as a result of pragmatic inferencing, which in this case is a metonymic process.

Two pragmatic inferences become more prominent with the presence of success markers. The first is the inference that the performance of an action by an agent has been completed. This inference is derived from the original meaning that there is a resulting event in the form of a change of location of an affected entity. The perfect and the resultative meanings can be regarded as direct metonymic "mirror-images" of the same event (Detges 2000, 361). Furthermore, the fact that a transitive motion or motion-implied verb occurring in the construction under investigation expresses an intentional action leads the hearer to infer that the agent has a further intention that his or her action will lead to a particular result and that the result has been attained. In other words, the hearer is inclined to infer that the agent has been successful in bringing about his or her desired result in the case of an affirmative and declarative sentence or that the agent has failed to do so in the case of a negative sentence. This analysis constitutes the second pragmatic inference, and it is why this type of grammaticalized marker is called a "success marker." This pragmatic inference is more or less subjective and evaluative in that it is grounded in the speaker/hearer's belief and attitudes. The two pragmatic inferences can be summarized as follows:

Original Meaning		***Pragmatic Inference***
(source meaning)		(target meaning)
(i) An affected entity changed its location.	→	An agent has completed his/her action.
(Resultative meaning)		(Perfect meaning)
(ii) The action has been completed, and the action was performed intentionally.	→	The agent was successful in accomplishing the desired result on the part of the affected entity.
(Perfect meaning and intentionality expressed by the verb)		(Success meaning)

When directional verbs co-occur with transitive motion or motion-implied verbs in this type of construction, they take on other meanings described above. Notice that if we delete success markers from sentences with motion or motion-implied verb phrases, the same situations expressed by the predicates still obtain. The presence of success markers, however, makes explicit the new location of the affected entities and the agent's successful performance of the action expressed by the predicate.

Conclusion

Success markers as a type of grammaticalized marker of directional verbs occur at early stages of the grammaticalization path and express many semantic properties that coexist synchronically. The conventionalized meanings of directional verbs that remain in success markers are the notions of motion and direction. The other meanings of success markers are derived from pragmatic inferences that were background knowledge associated with motion or motion-implied verb phrases. These pragmatic inferences are derived by means of metonymic processes and become more prominent when these directional markers appear in the syntactic context: NP1 TV NP2 DV, where TV stands for a transitive motion or motion-implied verb and DV stands for a directional verb, which is called a success marker in this context. Thus, the construction in which success markers appear can be said to be a type of transitive-based resultative construction whose resultative predicate expresses a change of location of an affected entity.

In the case of success markers, it is apparent that some aspect of the original meaning of their lexical sources coexists with the grammaticalized meanings. Hence, semantic bleaching does not play an important role in this case. This fact corresponds to Hopper and Traugott's (1993) claim that in the early stages of grammaticalization there is a shift in meaning of lexical words rather than bleaching, as researchers generally have believed. In a meaning shift, some meanings are promoted and some are demoted. At the present stage of grammaticalization of directional verbs into success markers, it seems that the new grammaticalized meanings have emerged while the original meaning has not yet bleached or disappeared.

Acknowledgments

In carrying out this research, the second author is partially supported by the Grant-in-Aid for Scientific Research for Japan Society for the Promotion of Science (No.15520241).

NOTES

1. According to Langacker (1987), the description of a location of an object involves recognition of some kind of asymmetrical relation between the object we want to locate and the object with respect to which we locate it. We may recognize asymmetrical relations with respect to size, containment, support, orientation, order, direction, distance, motion, or a combination of these criteria. In describing the asymmetrical relation between entities in a spatial situation, Langacker (1987) uses the terms "Trajector" and "Landmark" to label the object to be located and the reference object, respectively.
2. The pattern of sentence translation used throughout this study—"subject + tried to + VP but was not successful"—does not reflect the actual meaning of the Thai counterpart, in which a success marker appears. The latter literally means that an agent kept doing the action indicated by the transitive verb phrase, but the intended goal was not attained. For more details see the subsection "Syntactic Contexts of Success Markers."

3. Sentences (23b)–(25b) are unacceptable in unmarked contexts. They could become acceptable only in marked contexts. The usage of the directional verbs in (b) therefore is considered marginalized. In analyzing the directional verbs under investigation in this study, we take into consideration only unmarked contexts.

REFERENCES

Anttila, Raimo. 1972. *An introduction to historical and comparative linguistics.* New York: Macmillan.

Atlas, Jay David, and Stephen C. Levinson. 1981. It-clefts, informativeness and logical form: Radical pragmatics. In *Radical pragmatics*, ed. Peter Cole, 1–61. New York: Academic Press.

Detges, Ulrich. 2000. Time and truth: The grammaticalization of resultatives and perfects within a theory of subjectification. *Studies in language* 24, no. 2:345–77.

Givón, Talmy. 1989. *Mind, code and context: Essays in pragmatics.* Hillsdale, N.J.: Lawrence Erlbaum Associates.

Heine, Bernd. 2002. On the role of context in grammaticalization. In *New reflections on grammaticalization*, ed. Ilse Wischer and Gabriele Diewald, 83–101. Amsterdam: John Benjamins.

Hopper, Paul J., and Elizabeth Closs Traugott. 1993. *Grammaticalization.* Cambridge: Cambridge University Press.

Lakoff, George, and Mark Johnson. 1980. *Metaphors we live by.* Chicago: University of Chicago Press.

Langacker, Ronald W. 1987. *Foundations of cognitive grammar, vol. 1: Theoretical prerequisites.* Stanford: Stanford University Press.

Thepkanjana, Kingkarn, and Satoshi Uehara. 2004. Semantic types of resultative predicates in Thai. *Proceedings of the eleventh annual meeting of the Southeast Asian Linguistics Society.* May 16–18, 2001. Bangkok, Thailand.

———. In press. Directional verbs as success markers in Thai: Another grammaticalization path. In *The Tai-Kadai languages,* ed. Anthony Diller and Jerold Edmondson. London: Routledge.

Traugott, Elizabeth Closs. 1982. From propositional to textual and expressive meanings; some semantic-pragmatic aspects of grammaticalization. In *Perspectives on historical linguistics*, ed. Winfred P. Lehmann and Yakov Malkiel, 245–71. Amsterdam: John Benjamins.

———. 1986. From polysemy to internal semantic reconstruction. *Proceedings of the twelfth annual meeting of the Berkeley Linguistics Society,* 539–50. Berkeley, Calif.: Berkeley Linguistics Society.

———. 1988. Pragmatic strengthening and grammaticalization. *Proceedings of the fourteenth annual meeting of the Berkeley Linguistics Society,* 406–16. Berkeley, Calif.: Berkeley Linguistics Society.

———. 1989. On the rise of epistemic meanings in English: An example of subjectification in semantic change. *Language* 65:31–55.

———. 1990. From less to more situated in language: The unidirectionality of semantic change. In *Papers from the fifth international conference on English historical linguistics*, ed. Sylviv Adamson, Vivien Law, Nigel Vincent, and Susan Wright, 496–517. Amsterdam: John Benjamins.

Traugott, Elizabeth Closs, and Ekkehard König. 1991. The semantics-pragmatics of grammaticalization revisited. In *Approaches to grammaticalization, vol. 1: Focus on theoretical and methodological issues*, ed. Elizabeth C. Traugott and Bernd Heine, 189–218. Amsterdam: John Benjamins.

IV

Language and Identity

14

"Trying on" the Identity of "Big Sister": Hypothetical Narratives in Parent-Child Discourse

CYNTHIA GORDON
Georgetown University

RESEARCHERS IN A VARIETY of disciplines have suggested that individuals construct identities in interaction by telling narratives of personal experience. Linguists such as Schiffrin (1996, 2000) and psychologists such as Bamberg (1997) have considered identity from this narrative-constructivist perspective, drawing on Davies and Harré's (1990) discussion of positioning and/or Goffman's (1981) related concept of footing to do so. *Positioning* refers to "the discursive process whereby selves are located in conversations as observably and subjectively coherent participants in jointly produced story lines" (Davies and Harré 1990, 48). *Footing* relates to "the alignments we take up to ourselves and the others present as expressed in the way we manage the production or reception of an utterance" (Goffman 1981, 28). Past work that draws on positioning and/or footing in considering identity construction has examined narratives of past experience told by competent adult tellers. For example, Schiffrin (1996) examines stories told by two women in sociolinguistic interviews that describe past experiences with other members of their families and create "self-portraits" of the narrators as mothers.

Like Schiffrin, I examine a family identity as it is constructed in narrative discourse. However, I consider future-oriented narrative or narrative-like discourse that is co-constructed by a young child and at least one of her parents in everyday conversation. Specifically, I investigate how one expectant mother, her husband, and their daughter (age two years, eleven months) co-construct future hypothetical "narratives" that allow the young girl to "try on" the identity of "big sister" to her as-yet-unborn baby brother. The concept of "trying on" an identity as I use it is drawn from Bruner's (1990, 54) discussion of "subjunctive" stories, or stories through which narrators explore alternative possibilities. Bruner suggests that such stories allow individuals to "try on" identities "for psychological size." Although the excerpts of interaction I examine show parents socializing their child through everyday discourse—that is, they show "parenting" in action—the main purpose of this study is to consider how "minimal" hypothetical narratives permit one young child (with the aid of her parents) to construct or begin to construct a future identity that will soon be a real part of her life. In taking this focus, this study adds to past work that considers how children construct identities through narrative or narrative-like discourse in peer interaction (e.g., Kyratzis 1999, 2000) and to studies that identify functions of future-oriented discourse (e.g., Peräkylä 1993), while also examining positioning as it takes place in nonprototypical narratives.

The data for this analysis were drawn from a larger project that involved having adult members of four dual-income families carry digital audiotape recorders with them for approximately one week, taping nearly nonstop throughout the day.[1] I consider the tapes of one of the families, consisting of a couple in their early thirties (Janet, who was six months pregnant, and her husband, Steve) and their daughter Natalie (a very verbal child who was just under three years old). For this study, I searched the entirety of the family's transcripts (seven days of taping) for instances in which talk between Natalie and at least one adult "steps into the future," to use Ochs' (1994) phrase, and anticipates a time when Natalie's brother will be born.

The analysis that follows focuses on four excerpts of interaction between Natalie and at least one adult member of her family (her mother, father, or grandmother). I identified a total of nine excerpts of conversation with Natalie about "baby brother"; those I present here represent the range of "narrativity" I found and feature Natalie as an active participant. (In several instances, a parent constructs a minimal hypothetical narrative with little input from Natalie.) Before turning to the analysis, I briefly summarize how past research has defined narrative discourse and the types of discourse that have been considered "narrative." I also summarize Bamberg's (1997) application of Davies and Harré's (1990) notion of positioning to narrative discourse, as well as Bamberg's identification of three different types of positioning that lead to identity construction in storytelling: positioning between characters in the story, positioning of the narrator vis-à-vis the audience, and positioning of the narrator with respect to himself or herself as protagonist. Then I identify and discuss four aspects of the narratives I subsequently analyze (the *interpersonal*, *imaginative*, *action*, and *evaluative* dimensions) that allow storyworld positioning to occur. The analysis shows that positioning in hypothetical narratives works much as it does in past narratives. Furthermore, it illustrates that even minimal narratives—as long as they include the interpersonal, imaginative, action, and evaluative dimensions—are capable of doing identity work in interaction. Finally, the analysis shows how one young child, with the aid of her parents, is able to use narrative language to explore an identity that will soon become a part of her life.

Defining and Analyzing Narrative Discourse

Work in linguistics and other fields studying narrative to date has focused on narratives of the past told by competent adult tellers. Labov's (1972) influential work defines narrative as "one method of *recapitulating past experience* by matching a verbal sequence of clauses to the sequence of events which (it is inferred) actually occurred" (359–60; emphasis added).

Subsequent to Labov's seminal work, researchers have suggested that narratives not only can recapitulate past experience but also can project into the future (e.g., Beach and Japp 1983; Bruner 1990; Kyratzis 1999, 2000; Quigley 1999). Ochs

(1994, 107), focusing on family dinnertime discourse, notes that narratives that recapitulate the past project future time experiences as well in the sense that the "storyteller's recollections of past events have the potential to evoke for participating interlocutors ideas and talk about future events/circumstances." Peräkylä (1993, 292) suggests that future projections work much like narratives in that they create a "world" or "alternate reality" that is separate from the "reality" of conversation. Similarly, Beach and Japp (1983) argue that what they call "storifying" allows interlocutors to "time travel" in conversation.

Studies also have shown that future-oriented narrative or narrative-like discourse allows children to, among other things, plan for the future (Quigley 1999), "try on" an identity (Bruner 1990), and explore "possible selves" (Kyratzis 1999). These studies all take a relatively broad definition of narrative in that they explicitly suggest that narratives can be oriented toward the future. Those that consider the discourse of young children (e.g., Kyratzis, who considers the talk of preschool children) suggest that narratives need not include some of the elements found in adult narratives, such as an abstract and orientation.

In considering the discourse of a young child (age two years, eleven months) and at least one of her parents, the present study takes a fairly broad definition of narrative in that it allows "narratives" to be minimally developed and it allows narrative to be oriented toward the future (as Kyratzis 2000). In the following sections, I review positioning as it occurs in narrative and then identify and briefly describe aspects of the "minimal narratives" I examine that allow positioning to occur.

Positioning in Narrative

Bamberg (1997) and Talbot et al. (1996) use Davies and Harré's (1990) concept of positioning in the context of narrative discourse. The work of Bamberg and his colleagues points toward the fact that positioning in narrative can be accomplished in some capacity by both children and adults; more important, however, it identifies three levels of positioning that occur in storytelling and work toward identity construction in interaction.

These three levels of positioning answer the following questions: How are characters positioned in relation to one another in the reported events? How does the speaker position himself or herself to the audience? How do narrators position themselves to themselves? According to Bamberg (1997), Positioning 1 occurs where characters are positioned in relation to one another within the reported events. Positioning 2 takes place where narrators position themselves in relation to their audience. Positioning 3 happens where narrators position themselves as tellers vis-à-vis themselves as storyworld figures. Bamberg (1997) notes that identity claims occur on the level of Positioning 3 but that Positioning 3 in many ways is the sum of Positioning 1 and Positioning 2. Related to these findings is Schiffrin's (1996) work that shows how two narrators construct their identities as mothers by positioning themselves as storyworld figures vis-à-vis other storyworld figures and by positioning themselves as storytellers vis-à-vis themselves as storyworld actors. Significantly, Schiffrin (1996) identifies a range of linguistic features that create these alignments (or positions), including but not limited to syntax, repetition, reported speech, and speech acts.

Bamberg (1997) notes that in contrast to adults' discourse, the young children whose discourse he examined did not seem to accomplish Positioning 3, although "their choices of linguistic constructions to position themselves as characters in reported personal experiences reflect clearly the ability to construct scenarios in light of discursive purposes such as attributing blame or saving face" (1997, 340–41). Although the child whose discourse I examine primarily constructs positions at the levels of Positioning 1 and Positioning 2, my analysis shows that Positioning 3 also occurs in these excerpts of parent-child narrative discourse: The child collaboratively (with the help of her parents) evaluates herself as a storyworld character from her perspective as teller.

Some Features of Narrative that Allow for Positioning 1, 2, and 3

Through analysis of the excerpts and consideration of past work on narrative discourse, I identified four features of the "narratives" I examined that are precursors to storyworld positioning, or essential for doing identity work on the level of what Bamberg (1997) calls Positioning 3. One is the action dimension. By *action*, I simply mean something has to happen. This dimension has been identified and discussed at great length by others, most notably by Labov (1972), as well as by Linde (1993), Bruner (1990), and Georgakopoulou and Goutsos (2000), among others.

Another dimension of narrative discourse that is central to creating narrative and is linked directly to positioning is the *interpersonal* dimension. This dimension relates to the idea that identities are understood in relation to others. This aspect of narrative has been emphasized by several researchers, including Bruner (1990) and Polkinghorne (1991). Schiffrin (1996, 197) notes that "who we are is sustained by our ongoing interactions with others, and the way we position ourselves in relation to those others." Polkinghorne emphasizes that family members often are the others that help define the self: "My spouse, children, and other loved ones become indispensable partners within my story" (1991, 146).

The next dimension is the *imaginative* dimension. This dimension refers to the fact that telling a story, in any tense, depends on using the imagination. Bruner (1990, 55) notes that all stories, even "true" stories of the past, "remain forever in the domain of the midway between the real and the imaginary." Chafe (1994, 32) argues that the imagination (as well as the memory) plays an essential role in any instance of what he calls *spaciotemporal displacement*. Similarly, Peräkylä (1993), considering hypothetical "alternate realities" invoked in AIDS counseling sessions, suggests that imagination facilitates accessing possible future scenarios.

Finally, narratives that are capable of doing identity work through Positioning 3 have an *evaluative* dimension. Labov (1972, 166) identifies evaluation as "perhaps the most important element" of narrative (in addition to the narrative clause). Evaluation wards off the dreaded question, "So what?" Similarly, Chafe (1994, 77) remarks that narrative requires a "narrator's perspective." Georgakopoulou and Goutsos (2000) also identify evaluation as a critical feature of narrative, and Linde (1993,

122) suggests that the separation of narrator from protagonist is central to defining narrative in that it permits the narrator to "observe, reflect, and correct the self that is being created"—in other words, to evaluate.

The analysis that follows relates these four features (action, interpersonal, imaginative, evaluative) to the positioning that does (or does not) occur in the parent-child future co-constructions I identified. The presence of these features is important because they make Positioning 1, 2, and 3 possible, and through Positioning 3 (and to some extent through Positioning 1 and 2) identities are constructed in narrative. I identified in the tapes of the family whose discourse I analyze here a total of eight instances of parent-child conversation (and one instance of grandmother-child conversation) about a future time when "baby brother" is born; I present here four that are representative of the "range of narrativity" that I found.

Constructing an Identity through Minimally Developed Narratives

Excerpt 1 illustrates the kinds of identity work that occur in one of the "least narrative-like" segments I identified, where the four dimensions of narrative I elaborated above (action, interpersonal, imaginative, evaluative) are difficult to locate and Positioning 3 does not occur. In this excerpt, mother Janet and daughter Natalie are at home talking in the kitchen, and Natalie spontaneously brings up the topic of how big "baby brother" will be. It is evident from listening to the tapes that gestures in the form of hand movements take place in this segment, as Janet and Natalie collaboratively agree on how big baby brother will be.

Excerpt 1

(1) Natalie: Will my brother be this big?
((presumably holding out hands))
(2) Janet: <*laughs*>
(3) Well I don't know if he'll be THAT big!
(4) Natalie: Will he be this tiny big.
(5) Janet: Oh he'll be a little bit bigger than that.
(6) Natalie: Will he be this tiny.
(7) Janet: He'll be bigger than that.
(8) He'll probably be about . this big.
(9) Natalie: This big?
(10) Janet: A little bigger.
(11) Natalie: Like this big?
(12) Janet: Oh that would be a pretty big baby.
(13) Natalie: This big baby?
(14) Janet: Whoa,
(15) that's really big.
(16) Natalie: Or this tiny . baby.

(17) Or this big baby.
(18) Janet: I don't think he'll be quite that big.
(19) Okay I've got . things everywhere.
(20) Yikes. ((Janet begins to put things away))

Although this excerpt travels into a future time when Natalie's brother will have been born, it is quite nonnarrative. There are no *action* or *interpersonal* dimensions in a storyworld, though Natalie is comparing herself and her brother in terms of size. Although the *imagination* plays a role, there is no "story" here with a "point" created by evaluation. This excerpt seems more like a *description* than a narrative, and what little identity work is accomplished here is not done through storyworld positioning. By showing interest in her little brother, Natalie does send a message about herself, however: that she is interested in how big her brother will be (and probably what her relationship to him will be in terms of their physical sizes) and that she looks to her mother for this type of information.

Excerpt 2, like Excerpt 1, is durative rather than instantaneous. It has a few hints of narrativity, however. In this excerpt, Natalie and Janet are having dinner at home when Natalie asks why she can no longer sleep in the "cribby" (the crib she slept in when she was a baby). This inquiry begins a series of questions and answers.

Excerpt 2

(1) Natalie: Mom,
(2) Janet: Yeah?
(3) Natalie: Why I can't sleep in the cribby anymore.
(4) Janet: Why what?
(5) Natalie: Why can't I sleep in the cribby anymore.
(6) Janet: Because you've got your big girl bed.
(7) Natalie: Who's gonna sleep in the cribby.
(8) Janet: Nobody for a while.
(9) ((short pause))
(10) Natalie: Who's gonna sleep in there for a while.
(11) Janet: What?
(12) Natalie: Who's gonna sleep in there for a while.
(13) Janet: Well someday your baby brother will sleep in there.

A storyworld begins to take form in this excerpt in that there is some indication of not just "time-traveling" to the future (Beach and Japp 1983) but also a moving through time within that future world. The temporal gap formed between line 8, where Janet says that nobody is going to sleep in the crib for a while, and line 13, where Janet says that "someday" Natalie's baby brother will sleep there, creates temporal juncture. As in Excerpt 1, however, there is no protagonist, and also as in Excerpt 1, the conversation is primarily a question-answer exchange. However, Natalie's invocation of this topic and Janet's referring to her as-yet-unborn son in terms of his relationship with Natalie (line 13, "your baby brother") begins to construct a big sister identity for Natalie.

In contrast to Excerpts 1 and 2, in Excerpt 3 there is some sense of action and some sense of an actual scene or storyworld. The conversation in this excerpt occurs at home and involves Janet, Natalie, and Steve. At the beginning of the excerpt, Natalie is giving Janet and Steve "baby kisses," which seem to be kisses in which one does not pucker one's lips.

Excerpt 3

(1)	Janet:	(?) you give me a baby kiss?
(2)	Natalie:	I gave you a BA:BY kiss.
(3)	Janet:	Did you give me one of those silly baby kisses.
(4)		[(????)]
(5)	Steve:	[Can you show me.]
(6)	Janet:	That's how baby brother will give kisses.
(7)		We'll have to teach him how to give REAL kisses.
(8)	Natalie:	I will teach my baby brother how to give REAL kisses.
(9)	Steve:	Oh boy.

In this excerpt the participants use their *imaginations* to jump forward to a time when they can teach Natalie's as-yet-unborn baby brother to give "real kisses." Something also happens in this excerpt; thus, the *action* dimension is present. In line 6 the state of affairs is that baby brother will give "baby kisses," but in lines 7 and 8 "we" (Janet, Steve and Natalie) or just Natalie ("I") become storyworld characters who will teach baby brother to give real kisses. (Note that Natalie's participation in this excerpt is based on the scaffolding Janet provides.) The *interpersonal* dimension appears when the parents, and then just Natalie, are teachers to baby brother's position as novice; thus, Positioning 1 (between storyworld characters) occurs. The "so what" or *evaluative* dimension seems to point to the joint enthusiasm of sharing something intimate with baby brother, as well as Natalie's capability to participate in this activity, which relates to Positioning 2 (narrators vis-à-vis the audience). Positioning 3 also is hinted at in that both Positioning 1 and 2 occur. In addition, Natalie speaks with pride and enthusiasm as a teller about being a teacher to her brother, positively evaluating the storyworld events and herself as a storyworld actor, and Steve supports her by uttering "Oh boy."

In Excerpt 4, Natalie also does identity work for herself as a future big sister. This excerpt is one of the "most-narrative-like" excerpts I found. Here Janet and Natalie are at the playground, swinging on the swings. Identity work is even easier to find here than in the previous excerpts, and this excerpt seems more like a "narrative." In line 5, when Natalie mentions teaching baby brother to "go back and forth," she means teaching him to pump his legs to propel himself on the swing on which he hypothetically would be sitting.

Excerpt 4

(1) Janet: It won't be too long . before we take →
(2) baby brother with us to the playground.
(3) Natalie: I will take my baby (bether)—
(4) I will take my baby brother to the playground →
(5) and teach him how to [. go] back and forth.
(6) Janet: [<*chuckles*>]
(7) <*chuckling*> A::w.>
(8) [It'll be a little—]
(9) Natalie: [Can I do] that when I take my baby brother to the playground?
(10) Janet: Sure,
(11) but it'll be a little while before he can do that.
(12) Natalie: I'll teach him.
(13) Janet: Yeah!
(14) First he'll probably sit in the stroller while- →
(15) while you play though.
(16) Natalie: (Why.)
(17) Janet: Because he'll be too little.
(18) Do you want a push?
(19) Do you want me to give you a push?

Here Natalie, necessarily using her *imagination* and relying on her mother's input, creates a brief storyline in lines 4–5 (*I will take my brother to the playground and teach him how to go back and forth*); thus, there is an *action* dimension to this excerpt. As with Excerpt 3, the storyline is based in some way on the scaffolding provided by Janet in the line before. An *interpersonal* dimension also is present, and Natalie positions herself as a caregiver and teacher vis-à-vis her baby brother; thus, Positioning 1 (between characters) takes place. Positioning 2 (Natalie vis-à-vis Janet as her audience) occurs as Natalie speaks with pride in her voice and Janet appreciatively utters "Aw." Thus, the perspective or point of this story seems to be Natalie taking pride in displaying her intentions of being a teacher or parent-like figure vis-à-vis her baby brother. Positioning 3 (Natalie as teller vis-à-vis Natalie as storyworld character) occurs through the evaluation provided by Natalie's quality of voice (which might be described as "proud") as she narrates her hypothetical actions. Positioning 3 also is hinted at when Natalie asks Janet about whether she can teach her baby brother to swing when she takes him to the playground (line 9). Here Natalie shows some uncertainty about what can occur in the future storyworld—that is, what kind of figure she can be. Natalie looks to her mother for verification of the plausibility of her future playground scenario—that is, how Natalie as a storyworld actor should be evaluated from the perspective of the telling.

In responding to Natalie's uncertainty, Janet clearly aids her daughter in "trying on" the big sister identity and the playground scenario. She supports Natalie's suggestions, saying "Sure" when Natalie asks if she can teach baby brother to swing at the playground (lines 9–11) and supportively uttering "Yeah" when Natalie mentions "I'll teach him" (line 12). In addition, Janet adds information and with it a mediating layer of time between the events of "taking baby brother to the playground" and "teaching baby brother to swing" by remarking that baby brother at first will have to "sit in the stroller" because he'll "be too little" to swing.

It is interesting that Janet adds this intermediary layer in reference to baby brother's shortcomings (saying "he'll be too little") and not in reference to Natalie. Janet does not say "you'll be too little to take him to the playground" (despite the fact that Natalie would be less than three and half years old when the baby is born). Janet also does not say "you don't know how to 'go back and forth' yourself, how can you teach your brother?" This too would be a valid response; when I observed this family after they taped, I noted that Natalie could not pump her legs and swing by herself. In avoiding talking about Natalie's limitations as a three-year-old in talking about the big sister identity, Janet supports Natalie's "trying on" aspects of the identity that are presently out of Natalie's reach.

Discussion

In this analysis, I considered four instances of family members talking about a future time when Natalie's brother has been born. Although these excerpts highlight Janet's role in this endeavor, three examples not discussed here involved only Natalie and Steve, one involved Natalie and both parents, and another involved Natalie and her grandmother. Thus, all family members participate in socializing Natalie into the big sister identity and assist her in "trying on" this identity to some extent. The excerpts I show here in which the *imaginative, action, interpersonal,* and *evaluative* dimensions are all present are not only the most "narrative-like" intuitively; they also do the most identity work, allowing Positioning 1, Positioning 2, and to some extent Positioning 3 to occur. Analysis of these excerpts and the identity work accomplished within them relies on a fairly broad understanding of narrative that includes these dimensions (but not necessarily structural parts such as an abstract or a resolution) and encompasses future as well as past time. Thus, this study adds to the body of work that considers narrative as it is broadly defined.

This study complements past work that has examined how competent adult narrators construct identities (in particular, family identities—e.g., Schiffrin 1996, 2000) by narrating past events by considering "minimally developed" adult/child narrative-like future co-constructions. It adds to prior research that illustrates that children use narrative and narrative-like language at a young age and that children construct identities and social relationships through narrative discourse (e.g., Kyratzis 1999, 2000). The child whose discourse I analyze here, at just less than three years old, collaboratively used language to anticipate an upcoming change in her life and begin in some way to preexperience a future time when she would no longer be an only child. Her parents, in aiding her in this process, gave Natalie emotional and informational input as well as some skeletal narrative structure.

In sum, my analysis has shown that narrative positioning works in future narratives much as it does in past narratives. Although future-oriented discourse has been considered by linguists and others in the past, much more work has been done on narratives of the past than on narratives of the future. This work begins to address this discrepancy; it has shown that if narrative or narrative-like discourse includes certain features, it serves as a resource for constructing identities regardless of whether it looks to the past or the future. This analysis also suggests that even very young children create identities by using narrative language in their everyday interactions.

Acknowledgments

This research was funded by the Alfred P. Sloan foundation (grant #99-10-7 to Deborah Tannen and Shari Kendall). I am indebted to Heidi Hamilton and Deborah Tannen for their helpful comments on earlier versions of this paper.

NOTE

1. The purpose of the larger study was to consider the role talk plays in balancing the demands of work and family for dual-income couples. As a research team member for this project, I shadowed Janet for two days and logged all of her audiotapes; I have analyzed Janet and Natalie's talk in depth elsewhere (see Gordon 2002).

Transcription Conventions

These conventions were developed by Shari Kendall and Deborah Tannen for use in the research study "Balancing Work and Family: Creating Parental Identities through Talk," at Georgetown University, of which this study is a part.

((words))	Double parentheses enclose transcriber's comments
(words)	Single parentheses enclose uncertain transcription
carriage return	Each new line represents an intonation unit
→	An arrow indicates that the intonation unit continues to the next line
—	A dash indicates a truncated intonation unit
-	A hyphen indicates a truncated word
?	A question mark indicates a relatively strong rising intonation
.	A period indicates falling, final intonation
,	A comma indicates continuing intonation
.	One dot surrounded by spaces indicates a brief silence
CAPS	Capitals indicate emphatic stress
<*laughs*>	Angle brackets enclose descriptions of vocal noises
<*manner*>	Angle brackets enclose descriptions of the manner in which an utterance is spoken, e.g., high-pitched, laughing, incredulous
[words]	Square brackets enclose simultaneous talk

REFERENCES

Bamberg, Michael G. W. 1997. Positioning between structure and performance. *Journal of Narrative and Life History* 7:335–42.

Beach, Wayne A., and Phyllis Japp. 1983. Storifying as time-traveling: The knowledgeable use of temporally structured discourse. In *Communication yearbook VII*, ed. Robert N. Bostrom, 867–88. New Brunswick, N.J.: Transaction Books-ICA.

Bruner, Jerome. 1990. *Acts of meaning*. Cambridge, Mass.: Harvard University Press.

Chafe, Wallace. 1994. *Discourse, consciousness, and time: The flow and displacement of conscious experience in speaking and writing*. Chicago: University of Chicago Press.

Davies, Bronwyn, and Rom Harré. 1990. Positioning: The discursive production of selves. *Journal for the Theory of Social Behaviour* 20, no. 1:43–63.

Georgakopoulou, Alexandra, and Dionysis Goutsos. 2000. Revisiting discourse boundaries: The narrative and non-narrative modes. *Text* 20, no. 1:63-82.

Goffman, Erving. 1981. *Forms of talk*. Oxford: Blackwell.

Gordon, Cynthia. 2002. "I'm Mommy and you're Natalie": Role-reversal and embedded frames in mother-child discourse. *Language in Society* 31, no. 5:679–720.

Kyratzis, Amy. 1999. Narrative identity: Preschoolers' self-construction through narrative in same-sex friendship group pretend play. *Narrative Inquiry* 9, no. 2:427–55.

———. 2000. Tactical uses of narratives in nursery school same-sex groups. *Discourse Processes* 29, no. 3:269–99.

Labov, William. 1972. *Language in the inner city*. Oxford: Blackwell.

Linde, Charlotte. 1993. *Life stories: The creation of coherence*. New York: Oxford University Press.

Ochs, Elinor. 1994. Stories that step into the future. In *Sociolinguistic perspectives on register*, ed. Douglas Biber and Edward Finegan, 106–35. New York: Oxford University Press.

Peräkylä, Anssi. 1993. Invoking a hostile world: Discussing the patient's future in AIDS counseling. *Text* 13, no. 2:291–316.

Polkinghorne, Donald E. 1991. Narrative and self-concept. *Journal of Narrative and Life History* 1, nos. 2 & 3:135–53.

Quigley, Jean. 1999. Modality and tense in children's autobiographical accounts. *Narrative Inquiry* 9, no. 2:279–302.

Schiffrin, Deborah. 1996. Narrative as self-portrait: Sociolinguistic constructions of identity. *Language in Society* 25, no. 2:167–203.

———. 2000. Mother/daughter discourse in a Holocaust oral history. *Narrative Inquiry* 10, no. 1:1–44.

Talbot, Jean, Roger Bibace, Barbara Bokhour, and Michael Bamberg. 1996. Affirmation and resistance of dominant discourses: The rhetorical construction of pregnancy. *Journal of Narrative and Life History* 6, no. 3:225–51.

15

The Discourse of Local Identity in Postwar Bosnia-Herzegovina

AIDA PREMILOVAC
Georgetown University

National, Ethnic, and Local Identity

Recent investigations in national and ethnic identity have challenged earlier assumptions that such identities are relatively stable constructs, developed out of particular historical and sociopolitical circumstances. In their study of national identity in Austria, Wodak et al. (1999) propose that national identity is a discursive construct, continuously reevaluated through written and spoken narratives of a nation and its culture. In this framework, discourse is one of the most essential social practices that allows for the construction and manifestation of nations as symbolic and imagined communities (cf. Anderson 1991).

Barker and Galasinski (2001) suggest that ethnic identity also is best understood as continually shifting descriptions and actions achieved and manifested through social interaction. By studying discourse data from elderly Poles, the authors demonstrate that the speakers' construction of ethnic identity was changing with context-specific demands. Thus, depending on the interactional context, the speakers sometimes displayed their ethnic identity through adoption or negation of the same identity position; at other times they constructed multiple or conflicting ethnic identities.

Suggesting that national and ethnic identities are fluid and variable concepts does not imply that individuals can shift easily in and out of different national and ethnic identity categories. It simply suggests that such identities are affected by the situation in which they emerge and that they may still be "stabilized as categories through their embedding in the pragmatic narratives of our day-to-day conduct" (Barker and Galasinski 2001, 44). In other words, although national and ethnic identities are flexible social constructs, they still may be regulated and made invariable through specific discourses of sociopolitical and historical institutions. In instances of radical nationalism, for instance, we often observe extreme manifestations of the discourse and ideology, which rely on the idea that one group's national or ethnic identity is more unique and rooted in distinct norms, culture, history, and practices than that of another group. A radical nationalist group may portray itself as a historical victim at the hands of another ethnic or religious group, thereby legitimizing its claim for autonomy or full sovereignty as well as justifying the marginalization of those who are perceived as a threat to the group's survival and prosperity.

In this chapter I investigate the discursive notions of ethnic and national identity by emphasizing a largely overlooked construct of local identity, which can buttress or contest identification along the national and ethnic lines. Local identity can be defined as an identity position that centers on the significance of place (e.g. urban versus rural settlements) and its residents' shared everyday practices. For instance, what it means to be a dweller of New York or Sarajevo may significantly affect, compete with, or reinforce what it means to be American or Bosnian (in nationality terms) and Italian American or Bosniak (in ethnic terms). Within geographic boundaries of one region, one way in which local identity may be manifested is through the discursive construction of village versus town, town versus city, or village versus city identity positions.

The purpose of this analysis is to indicate the importance of the local identity construct for communities such as those in Bosnia-Herzegovina, which have been affected by radical nationalism. In that country, radical groups were mobilized to destroy and ethnically cleanse others. In the aftermath of such events, questions often are raised about the extent to which strong national and ethnic affiliations in such communities will continue to exist, in what form, and how they will affect the expression of other kinds of identities (e.g., personal, social, cultural, political). In this essay I examine the ways in which the discursive construction of local identity can serve as an important indication of how members of different ethnic groups are attempting to deal with earlier massive disruptions of their daily practices and identities. Because the construction of local identity can cut across ethnic and national boundaries, this position allows for accentuating similarities among groups and can serve as a basis for rebuilding communities' multi-ethnic composition.

In my analysis of local identity I focus on everyday interactions among two ethnic Croats and two ethnic Bosniaks from Stari Grad, a town in Bosnia-Herzegovina.[1] After briefly discussing the recent history of war in Bosnia-Herzegovina, particularly the Croat-Bosniak conflict in Stari Grad, I offer background information about the data and the speakers. I proceed with a micro-level analysis of an interaction, in which I demonstrate the ways in which a shared local identity among Croats and Bosniaks is constructed through the speakers' use of personal (e.g., pronouns), spatial (e.g., toponyms), and temporal (e.g., temporal adverbs) reference. In conclusion I offer a summary of my findings and their relevance for the community studied and the research on ethnic and national identity in general.

Bosnia-Herzegovina and Stari Grad during the 1992–1995 War

In the period from World War II until 1992, Bosnia-Herzegovina was one of the six republics that formed the Socialist Federation of Yugoslavia. The other republics in the federation were Croatia; Macedonia; Montenegro; Serbia, with two autonomous provinces of Vojvodina and Kosovo; and Slovenia. The Yugoslav federation was run by socialist leader and President Josip Broz Tito from World War II until his death in 1980. Despite constitutional assurances of equality among the Yugoslav republics and provinces during Tito's reign, in reality these rights were not easily maintained. For that reason, after Tito's death the presidential post was transformed into a seven-member body, representing the republics that constituted Yugoslavia. Rotating presidential terms of the new political body were intended to preserve Tito's longstanding goal of maintaining political balance among the republics and ethnic groups, whose size and economic and social affluence differed.

The delicate balance began to shift, however, as Yugoslavia's largest ethnic group, the Serbs, began to dominate the political, military, and economic leadership of the country. The domination was apparent on the federal level as well as on some state levels. As a result, the republics of Slovenia and Croatia struggled to break away from Serbian domination and eventually declared independence in 1991. Bosnia-Herzegovina followed their example in April 1992. As the Yugoslav federation disintegrated, the ethnic Serbs' goal of dominating Yugoslavia was transformed into the goal of creating a "Greater Serbia" in which Serbs from all parts of Yugoslavia would live. However, this new goal could be achieved only through armed aggression across the borders of Serbia and Montenegro. This new political reality led to the short Serb invasion of Slovenia; a six-year invasion of small parts of Croatia; and three years of aggression, ethnic cleansing, and genocide against non-Serbs, particularly Bosniaks, in Bosnia-Herzegovina (for more, see Gutman 1993; Malcom 1994; Silber and Little 1995; Sells 1996).

The town of Stari Grad and its multiethnic population were affected and changed by these events. According to prewar census figures for Bosnia-Herzegovina, the Stari Grad municipality comprised 44 percent Bosniaks (then known as Bosnian Muslims), 33 percent Serbs, 22 percent Croats, and a few people who identified as themselves as Yugoslav or other (Statistički bilten no. 234 1991). These figures reflected what residents of the Stari Grad region were proud of: a multiethnic community with a longstanding social and cultural history that was particularly apparent in an exceptional blend of different architectural styles (cf. Filipović 1990). The significance of the shared multiethnic history of residents in the Stari Grad area changed, however, with the impact of ultranationalist ideologies, war, and genocide.

In Stari Grad, the 1992–1995 conflict had two phases: the occupation and aggression of Serb forces against Croats and Bosniaks in the interest of creating a Greater Serbia, and the aggression of Croat forces against Bosniaks in the interest of creating a Greater Croatia. The first phase took place in the spring of 1992 and was over in the summer of 1992 once Croat forces advanced from the south, breaking a three-month siege and pushing Serb forces to the surrounding hills. Serb residents of Stari Grad had left the town voluntarily long before the Serb aggression started; Bosniak and Croat residents remained in town until the end of siege. Even after Serb aggression had been stopped, however, the town was still considered to be on the frontline. For that reason, most Bosniak and Croat women, children, and elderly persons relocated to the surrounding villages and towns. Some left the country altogether.

The initial unity of Bosniak and Croat forces was broken off in 1993 when nationalist Croats mobilized their forces against Bosniaks, committing crimes first in central Bosnia-Herzegovina and then in other communities where Croats outnumbered Bosniaks—including Stari Grad. In the summer of 1993, architecture that symbolized Bosniak heritage was damaged or completely destroyed, and the majority of Bosniak homes were looted (Sells 1996). Furthermore, Bosniak men from Stari Grad and nearby communities were taken to concentration camps, and remaining women, children, and elderly persons were driven out to nearby towns. Even after the Dayton peace accords were signed between November 1995 and February 1996, marking the end of the war, the destruction of Bosniak houses continued.

During this period of Croat-led ethnic cleansing, Croats from other regions were resettled to Stari Grad as part of a nationalist project for the purpose of increasing, condensing, and solidifying their presence in town. Consequently, the Croat population in Stari Grad comprised three different groups: prewar and long-time Croat residents of Stari Grad, new Croat residents from villages in central Bosnia-Herzegovina, and new Croat residents from villages in southern Bosnia-Herzegovina. The new Croat settlers were given remaining Serb or Bosniak homes, or they were given property and funds to build homes in Stari Grad—mostly without any legal authorization.

Even though the war was over in 1995, large-scale repatriation of Bosniaks was not possible until the summer of 2000 because Croat nationalists did not allow it. One of the major obstacles was that repatriation would have enabled Bosniaks to reclaim their property, but a substantial number of the resettled Croats were still occupying the houses of the Bosniak returnees. In addition, Croat individuals who had committed crimes against Bosniaks during the war were living in the community, but local Croat authorities at the time were not committed to having them sent to court. These problems continued in 2001 when I was doing my ethnographic work and collecting the discourse data presented here.

Although Bosniak refugee return is now unobstructed, Stari Grad continues to be a largely divided town. The conditions and politics of segregation are ongoing and are particularly apparent in the organization of life in schools, employment, and the toleration of nationalist Croat insignia such as flags, crosses, and crucifixes (cf. Hart and Premilovac 2002).

Against the backdrop of this recent history of Bosnia-Herzegovina and Stari Grad, I introduce my data and the speakers.

Data

Data used for my analysis of local identity come from a set of naturally occurring conversations I audiotaped in Stari Grad in the summer of 2001. The excerpts analyzed here are taken from a ninety-minute interaction among Ana, Mirsad, Boro, and myself.[2] Ana (female) and Boro (male) are ethnic Croats; Mirsad (male) and I (female) are ethnic Bosniaks. I have been friends with the participants for a long time. Because of our different ethnic backgrounds, we had distinct experiences during the recent war and did not have much contact during that time. The summer of 2001 was the first time after the war that we all met in Stari Grad.

The taping of the interaction came about as I was having drinks with Ana, Mirsad, and Boro at a local restaurant. I had told the participants about my audio data collection and research in the community on an earlier occasion, and I asked for their consent to tape-record our interaction in the restaurant. The group approved of the taping and my use of the interaction in scholarly analyses. The conversation took place in Bosnian.

The Discursive Construction of Local Identity

My analysis of local identity focuses on the speakers' use of personal, spatial, and temporal reference. More specifically, I demonstrate the ways in which these linguistic units are used as discursive acts to promote speakers' similarity and sameness in the aftermath of a war and ethnic cleansing (cf. Wodak et al. 1999). I suggest that all three types of reference work together in speakers' construction of a shared local identity. This local identity is achieved primarily through the positioning of the Croat and Bosniak speakers as townspeople and long-time residents of Stari Grad against a certain kind of ethnic Croats—namely, those who had resettled to town from rural areas during the recent conflict. In other words, rural Croats are constructed as the main cause of disruption in postwar everyday practices, rendering Croat and Bosniak speakers as equal victims of the new social order.

The relevance of the speakers' construction of local identity is highlighted against the fact that ethnic identity remains the most salient descriptor and divider of Croat and Bosniak residents in postwar Stari Grad. Consequently, this discursive act—in which the speakers' identities as ethnic Croats and ethnic Bosniaks become overshadowed by forefronting their joint identities as original residents in contrast to newcomers—allows the speakers to contest the lingering nationalist discourse and ideology.

Let us now look at specific discourse examples, which demonstrate the speakers' use of personal, spatial, and temporal reference in the construction of local identity. The analytical units are marked with boldface for easier reference.

The first example is occasioned by the participants' talk about Stari Grad after the war. Mirsad and Boro, who were residing in the community for months prior to our meeting, describe how empty the town is, especially in wintertime. Ana follows up with the following comment:

Example 1

Bosnian

(1)	Ana:	A neka, kojima danima zimi bude ovako **ljudi** ono.
(2)		**Subotom.**⌉
(3)	Boro:	⌊**Subotom i petak naveče.**
(4)	Ana:	**I nedjeljom oko jednaest, dvanaest.**
(5)	Boro:	Aha.
(6)	Mirsad:	Tad se **mi** pomamimo.
(7)	Boro:	Nema, ne moreš nas naći nikako.

English

(1)	Ana:	And so, what days during winter are there **people** like.
(2)		**On Saturday**.⌉
(3)	Boro:	⌊**On Saturday and Friday evening**.

(4) Ana: **And on Sunday around eleven, twelve.**
(5) Boro: Uh-huh.
(6) Mirsad: **We** go wild then.
(7) Boro: Right, you can't find us at all.

In example 1, the construction of local identity is accomplished primarily through personal and temporal reference. In Ana's self-posed question in line 1 ("And so, what days during winter are there people like"), she uses the personal referent "people" to refer to a *specific* rather than an indeterminate group of people—namely, Croats. That "people" can only refer to Croats is substantiated by the fact that Stari Grad at that time, particularly in the winter, had hardly any non-Croat residents. The few Bosniak families who had returned were excluded from the town's life.

The referential scope of "people" is narrowed further by Ana's use of the temporal referent "On Saturday" in line 2. By providing this answer to her own question, Ana not only indicates her existing knowledge of the "people's" activities in town, she also evokes the participants' knowledge of prewar practices that can be linked to rural Croats. In prewar times, Croat villagers were regarded as outsiders by Stari Grad residents because they did not participate in the town's practices on a daily basis. The villagers would pour into Stari Grad only on weekends and flaunt their money during Friday and Saturday activities such as shopping and drinking in selected bars. Thus, by linking the presence of "people" to "Saturday" Ana invites the other participants to co-construct a shared local identity that is easily distinguishable from that of nonresident Croats. Indeed, Boro latches onto Ana's utterance in line 3 ("On Saturday and Friday evening"), elaborating the temporal reference and specifying further the practices of the "people."

Of particular interest here is Ana's use of the temporal referent in line 4 ("And on Sunday around eleven, twelve"). The temporal reference, linked to the time when Catholic mass takes place, is especially powerful because the Croats are Catholics and may observe such services. The force of Ana's reference lies in evoking prewar practices of rural Croats who, in addition to pouring into town Friday and Saturday evenings, also would come for Sunday church services and head toward the town's bars around 11:00 or 12:00. Because Catholic religious services in the Stari Grad community often have been used as a vehicle for the expression of Croat radical nationalism, the attempt to link nonlocal Croats to such practices and political tendencies allows the Croat speakers to background their own ethnicity and emphasize practices they share with the Bosniak speakers. That these weekend activities are not what actually constitutes the expression of local identity for the speakers is indicated by Mirsad's use of the referent "we" in line 6 ("We go wild then"), which positions him and Boro as protesters of such events.

Because I was not quite sure if Ana, Mirsad, and Boro were associating the weekend activities to all nonlocal Croats, I asked for a clarification regarding the "people's" origin (line 8 below) to find out which group of nonlocal Croats was most dominant. My clarification request instigated the following sequence:

Example 2

Bosnian

(1) Aida: Šta, dolaze **ljudi sa strane** ⌉ ovdje ili . . .
(2) Boro: ⌊**Livadari.**
(3) Aida: Ozbiljno?
(4) Boro: **Oni** su **sad** najrazvijeniji **građani** na svijetu.
(5) **Oni** imaju cash,
(6) **oni** imaju radna mjesta,
(7) **oni** imaju zemlje,
(8) razumiješ.
(9) Od svakle lovu kupe,
(10) šta ćemo **mi**,
(11) **mi** nemamo kapi zemlje.
(12) Ono cviječnjaka što imaš,
(13) ⌈to ti je.

English

(1) Aida: What, **people from elsewhere** ⌉ come here or . . .
(2) Boro: ⌊**Livadars**.
(3) Aida: Really?
(4) Boro: **Right now they** are the most developed **city dwellers** in the world.
(5) **They** have cash,
(6) **they** have work positions,
(7) **they** have land,
(8) {you} understand.
(9) {They} gather money from everywhere,
(10) what can **we** do,
(11) **we** don't have a drop of land.
(12) That bit of a flower garden you have,
(13) ⌈that's all.

In example 2, the construction of local identity is continued through positioning of the speakers as "we" against the nonlocal Croats, who are now implied in the personal references "people from elsewhere" (line 8), "Livadars" (line 9), "city dwellers" (line 11), and "they" (lines 12–14).

Instead of asking "Croats from X region come here or," I continue to use the referent "people," thereby deemphasizing the speakers' ethnic identity and participating in the construction of local identity. In line 9 Boro defines "people" as "Livadars" via the toponym Livade, which stands for an entire region of many previously multiethnic villages south of Stari Grad. During the Croat-Bosniak conflict, the region of Livade also was ethnically cleansed by Croats. The significance of the referent

"Livadars" is that it allows Boro to reemphasize the rural identity of the "people"—that is, of a certain kind of Croats whose prewar and postwar identities are to be distinguished from those of the speakers. Ironically, the rural Croats in Stari Grad also are defined with the referent "city dwellers" (line 11) and repetitiously and impersonally marked as "they" (lines 12–14). Following Tannen's (1989) work on repetition, I suggest that the repetitious use of the pronoun "they" in this sequence establishes a powerful contrast. In other words, the utterances with "they," which list what the newcomers have, set up the ground against which the lack of what "we" have (lines 17–18) is dramatized.

As in example 1, temporal referents in example 2 further intensify the speakers' construction of local identity. Boro's use of "right now" in line 11 ("Right now they are the most developed city dwellers in the world") clearly delineates different experiences and identity constructions in Stari Grad before and after the war. The marker separates the roles of nonlocal Croats from the Croat and Bosniak speakers, all of whom are "right now" the victims of the new social order in which the nonresident population dominates.

Finally, example 3, which is a continuation of the preceding excerpts, illustrates how spatial reference was used together with personal and temporal reference in the speakers' construction of local identity:

Example 3

Bosnian

(14) Anna: ⌊Nema, imaš onaj . . .
(15) recimo, **tamo, u zgradama,**
(16) **ono** su **Livade** uglavnom jel' de?
(17) Ono . . .
(18) Aida: Ne znam.
(19) Ana: **Populacija** je uglavnom,
(20) **Livade** sada,
(21) a **ov- ovi Bosanci** što su došli
(22) ⌈**oni** su **po kućama, je li tako?**
(23) Boro: ⌊**Bosanci** su smješteni dole, **u onim poljima**,
(24) i **po kućama**.
(25) Ja, tamo prave, onaj, kuću.
(26) Aida: (*kroz smijeh*) Ima **jedan** u Arke što gange uvijek sluša.
(27) Mirsad: (*smijeh*)
(28) Ma ludnica.

English

(14) Ana: ⌊Yeah, you have . . .
(15) for example, **there, in the buildings**,
(16) **those** are **Livade** mostly, right?

(17) Like . . .
(18) Aida: I don't know.
(19) Ana: **The population** is mostly,
(20) **Livade** now,
(21) and **th- these Bosnians** that came
(22) ⌈they are **in the houses**, right?[3]
(23) Boro: ⌊**The Bosnians** are located down, **in those fields**,
(24) and **in the houses**.
(25) Ana: Yeah, there they are building, like, a house.
(26) Aida: (*laughingly*) There is **one** living at Arko's who is always listening to *gange*.
(27) Mirsad: (*laughs)*
(28) Yeah a madhouse.

Ana continues with the local identity construction by using the spatial reference "there, in the buildings" in line 22 to point to one of the Croat newcomers' residences in Stari Grad. The expression "in the buildings" presupposes the participants' shared knowledge of the neighborhoods of Stari Grad before the war, as well as a specific language used by locals to refer to such residences. In prewar Stari Grad, residents used "the buildings" to refer to the most recently built neighborhood, consisting of a cluster of highrises. As such, the expression implies that only townspeople used to inhabit such places. As a prewar and postwar resident of "the buildings" herself, Ana is familiar with the composition of the neighborhood but invites others to co-construct her stance toward the newcomers by asking questions about them.

Notice the way Ana points to a reversal in the town's social order: She uses the spatial referent "Livade" to mark the presence of nonrural people who are occupying "the buildings." Ana does not say or imply that, in fact, Croats from Livade and other places were illegally occupying Bosniak and Serb property in the buildings. Instead, she uses the ethnically indeterminate referents "those" (line 23) and "the population" (line 26) to speak of these new Croat residents. These referents background the Croat residents' ethnic identity and reemphasize the speakers' local identity.

It also is interesting to note that instead of saying "the population is mostly *from* Livade now," Ana exaggerates her position by saying "the population *is* mostly Livade now" (lines 26–27). The latter utterance constructs an image of the entire group of Livade villages that seemed to have relocated to Stari Grad, changing its demographic composition. The temporal reference "now" in this sequence signals the current level of disruption in the community caused by the presence of "the population" and further intensifies the existing local connection among the speakers.

Ana and Boro also use the personal referent "the Bosnians" (lines 28 and 30) to refer to the Croat newcomers and the spatial referents "in the houses" (line 29 and 30) and "in those fields" (line 30) to refer to the residence of "the Bosnians." Like the expression "Livadars," the expression "the Bosnians" is a regional marker, signifying persons living in the Bosnia part of Bosnia-Herzegovina. At the same time, the expression evokes a set of stereotypes that people living in Herzegovina have toward Bosnians—such as, among other things, that Bosnians are backward peasants. Thus, by referring to the Croat newcomers as "the Bosnians," Ana and Boro are able to align themselves with the Bosniak speakers by accentuating their identity as townspeople and contrasting it to that of "the Bosnians."

This alignment is further intensified through the spatial referents "in the houses" and "in those fields," which presuppose an agreed-upon knowledge of the speakers about the changes that happened in Stari Grad during and after the war. In other words, "the houses" located "in those fields" stands for a whole new residential addition to the town, built illegally by nationalist Croats on municipally owned fields. Because the settlement is entirely Croat owned and was built for the Croat newcomers, it is one of the most visible and lasting changes in Stari Grad brought about by nationalist ideologies, war, and ethnic cleansing. Although the presence of this settlement and its residents is bound to evoke different associations and war experiences for Bosniaks and Croats in Stari Grad, in the interaction analyzed here the spatial referents "the houses" and "those fields"—together with the personal referent "the Bosnians"—allow the Croat speakers to distance themselves from the Croat role in the recent ethnic cleansing and to construe the postwar reality as a conflict of local versus nonlocal origins and identity.

The Croat speakers' position is finally affirmed by my comments and Mirsad's comments. I use the indeterminate referent "one" ("There is one living at Arko's who is always listening to *gange*") to speak of a Croat who was living illegally in my relative Arko's house and was always listening to *gange*—a type of music typical of the country's peasant communities. The daily practice of this rural Croat exemplifies not only his nonlocal belonging but also the lingering postwar nationalist discourse, ideology, and order in Stari Grad, which Mirsad describes as "a madhouse" (line 34).

Conclusion

In this chapter I investigate samples of postwar discourse among two Croats and two Bosniaks from Stari Grad in Bosnia-Herzegovina, where Croats nationalists were in charge of ethnic cleansing against Bosniaks during the recent war. I demonstrate how the speakers' use of personal, spatial, and temporal reference points to the delicate construction of local identity, which promotes the speakers' similarity and sameness as townspeople and long-time residents of Stari Grad by deemphasizing their ethnic identities. The speakers position themselves as locals by establishing a contrast between their resident practices and the presence and practices of nonresident Croats who resettled to Stari Grad during the war.

Identifying the discursive construction of local identity is extremely relevant for research on ethnic and national identity in Bosnia-Herzegovina and in general because this form of self- and other-representation can compete with, reinforce, or contest one's sense of ethnic and national identity and belonging. Using Stari Grad as an example, in this chapter I show how local identity also can reveal how individual members of a former multiethnic community attempt to deal with massive disruptions of their earlier shared practices. In this process, we can study local identity as an important discursive and social act because of its potential to contest current nationalist discourse and ideology of homogenous ethnic and national groups through everyday discourse. Furthermore, the construct of local identity can be essential for reviving communities such as Stari Grad because its discourse allows the speakers to construct a sense of continuity with the diverse and shared practices from before the war, signaling a possibility for their future coexistence.

Acknowledgments

I thank Shari Kendall, Deborah Tannen, and Vanja Filipovic for their comments on earlier drafts of this chapter.

NOTES

1. I use the term "Bosniak" to denote an ethnic group formerly referred to as Bosnian Muslims. "Stari Grad" and "Livade" are pseudonyms for places referred to in this chapter. "Stari Grad" replaces the name of the researched community, and "Livade" replaces the name of a neighboring region.
2. Except for mine, the names of the speakers and people they talk about have been changed.
3. In the original line "oni su po kućama," the preposition "po" (around) rather than "u" (in) is used to describe the location of people as "in the houses." This construct is found mostly in the spoken language. Its use to specify the location of people as "in" the houses is a stylistic choice that allows the speakers to signal another layer of meaning: the oddness of how the houses in the settlement were acquired. That is, the newcomers have been "strewn around the houses," inhabiting the property without a legal order.

Transcription Conventions

.	falling intonation
[[	overlapping speech
] [	no perceptible pause between utterances
{ }	covert referent
-	false start
,	continuing utterance
?	rising intonation

REFERENCES

Anderson, Benedict. 1991. *Imagined communities: Reflections on the origin and spread of nationalism*. London, New York: Verso.

Barker, Chris, and Dariusz Galasinski. 2001. *Cultural studies and discourse analysis: A dialogue on language and identity*. London: Sage Publications.

Filipovic, Mirza. 1990. *The art of Bosnia-Herzegovina*. Sarajevo: Svjetlost.

Gutman, Roy. 1993. *A witness to genocide: The 1993 Pulitzer Prize-winning dispatches on the "ethnic cleansing" of Bosnia*. New York, Toronto: Macmillan Publication Co.

Hart, Laurie, and Aida Premilovac. 2002. Reconstruction, pluralism and syncretism in post-war Bosnia. Paper presented at American Anthropological Association, New Orleans.

Malcom, Noel.1994. *Bosnia: A short history*. New York: New York University Press.

Sells, Michael. 1996. *The bridge betrayed*. Berkeley: University of California Press.

Silber, Laura, and Allan Little.1995. *The death of Yugoslavia*. London: Penguin Books.

Statisticki bilten [Statistical Bulletin] no. 234. 1991. Sarajevo: DZS BiH.

Tannen, Deborah. 1989. *Talking voices: Repetition, dialogue, and imagery in conversational discourse.* Cambridge: Cambridge University Press.

Wodak, Ruth, Rudolf de Cillia, Martin Reisigl, and Karin Liebhart. 1999. *The discursive construction of national identity.* Edinburgh: Edinburgh University Press.

16

Immigration Geographies, Multilingual Immigrants, and the Transmission of Minority Languages: Evidence from the Igbo Brain Drain

RACHEL R. REYNOLDS
Drexel University

THIS CHAPTER OUTLINES the linguistic repertoire of one migration network to the United States and the six sites in which the repertoire is partially reproduced. An outline of the repertoire and the contexts or sites under which that repertoire is reproduced represent a first step toward trying to take account of the new and changing sociogeographical settlement patterns of multilingual immigrants, such as many African immigrants, to analyze the process of transmission of minority languages to future generations.

The group of Nigerian Igbo-speaking immigrants described here and with whom I conducted ethnography of communication fieldwork for six years in the late 1990s are members of the "New Ethnics" (Saran and Eames 1980; Sridnar and Sridnar 2000). Such new ethnics are post-1965 immigrants who are largely professional, arriving in the United States already with advanced degrees or with student visas to obtain postsecondary training.[1] Many also begin the processes of obtaining citizenship by starting off as H1B visa immigrants—that is, highly skilled people whose immigration status is linked to their professional positions in corporations, schools, and nonprofits. Nigerians in Chicago typically work as electrical engineers, accountants, venture capitalists, social workers, pharmacists, professional salespeople, administrators, college professors, and paraprofessionals. Despite the fact that all of the informants in my network were college graduates, several with foreign diplomas had difficulty getting U.S. institutions to accept the validity of their degrees or had problems finding employment. In these cases, most people underwent paraprofessional training in the United States in fields such as respiratory therapy or radiology to facilitate quick and steady employment. Besides their educational and workplace experiences, it also is important to note that many new ethnics in the United States speak English with native or near-native fluency, usually because they came from former Anglophone colonies. Likewise, their political affiliations often fall in line with global political movements, ranging from behind-the-scenes work to influence world trade policy to international human rights work. Some of my informants engage in political work abroad designed to influence events in their home country.

The association of immigration status with employment means that group members frequently settle near places of work or places of status associated with their professional work—rather than, for example, settling in one of Chicago's many ethnic enclave areas. Igbo speakers of the elite migratory class tend to settle along the byways of what they explicitly refer to as a "route" along the path to success. They live in Chicago neighborhoods with easy access to the financial and global economic district known as the Loop, near the universities, near the hospitals, near the suburban corporations where many work, and among their American native-born customers and constituents. For example, in the group with which I worked, in 1999 there were 175 member families living in 67 different zip codes in four states and distributed across all five counties of the Chicago area.

This widespread distribution of members of this group means that they must actively seek reasons and structures to come together. They do so through a group called ONI, the "Organization for *Ndi Igbo*/Igbo People" (a pseudonym), which is a registered Illinois nonprofit cultural association. The group meets monthly to discuss political events; to plan cultural programs including ethnic festivals sponsored by ONI; and, in general, as a means to bring together far-flung group members to socialize and stay up-to-date with other Igbo speakers in the area.

Linguistic Repertoire of ONI Group

Members of this immigrant group, as is typical of elite Nigerians from the southern part of that country, are multilingual and multidialectal. Moreover, African contexts—on the continent or elsewhere—usually are considerably more multifarious than the situations on which most studies of first-language maintenance have been based. With the deep and long-running politicization of ethnic identities, indexed directly through multiple linguistic codes in places such as Nigeria where conservative estimates delineate about 240 ethnic groups—each understood as speaking a distinct ethnic language—it is difficult for Westerners to grasp such linguistic behavior (Williamson and Blench 2000). As such, the binary concept of diglossia also has limited utility because so many codes are constantly in use and they index so many interrelated culture groups and streams of power and prestige. Code-switching, lexical borrowing, and convergence among or between linguistic codes also are normative (Eze 1998; for an overview, see Myers-Scotton 1993).

Entering the field, I was surprised that the professional status of this migratory elite predicated that they were all native speakers of something like Received Pronunciation or British Received Pronunciation and usually a Nigerian pidgin English (i.e., nearly all ONI group members spoke at least one variety of English in the home in early childhood, as well as an Igbo dialect). Until the 1970s this generational cohort, born between the late 1940s and the early 1970s, was raised by parents in the upper levels of education, government, and the private sector in either colonial or postcolonial Nigeria, who stressed British-English alphabetic and cultural literacy as the key to success. Igbo speakers from the southeast portion of the country were missionized earlier than other groups, and during the colonial period many obtained

Western education and employment within the colonial enterprise. Moreover, many Igbo speakers come from migratory families within Nigeria. Elite families in particular may have moved outside Igbo-speaking areas to work as clerks, educators, and traders beginning in the 1920s and continuing today. Because of this mobility, most of my informants speak at least one other major Nigerian language, learned from playmates while their families lived outside of Igboland; many learned Nigerian languages from classmates in boarding school. In sum, the members of my fieldwork group in particular grew up speaking in their daily lives a minimum of three genetically distinct languages—Igbo, English, and usually Yoruba, Hausa, or another Nigerian language. In interviews about linguistic background, most of the respondents said that they attained competence in such languages before adolescence and that they developed near-native proficiency in them. (I also have frequently witnessed conversations in Yoruba in this network, for example.) Table 16.1 outlines the rich linguistic repertoire of my informants.

Add Nigerian multilingualism to transnational (or globalizing) contexts, and the task of describing and analyzing the patterns of deployment of African linguistic repertoires becomes considerably more difficult. Such complexity defies descriptive models of immigrant language use, which tend to rely on a place-bound concept of domain.

Conceptualizations such as domain often develop data from institutional categories such as the schoolhouse, the home, the church or synagogue, the courthouse or

Table 16.1
Languages spoken by Igbo immigrants in ONI group

Language(s)	Varieties
Igbo	• Home village (father's), home village (mother's), other village (place of residence) • "Central" Igbo • Market Igbo
English	• Pidgin English (a distinct Nigerian creole), which informants also call "Broken English" • Nigerian Standard English (similar to British R.P.)
Other Nigerian languages genetically distinct from Igbo (Northern)	• Hausa (for those who grew up in the North) • Other northern language like Born
Other Nigerian languages genetically similar to Igbo (Southern)	• Dialects of Yoruba (especially in high schools in Lagos, etc.) • Other southeastern languages (Itsekiri, Urhobo)
Other African languages	• Swahili, Akan, KwaZulu (learned while living outside Nigeria)
Other European languages	• French, German, Spanish (usually for international business)

Sources: Field notes and linguistic background questionnaires.

post office, the ethnic neighborhood, and possibly the ethnic workplace in determining who speaks what to whom and where and why. The problem of dispersed geographical settlement of new ethnics and highly mobile professional immigrants means that a researcher cannot find informants speaking a language such as Igbo at the post office, at the church, or in the ethnic neighborhood. In such cases, the concept of domain has limited utility in describing language planning efforts, as well as analyses of linguistic maintenance among the second generation within professional immigrant communities. Therefore, the difficulty at hand is to find the right analytical term to determine the nature of linguistic code choice among speakers—a term that is more appropriate to the sort of immigrant geographical settlement patterns caused by recent effects of globalization. Such a term, importantly, also must be able to encompass the striking mobility and use of contemporary communications technologies among such immigrant groups (Reynolds 2004).

To find a term for domain that can methodologically encompass Igbo immigrants' engagement with space and time compression, I have drawn on work by Susan Philips, linking my analysis of language to the notion of "key sites." The value of the term is that key sites are not necessarily places—although they can be—but conceptual moments and locations in which community is pointedly imagined (Stuart Hall, cited in Philips 2000, 232–33). In other words, one can use this term to determine when, where, and how community is created, as well as how community is sustained and maintained, by focusing on the interactivity of language and symbols rather than focusing on the physical place where language is used. Through key sites, we can see how language use joins with the way informants' linguistic performances are a process of multi-sited experiments of linguistic reproduction and verbal representation. Such verbal pratice should be analyzed because it runs directly along the fluctuating economic and geographic dimensions of new ethnic communities.

For example, the ability to capture the influence of newspapers in print and online as contributing to linguistic shift in this community is important. Because much of the oral discourse in ONI immigrant group meetings is both deeply intertextual and professional, understanding a conversation may require that everyone has read the morning's *Guardian* newspaper out of Lagos (http://www.ngrguardiannews.com) and the *Chicago Sun Times*, both of which are in English. Nearly all of the political and social aspects of literacy in Igbo speakers' lives anywhere in the world outside of Igboland (and often within it) occur in English; this fact explains why informants switch codes to English when they speak overtly about politics or the problems of being a global professional. This factor, combined with the personal linguistic history of Anglophone elite Nigerians of the 1950s, 1960s, and 1970s, as outlined above, and the groups' immense personal stake in contemporary development politics compels my informants toward using standardized English such as Standard American, British R.P., or Nigerian Standard English (Banjo 1997).

Examination of key sites—in this case, the key site of print and media cultures of the Anglophone Nigerian diaspora—can help a researcher move the level of data collection and analysis to sites where ideology is associated with the code. Moreover, such key sites, like the domains concept they are intended to replace, are empirically verifiable entities of utility in conducting fieldwork.

Through coding and analysis of recordings, a collection of written artifacts, and field notes collected over the six years of my ethnography of communication fieldwork, I have designated six key sites—primary sites in which Igbo speakers came together to reproduce African varieties or codes, usually varieties of English or Igbo. These key sites were as follows: (1) ONI immigrant group meetings, which are official immigrant association gatherings; (2) social ritual gatherings such as wakes, funerals, and harvest festivals; (3) ethnic establishments, especially Nigerian commercial establishments;[2] (4) Igbo and Nigerian print media and culture, which is vast, complex, and keenly lived by my informants; (5) the Igbo home; and (6) the return from diaspora. I was able to witness the first four of these key sites first-hand; I was less able to witness the other two sites first-hand.

Table 16.2 roughly outlines the four key sites I was able to witness by taping community meetings or through field notes. Each category or key site enumerated has an estimate of percentage of time that a specific linguistic code is used in oral or written discourse among community members. The fieldwork took place between 1996 and 2002; it generated more than 2,340 minutes of taped immigrant association meetings.

Estimates under key site 1 (immigrant association meetings) are based on five ninety-minute tapes I transcribed and coded for topic of discourse, language, and speaker. Because meeting formats are formulaic, following Roberts' Rules of Order and lasting always about 1½ to 2 hours, estimates are very accurate. The same assessment of accuracy applies to my collection of print materials (key site 4). The other two key sites, ethnic establishments and social ritual gatherings, were nearly impossible (or very impolite) to audiotape. To gather this data, I attended nightclub events, street festivals, and social service gatherings and spent many hours chatting with people at commercial establishments such as restaurants, nightclubs, and stores that were owned or frequented by Igbo speakers (and other West Africans). The category of key site 2—social ritual gatherings—included wakes, funerals, christenings, house-blessings, and Biafra-Nigeria war memorial services. In all cases, I wrote field notes within two or three hours of leaving a site, with particular attention to literacy and orality practices (which was the fieldwork focus for my dissertation). Therefore, for both of these key sites I provide field note–based estimates for how frequently various codes are deployed.

Unfortunately, I was not able to well document the fifth key site, Igbo homes, because of limited access. The sixth key site, "return from diaspora," is an ideology that backs up linguistic practices among certain parents. For example, my informants sometimes send their preteen children to Nigeria for summers or for schooling in the hope that their children will absorb both Igbo language and desired cultural values. Likewise, Igbo ritual requires that one is versed in the language of the ancestors, so parents who wish to foster cultural pride and the necessity to fulfill ritual obligations teach their children that the Igbo language is to be highly valued. The fact that arranged marriages can occur even among second-generation children also has a direct impact on the continued acquisition of Igbo language proficiency in the Igbo diaspora; the few adult children of my informants raised in the United States who have

Table 16.2
Key sites for bringing together Igbo communities among ONI immigrants, arranged by use of language varieties

	Key Sites (% of time)			
Language variety	(1) Official Immigrant Association Gatherings	(2) Social Ritual Gatherings	(3) Ethnic Establishments	(4) Print Media and Culture
Standard or Nigerian English	70	20	10	95
Central Igbo	20	40	50[c]	2.5[a]
Village Igbo	5[a]	20[b]	Rarely	Never
Other African languages	Never	5	30[c]	Never
"Broken English"	5[a]	15	30[c]	2.5[a]
Code-mixing[d]	Frequent/ normative	Frequent/ normative/	Frequent/ normative sometimes metaphorical	Frequent use of particles and proverbs; highly metaphorical

Sources: From coded transcripts of taped audio discourse (site 1), a collection of print materials (site 4), and estimates derived from field notes (sites 2 and 3).

[a] Use of code is highly marked where language code is deeply connected to verbal arts and performance. For example, Igbo village code choices index relationships between people in the room who are of differing villages of origin. Likewise, performances in Broken English index city life, working-class consciousness, and a Nigerian group identity under which Igbo identity is subsumed.

[b] Between individuals from the same village.

[c] Depends on the function and the individuals present. It is only at these commercial establishments, however, that Igbo speakers from a wide range of homelands might come together—for example, to see a popular West African high-life singer on tour. Likewise, such social events are the sorts of situations where speakers of Yoruba, Urhobo, or other languages might be in attendance. Usually, Yoruba and Broken English were the languages other than Igbo I heard.

[d] Code mixing is *de rigueur* among Nigerians; it occurs at the intrasentential level and can even vary at the grammatical or lexical level. Highly marked metaphorical code switching, however, is employed performatively to index in-group and out-group relationships.

become old enough to get married and have assented to arranged marriage do indeed speak Igbo with native or near-native proficiency.[3] Finally, also included in the "return from diaspora" category is the tendency to engage in extended periodic phone conversations. These long talks among relatives who are "back home" reportedly are always in a village dialect, and children absorb the gravity and importance of these all-day special conversations, even if the acquisition of a home dialect is not feasible through phone conversations.

Conclusion: On Multilingualism, New Ethnics, and Language Planning

What do tables 16.1 and 16.2 and my use of key sites tell us about language ideologies and language transmission, multilingualism, and language planning in general?

Ideologies and Language Transmission

Analyzing ideologies associated with specific Igbo linguistic codes and key sites leads to interesting patterns of linguistic socialization—or the lack thereof. Because of the far-flung geography among ONI immigrants, language code choice becomes linked especially to key sites where adults come together in moments of heightened performances of identity—for social ritual gatherings, at official immigrant group meetings, or in important phone calls from back home. In these cases, children generally are not exposed to enough Igbo to learn it with any fluency, yet through exposure to the gravity of language associated with key sites they are socialized into a deep cultural respect for the language and for the elders who speak something they know is an Igbo language. Many such "Igbo-born" monolingual American English-speaking children become heritage language learners in college, and although my research did not include formal interviews with children, I never encountered even vaguely negative or stigmatized attitudes toward the Igbo language among the several dozen Igbo children I know. Most, in fact, seem to have strongly internalized a positive attachment to the Igbo language, even if they only vaguely understand it. Coming into or exploring an Igbo "identity" for these second-generation children often entails learning Igbo as a second language.

Multilingualism

The use of multiple linguistic codes militates against children's acquisition of Igbo. Igbo speakers abroad lack enough fellow villagers to replicate an Igbo village dialect *in toto*; however, village dialects are deployed in performances about familial-village ritual and in verbal arts that highlight political-regional conflict in Nigeria. The result is that no single "default" Igbo dialect comes to the fore in any key site. Instead, village dialects often are used at moments of formally rigid religious performance or at moments of breakthrough to performance (Hymes 1981) in verbal art when dialect is associated with politics (as in Nigeria, the choice of specific dialects in public talk is deeply politicized within communities abroad).[4] One exception should be noted. In a few Igbo families there are parents who work assiduously to impart to their children their local village dialect. In such cases, either both parents are from the same village and therefore use the same code constantly around children or they are language practitioners like linguists or teachers.[5]

There is a second consequence to the problem of multiple codes in this immigrant community. Because the habitus of multilingual language use—and the African audiences appropriate to sustaining multilingualism—cannot be replicated in the United States, and because of these immigrants' status as Anglophone elites in diaspora, a functional shift toward English is occurring abroad among ONI group members. Such examples show that in multilingual immigrant groups, the transmission of language and cultural habitus to the second generation will take a different shape than it will among first-generation monolingual or bilingual immigrant groups.

Language Planning

A final reason for examining key sites for language use in immigrant communities is that they may earmark when and how codification and institutionalization of a single code will come about. Geography and language transmission are important among Igbo speakers in that in a generation or two, much will depend on this new and growing diaspora in terms of Igbo language codification (textbooks) and maintenance (regularized language courses). I propose that it would be valuable to pay attention to the mechanisms by which certain dialects of Igbo gain international prominence along the lines of middle-class migratory groups and the ways they become active in language politics; such middle-class immigrants, after all, are likely to attend universities where formal language programs emerge.

For example, for the first time in many years the University of Pennsylvania has had sufficient demand to offer Igbo courses in a regular and consistent yearly curriculum to undergraduate learners. Although a few universities advertise that they will teach Igbo as courses on demand or that they offer intensive Igbo through summer programs or scholarships in the federally funded program in foreign language area studies, the University of Pennsylvania appears to be the only institution offering the language consistently. Demand may rise as the children of the growing waves of Igbo immigration reach maturity and matriculate at American universities. The instructor's region of origin therefore is quite important because it will affect which Igbo dialects are made paramount in the minds of the instructor's largely heritage learner students. Even among immigrants, if this new elite finds the means by which to recast the value of either multiple Igbo codes or a single standardized Igbo code (for example, by creating a market for textbooks that will inevitably privilege one Igbo dialect over another), the children of this same elite will be preserving and promoting such codes into the future.

The foregoing discussion has attempted to raise two important issues for the methodologies by which linguists study minority language acquisition. The first is that with important studies in the role of language ideologies in language maintenance and transition, we would do well to examine and try to understand the key sites in which minority languages are valorized by new migrants. With populations that are highly mobile and tend to live outside ethnic enclaves, key sites are an important concept for understanding language transmission and are of potentially greater utility than the place-bound concept of domain. The second issue is that immigrant groups with extraordinary levels of multilingualism/multidialectism in the societies where they were socialized to language are potentially less likely than merely bilingual/diglossic immigrants to successfully reproduce the richness of linguistic repertoires among their young language learners. In such situations, it is important to keep track of the second generation's experiences with language learning, language socialization, and the absorption of attitudes toward their parents' languages, especially with an eye to understanding how such children may come to experience and possibly influence new heritage language programs in Western schools' language curricula.

NOTES

1. See also the Balch Institute for Ethnic Studies (2001) report on immigrants in Philadelphia, which estimates that more than half of the area's African immigrants have baccalaureate degrees. My sense of this picture, however, is that as of 2003 the level of educational attainment among African immigrants is beginning to change. For example, there is a growing influx of refugees from Africa,

especially from Sudan, and an increase in low-skilled traders migrating (but not necessarily immigrating) from Francophone countries.

2. Ethnic establishments often are sites of intraethnic discourse among a broad array of members of different Nigerian ethnolinguistic groups. Examples of such ethnic sites include nightclub performances by high-life artists or midday conversations at the African restaurants where men socialize.
3. Sridnar and Sridnar (2000, 377) note that, following Gumperz and Wilson, "ethnic separateness of home life, separation between the public and private (intrakin) spheres of activity are the central variable" in how language or other cultural attributes are maintained into a second generation. Sridnar and Sridnar are speaking explicitly about assimilation and South Asian immigrants. There is a strong tendency among Igbo speakers abroad and in Nigeria, however, to press their daughters to marry into Igbo families (successfully), whereas the expectation for sons to marry endogamously is not as stringent. Women, not surprisingly, are charged most directly with imparting "traditional values" to young offspring, and in that sense they are referred to as guardians of Igbo culture. Both men and women in my network assert that this is the case, although they emphasize, of course, that fathers also have important roles; among younger couples, the father often has a prominent role in childrearing.
4. Elaboration and codification of a single Igbo variety in Nigeria is thwarted by numerous factors. Not only is the orthography of this tonal language difficult to manage, but the use of any given dialect is, in various contexts, a political issue (see Van den Bersselaar 1998). The principal reason is that village codes are deeply connected to ritual and to political-social identity linked to the land. Giving up one's village code is like giving up one's family. Other reasons for the continued presence of a wide variety of spoken Igbo and other Nigerian indigenous codes is that English steps in to serve, in a sense, as a "neutral" language. As Chinua Achebe put it, "English is the thing that makes the idea of Nigeria possible" (quoted in an interview by Egejuru 1978, 101).
5. Interestingly, however, in ritual contexts my youngest informants do learn some "social" Igbo. I am designing a questionnaire for heritage learners of Igbo to find out if these social-ritual contexts influence their decisions to study Igbo as adults.

REFERENCES

Balch Institute for Ethnic Studies. 2001. *Extended lives: The African immigrant experience in Philadelphia.* Special Publication. Philadelphia: Balch Institute for Ethnic Studies.

Banjo, Ayo. 1997. On codifying Nigerian English: Research so far. In *New Englishes: A West African perspective*, ed. Ayo Bamgbose, Ayo Banjo, and Andrew Thomas, 232–47. Trenton, N.J.: Africa World Press.

Egejuru, Phanuel Akubueze. 1978. *Black writers, white audience: A critical approach to African literature.* Hicksville, N.Y.: Exposition Press.

Eze, Ejike. 1998. Lending credence to a borrowing analysis: Lone English-origin incorporations into Igbo discourse. *International Journal of Bilingualism.* 2, no. 2:183–202.

Hymes, Dell. 1981. *"In vain I tried to tell you": Essays in Native American ethnopoetics.* Philadelphia: University of Pennsylvania Press.

Myers-Scotton, Carol. 1993. *Social motivations for code-switching: Evidence from Africa.* Oxford: Clarendon Press.

Philips, Susan. 2000. Constructing a Tongan nation state through language ideology in a courtroom. In *Regimes of language: Ideologies, politics and identities*, ed. Paul Kroskrity, 229–57. Santa Fe, N.M.: School of American Research Press.

Reynolds, Rachel R. 2004. The constitution of a Nigerian diaspora along the contours of global economy. *City and Society* 16, no. 1:15–37.

Saran, Parmatma, and Edwin Eames. 1980. *The new ethnics: The Asian Indians in the U.S.* New York: Praeger.

Sridnar, Kamal K., and S. N. Sridnar. 2000. At home with English: Assimilation and adaptation of Asian Indians in the United States. In *New immigrants in the United States: Readings for second language educators*, ed. Sandra McKay and Sau-ling Cynthia Wong, 369–92. Cambridge: Cambridge University Press.

Van den Bersselaar, Dmitri. 1998. *In search of Igbo identity: Language, culture and politics in Nigeria, 1900–1966*. Leiden, The Netherlands: Leiden University Dissertation Service.

Williamson, Kay, and Roger Blench. 2000. Niger-Congo. In *African languages: An introduction*, ed. Bernd Heine and Derek Nurse, 11–42. New York: Cambridge University Press.

www.ingramcontent.com/pod-product-compliance
Lightning Source LLC
LaVergne TN
LVHW090807070826
844660LV00022B/1108

* 9 7 8 1 5 8 9 0 1 0 4 4 4 *